Society and Economy

Society and Economy

FRAMEWORK AND PRINCIPLES

Mark Granovetter

The Belknap Press of Harvard University Press

Cambridge, Massachusetts, and London, England   2017

Second printing

Library of Congress Cataloging-in-Publication Data
Names: Granovetter, Mark S., author.
Title: Society and economy : framework and principles / Mark Granovetter.
Description: Cambridge, Massachusetts : The Belknap Press of Harvard University Press,
    2017. | Includes bibliographical references and index.
Identifiers: LCCN 2016043756 | ISBN 9780674975217
Subjects: LCSH: Economics—Sociological aspects. | Social institutions—Economic aspects.
Classification: LCC HM548 .G73 2016 | DDC 306—dc23
LC record available at https://lccn.loc.gov/2016043756

Contents

Acknowledgments   vii

1   Introduction: Problems of Explanation in Economic Sociology   1

2   The Impact of Mental Constructs on Economic Action: 26
Norms, Values, and Moral Economy

3   Trust in the Economy   56

4   Power in the Economy   91

5   The Economy and Social Institutions   135

6   The Interplay between Individual Action and Social Institutions   171

Notes   207

References   215

Index   235

Acknowledgments

When a book has been as embarrassingly delayed as this one, it is hard to keep track of all those to whom you are indebted, so my apologies in advance to any and all whom I thoughtlessly omit here and whose good advice I have received and most likely neglected. I first offer my heartfelt thanks to my long-suffering editor emeritus, Michael Aronson, who bore with me over the years through numerous changes of direction, format, and content, and finally made good his longstanding threat to retire if I did not soon finish. Despite this, I hope that he will recognize some fruits of all his good advice over the years. My new Harvard Press editor, Ian Malcolm, has gamely stepped in to pick up the remaining pieces and help me shepherd them through to publication.

I am greatly indebted to the many current and former colleagues and students who have commented on ideas and drafts, including Michael Bernstein, Bob Eccles, Peter Evans, Ben Golub, Nitin Nohria, Steve Nuñez , Paolo Parigi, Woody Powell, James Rule, Michael Schwartz, Richard Swedberg, Ezra Zuckerman, and one anonymous reader. I have made many presentations over the years that contained pieces of these materials, and I am grateful to those who offered their thoughts. At the Russell Sage seminar on economic sociology, I received wise advice from Harrison White, Ron Burt, and Chuck Sabel, among others. I should say here that while the style of this work diverges widely from Harrison White's brilliant *Identity and Control*, Harrison's imprint on my work from the time he was my doctoral adviser to the present has been incalculable, and he is truly the scholar's scholar, operating on a cosmic plane that few of us can hope to attain.

At talks I gave at the Institute for Advanced Study and in conversations during my visiting year, Albert Hirschman and Clifford Geertz offered counsel born of their respective deep knowledge of many fields. During my time at the Wissenschaft Zentrum Berlin (WZB), I benefited especially from the comments of Gernot Grabher and Egon Matzner. Multiple conversations with Bob Gibbons have made me aware of parallel work in economics that I have probably done too little to address with the excuse that it would have required more serious work in the integration of disciplines and models than I could undertake in a relatively brief exposition. My thinking has nevertheless been informed by thinking about relevant models and I hope become more welcoming to those who want to build my arguments in formal directions. In talks I have given over the years at Columbia University, I have received immensely helpful feedback from Peter Bearman, Herb Gans, Dick Nelson, David Stark, and Diane Vaughan, and benefited particularly from a series of conversations with Josh Whitford, who kindly and astutely commented on draft chapters and engaged me in my first serious discussions on the proposal to divide this work into two books, so that this first and more theoretical one could see the light of day in a more timely fashion than had I held out for a single volume with both theory and applications. I am also grateful to Josh for his guidance in grasping the value of pragmatist epistemology in the study of human economic action and institutions.

I thank the Russell Sage Foundation for its support in the early years of my work on this book, encouraged especially by Eric Wanner during his tenure as president.

To my daughter Sara, who, as a child, referred to me as an "economical sociologist," I hope that in this volume I have dispensed with enough words to fulfill that elusive goal. And surely the longest suffering of all has been Ellen, who, I seriously hope, will view the appearance of this first volume as a glass half full rather than that famous other alternative.

Society and Economy

1

Introduction: Problems of Explanation in Economic Sociology

1.1 Scope of the Enterprise

In this book I present arguments about economic action and institutions that emphasize social, cultural and historical considerations in addition to purely economic ones. This may therefore be considered a contribution to "economic sociology," a subfield that has grown vigorously in the past thirty years.[1] But more fundamentally, I hope to contribute to an understanding of the economy in a way that transcends disciplinary boundaries and thus have little concern about the intellectual origins of useful ideas.

In this introductory chapter, I set out general arguments on the nature of social science; the meaning of explanation for economic action, outcomes, and institutions; and the relation between social structure and the economy. Subsequent chapters deal with important theoretical elements of my argument: the role of norms and other mental constructs in the economy, trust and cooperation, power and compliance, and the interplay between institutions and human purposive action. A sequel volume will treat a series of empirical cases analyzed within the proposed framework.

I distinguish three levels of economic phenomena to be explained. The first is individual economic action. Max Weber defines such action as occurring when "the satisfaction of a need depends, in the actor's judgment, upon some relatively *scarce* resources and a *limited* number of possible actions, and if this state of affairs evokes specific reactions. Decisive for such rational action is, of course, the fact that this scarcity is subjectively presumed and that action is oriented to it." ([1921] 1968: 339). These needs, Weber continues, "may be of any conceivable kind, ranging from food to religious edification, if there is a scarcity of goods and services in relation to demand" (339). This closely parallels economist Lionel Robbins's classic definition of economics, reprised in most current elementary textbooks, as "the science which studies human behavior as a relationship between ends and scarce means which have alternative uses" (1932: 15). These differ only in Weber's insistence on the importance of the actor's subjective orientation to the means-end situation.[2]

Having adopted this broad definition of economic action, I could then logically discuss a wide range of subjects, including marriage, divorce, crime, and the allocation of time, as in the program of "economic imperialists" such as Gary Becker (cf. Hirshleifer 1985). Instead I confine attention to examples that are "economic" in the usual sense of having to do with the production, distribution, and consumption of goods and services—what we might call the "hard core" of economic activity. But my goal is not the parallel one of "sociological imperialism" but rather of understanding the economy with whatever means and ideas are required, from whatever source.

A second level of economic analysis concerns patterns of action *beyond* the realm of single individuals—what I call "economic outcomes." Examples of "outcomes" would be the formation of stable prices for a commodity or of wage differentials between certain classes of workers. So these "outcomes" are regular patterns of individual action.

A third level refers to economic "institutions." These differ from "outcomes" in two ways: (1) they typically involve larger complexes of action, and (2) individuals come to see them as the way that things *should* be done. Institutions convey, as is well captured in the sociology of knowledge, a deceptive impression of solidity, they become reified, experienced as external and objective aspects of the world rather than as the products of social construction, which they are (see, e.g., Berger and Luckmann 1966). This social-constructionist perspective is highly relevant for economic institutions. Examples are entire systems of economic organization, such as capitalism or, at lower levels, the way particular organizations, industries, or professions are constituted. Chapters 5 and 6 discuss the nature of institutions more fully.

These three correspond closely to what are usually called micro, meso and macro levels of analysis. While each requires some principles that apply exclusively to its own level, it is important to attempt a synthesis that brings all these levels into a common framework and illuminates the way influences at one level affect results in others without giving one level causal priority over the others. Roughly speaking, the substantive chapters, beginning with Chapter 2, begin at the micro level of individuals, progress through meso-level issues, and end with more macro-level or institutional concerns.

1.2 "Human Nature," Null Hypotheses, and Levels of Analysis: Beyond Reductionism

Null hypotheses, typically unspoken, lurk beneath most social science accounts of the economy. I refer to underlying baseline assumptions about how humans behave and how society is organized—the conceptual starting point for scholars who try to understand a set of phenomena. These baselines underlie much of the rhetoric of the social sciences and have a strong psychological effect on who is persuaded by which arguments (as eloquently argued by McCloskey 1983).

Null hypotheses typically contain assumptions about "human nature," and because "nurture" trumped "nature" in most twentieth-century social science, it looks old-fashioned to make such assumptions explicit; yet they are pervasive, even when barely whispered. The null hypotheses of economists and sociologists differ markedly. Most economists explain by assuming that individuals pursue their interests, guided by quantifiable incentives. While few endorse the stereotypical rational calculator, *homo economicus*, models based on individual interests and explicit or implicit calculations still take priority over those that invoke more "complicated" social factors not amenable to simple and elegant models. As Elster points out, a typical practice in "applied rational choice theory" is to construct a model in which "the observed behavior of the agents maximizes their interests as suitably defined, and one assumes that the fit between behavior and interest explains the behavior." But, he notes, without explicit evidence for a causal relation, the "coincidence of behavior and interest may be only that—a coincidence"

(Elster 2000: 693). The null hypothesis in play here is so strong that the coincidence is automatically assumed to reflect causality.

Sociologists are even less likely to make explicit their ideas about human nature, but more than a century of social theory has disposed many to assume that individuals are constituted by their social environment and cannot even imagine what they are like or who they are without having absorbed impressions of themselves from significant others as well as a more general sense of where they fit into society, provided by socialization into a particular milieu. Thus, sociologists portray individuals as guided by social influences, including their own social circle and beyond, social norms or ideologies, social class, or social institutions based on such social complexes as religion, economy, or politics.

All scholars endorse parsimony in explanation, but criteria for what is parsimonious are not objectively given. They follow from which null hypothesis you favor, as this determines what levels of analysis you think critical, and whether you consider reductionist projects in the social sciences feasible or feckless. In the history of science, attempts to link disciplines frequently entail such projects, which aim to show how one conceptual framework is more fundamental than the other and can therefore subsume it. The successful reduction of much classical biology to a molecular basis has encouraged many other such attempts.

Though most sociologists still subscribe to Emile Durkheim's turn-of-the-twentieth-century insistence on society as a reality *sui generis,* sociological arguments and theories are sufficiently diffuse to make the discipline a popular takeover target. B. F. Skinner was perhaps the first psychologist to argue that social life could be fully explained in terms of behavioral regularities induced by reinforcement contingencies, but this view has attracted only a few sociological adherents (e.g., Homans 1971). Reduction of social behavior to biology is one of the main projects of sociobiologist E. O. Wilson and his followers (Wilson 1975), where the mechanism assumed to generate social relations is natural selection at the individual genetic level and less frequently (and more controversially) at that of groups. As I have noted, some economists have framed their reductionist project as "economic imperialism," beginning with Gary Becker's incursions into such sociological subjects as love, marriage, crime, and the allocation of time (e.g., Becker 1976) and reflected in claims like that of Jack Hirshleifer that "economics really does constitute the universal grammar of social science" (1985: 53).

Because of their alleged parsimony, reductionist projects attract more adherents than their epistemological opposite, the projects of (w)holism, which in various contexts have claimed that individual units in their discipline are quite uninterpretable without an understanding of the larger context in which they are found, including proponents of various flavors of systems theory and functionalism.[3]

Kontopoulos (1993) shows that in many scientific fields, reductionism and wholism have given way to far more complex and nuanced projects that seek to understand how various levels of analysis in the phenomena under study fit together and that argue that none should be privileged in explanation. The reader should understand my book as such a project. At every point in my argument, I will try to understand how micro and macro levels of analysis are connected and how what some have called a "meso" level of analysis is critical in understanding the dynamics of such relationships. It is only because of the criticality of this middle level of analysis that "social networks" occupy at times a pivotal role in my argument. I want to emphasize that they are not a privileged causal concept and by themselves have only modest explanatory value in most situations.[4]

1.3 Functionalism, Culturalism, and History

Because reductionism to the level of individuals is often unsatisfactory in its explanatory power, its proponents typically supplement it with other arguments. In the social sciences, two of the most prominent are functional and cultural explanations. This is ironic since these might be imagined to belong most appropriately to the toolkit of wholists.

"Functional" explanations account for a behavior, practice, or institution by reference to the "problem" it solves. Thus, one might propose that the institution of limited liability in the corporate world can be explained by the fact that few will undertake substantial entrepreneurship if their own private resources can be entirely wiped out by a company's failure. Separation of individual from corporate resources "solves" this problem and makes entrepreneurship more likely. But any inference that this explains the origins of limited liability cannot be sustained without a careful investigation of its actual history and its consequences as well as comparison of entrepreneurship between countries that did and did not develop such a legal pattern. In this case, there is much more to the story, and some would argue that this practice developed not as a way to improve entrepreneurship in general but rather to serve a particular set of interests.[5] In Chapter 6, I offer the more complex example of the medieval Florentine partnership system. More generally, it is hazardous to assume that every economic institution can be explained as the solution to some problem. Thus, Schotter suggests as a task for economists to develop an "economic theory of social institutions," in which understanding any institution requires that we "infer the evolutionary problem that must have existed for the institution as we see it to have developed. Every evolutionary economic problem requires a social institution to solve it" (1981: 2).

This proposal resembles the practice of sociobiologists, who explain any feature of a species as having evolved to solve some problem in its environment. Here, the creative scientific enterprise is to imagine what that problem might have been. In their wide-ranging critique, Gould and Lewontin call such explanations "adaptive stories" and comment that "the rejection of one adaptive story usually leads to its replacement by another, rather than to a suspicion that a different kind of explanation might be required. Since the range of adaptive stories is as wide as our minds are fertile, new stories can always be postulated. And if a story is not immediately available, one can always plead temporary ignorance and trust that it will be forthcoming. . . . Often evolutionists . . . consider their work done when they concoct a plausible story. But plausible stories can always be told. The key to historical research lies in devising criteria to identify proper explanations among the substantial set of plausible pathways to any modern result" (1979: 153–154).

As Gould and Lewontin suggest for biology, one problematic element of "adaptive stories" is that while in principle appealing to an historical account, they actually skip over historical research by appealing to a speculative idea about what "must" have happened. Similarly, when you explain an economic institution in terms of the problem it "must" have evolved to address, you implicitly choose to remain within the comparative statics of equilibrium states rather than studying the dynamics of how the institution was actually created over time. The argument assumes, moreover, that the system is now in equilibrium because a still-evolving institution could not reveal by inspection what problem it had evolved in order to solve.

This explanatory strategy is usually supported by explicit or implicit reference to a selection mechanism, such that units unable to solve the environmental problem fall by the wayside, and only those with the observed institutional solution remain. The classic exposition of this argument is in Milton Friedman's influential 1953 essay "The Methodology of Positive Economics" (1953: 16–22). The argument has evolved in economics into the idea that unsolved problems present the possibility of profit, and such opportunities will always be taken by rational individuals. Inefficiencies are arbitraged away, and part of the rhetoric of modern economics is that "you won't find dollar bills lying in the street."[6] The assumption that one should explain an institution by showing in what way it creates efficiencies has entered the economic lexicon especially in the New Institutional Economics, where "efficiency analysis" means telling an adaptive story about some institution. In part, this is a reaction against the "old institutional economics," which often gave legal, sociological, or historical accounts of institutions' origins.[7]

Even in biology, where the genetic mechanism of Darwinian selection is clear, Gould and Lewontin (1979) note that any particular adaptive story is merely speculation and may in fact be quite inconsistent with what actually occurred. They nicely catalogue the errors that result. In the economy, the mechanism of selection would most plausibly be the discipline of competitive markets; yet few markets entail competition so stringent that all inefficiencies are rooted out and all problems solved.[8] Instead, I argue here that economic action and institutions typically result from a variety of goals implemented by complex networks of actors and that without an understanding of the historical sequence and networks of relevant actors, these outcomes can easily be misinterpreted.

Cavalier invocation of Darwinian rhetoric careens toward a Panglossian view of behavioral patterns or institutions. The pitfalls of functionalist explanations have been catalogued many times (e.g., Merton 1947; Nagel 1961; Hempel 1965; Stinchcombe 1968; Elster 1983), and rigorous accounts have been given of the requirements that must be met for an *explanandum*[9] to be properly explained by reference to problems it is claimed to solve. Rather than recapitulating these accounts, I simply suggest a sequence of four practical questions one must be able to answer about a functionalist explanation before it can be accepted. (1) In what sense was the "problem" really a problem? If the problem a pattern is alleged to have solved was in fact no problem at all, the explanation fails immediately. (2) Was the "solution" a solution? Even if the problem is admitted to be genuine, the institution under scrutiny had better really solve it; otherwise the functionalist account is not persuasive. (3) Do we understand the process by which this solution has arisen? To avoid this question is to assume that all problems that arise are automatically solved, a proposition that, once stated, hardly anyone would endorse.

Part of a functional explanation should thus be to account for why and how the stipulated problem was indeed solved. But once we know how this solution can arise, we also understand under what circumstances it cannot. In practice, this means that the solution will not arise in all instances where the problem does, but only in some. The explanation of the pattern then will require us to know more than just the problem it solves but also the conditions that are required for this solution to emerge. This leads then to (4) Why this *particular* solution? What is the range of possible solutions for this problem, and under what circumstances might others arise? Like the answers to (3), a response to this question distances us from crude functionalist accounts and reduces the gap between a static functionalist explanation and one based on historical sequences.

Functionalist accounts often seem plausible because an economic institution appears well matched to its economic environment. But this may occur because institutions have modified their environment so as to *create* greater compatibility. Comparative statics will not reveal such a process and may instead persuade the suggestible that environmental exigencies created the institution. While economic environments certainly limit institutional configurations, these limits may be wider than we typically imagine and encompass multiple stable institutional equilibria. The historical trajectory of the system may determine which of these occurs, making the study of dynamics indispensable.

Related arguments have been made for technology by students of economic history under the heading of "path dependence." Paul David, for example, has argued that because of some specific initial conditions, the highly inefficient QWERTY typewriter keyboard became the standard of the industry by the 1890s, despite the existence of more efficient designs. QWERTY became established as the technical standard and was "locked in" by the large base of existing machines and users (1986). More generally, Brian Arthur has proposed a stochastic model of how random events in the early stage of a process can fix an outcome independent of its overall efficiency. In these "path-dependent" processes, one sees increasing returns to scale since once one of several competing technologies has a temporary lead in the number of users, this lead makes it profitable for various actors to improve it and to modify the environment in ways that facilitate further use. This further use then again spurs improvements and reduces the profitability of improving competing but less-adopted technologies. Eventually, technologies that were originally less efficient may be locked in by this train of events (Arthur 1989).

To the extent this is so, only historical analysis can explain outcomes. If, by contrast, we could assume diminishing returns to adoption of a technology, then static analysis would be sufficient; the outcome is unique and does not depend on small events in market formation or the order in which choices are made. "Under increasing returns, by contrast, many outcomes are possible. Insignificant circumstances are magnified by positive feedbacks to 'tip' the system into the actual outcome 'selected.' The small events of history become important. Where we observe the predominance of one technology or one economic outcome over its competitors we should thus be cautious of any exercise that seeks the means by which the winner's 'innate' superiority became translated into adoption" (Arthur 1989: 127)

These arguments mainly concern technology, but I argue in subsequent chapters that many other economic outcomes and institutions are also "locked in" by processes that need not be confined to random "small events" but rather can be analyzed as evolving from purposive networks of action mounted by interested actors rather than as solutions to problems. And what appear to be "random" events from an economic frame of reference can often be systematically treated in a sociological account. The technical concept of "lock-in" is in fact analogous to the sociological idea of "institutionalization." Just as the technical developments that never took hold are forgotten or dismissed as technically inferior, institutional alternatives that did not occur are forgotten, and adaptive stories are told about how the existing form was inevitable given the environment. A central question for a sociology of economic institutions is under what circumstances such stories might be correct. In the sequel volume, my account of the electricity industry in the United States fits this description well.

It is notable that scholars who endorse methodological individualism in general nevertheless often endorse functionalist explanations that rely on homeostatic system properties only tenuously linked to individual action. The attraction may be that by doing so, one avoids the need for detailed historical accounts of how action and institutions evolve. A closely related explanatory strategy, which may appeal for similar reasons, is the reliance on cultural differences to explain outcomes and institutions.

The "culturalist" position does not derive from economic logic but rather explains some outcome or institution by arguing that the group that produced it has cultural beliefs, values, or traits that predispose it to the observed behavior. Building on recent theory, such beliefs are often characterized as "social capital." Groups characterized by a "Protestant ethic" will work harder and produce more successful firms or other outcomes; those with a culture oriented to cooperation in a hierarchical setting, where individuals are subordinated to the society, will develop smoothly functioning industrial enterprises (as is often claimed for Japan, e.g., Ouchi 1981), and societies where culture confines trust to a small circle of friends and relatives will have difficulty managing economic enterprises of any substantial size (Fukuyama 1995).[10] At a sub-societal level of analysis, different organizations are said to have distinct cultures that resist merger or at least raise its cost.

If groups really did behave in ways so closely determined by their cultures, we could safely neglect the detailed historical evolution of institutions; indeed, there would be little such evolution so long as the culture remained stable. As with many functionalist arguments, however, this one hovers uncomfortably close to circularity, since the causal tie between cultural beliefs and observed patterns is usually inferred from behavior rather than shown explicitly.

Moreover, this treatment of culture as an influence on individual behavior is static and mechanical: once we know the well-socialized individual's social location, everything else in behavior is automatic. Individual actors are stripped of agency, which is odd for methodological individualists for whom agency should be of prime importance. Culture is an external force that, like the Deists' God, sets things in motion and has no further effects. Once we know in just what way one has been affected, purposive action and ongoing social relations and structures are irrelevant. Social influence is all contained inside an individual's head, so in actual decision situations, he or she can be as atomized as any *homo economicus,* but with different rules for decisions. Yet more sophisticated analyses of cultural influences (e.g., Fine and Kleinman 1979; Cole 1979, Ch. 1; Swidler 1986; DiMaggio 1997) make it clear that culture is not a once-for-all influence but an ongoing process, continuously constructed and reconstructed during interaction. It not only shapes its members but also is shaped by them, in part for their own strategic reasons. Thus, I do not mean here to denigrate the importance of culture as a force in human affairs, only to object to its misuse as a near-tautological and merely residual explanation. I delve into these questions further in Chapter 2, on the influence of culture, norms, and other mental constructs on economic action, and again in Chapters 5 and 6, which consider the relation between culture and institutions.

1.4 Under- and Oversocialized Conceptions of Human Action

Null hypotheses and their associated conceptions of human nature lead to unstated but consequential ideas about the nature of human action. When pushed too far, such conceptions distort. The sociological conception of actors as highly responsive to their social setting, for example, was famously criticized by sociologist Dennis Wrong as the "oversocialized conception of man in modern sociology" (1961)—a conception of people as so overwhelmingly sensitive to the opinions of others, and hence obedient to the dictates of consensually developed norms and values, internalized through socialization, that obedience is not burdensome but unthinking and automatic.

Wrong noted that it is "frequently the task of the sociologist to call attention to the intensity with which men desire and strive for the good opinion of their immediate associates in a variety of situations, particularly those where received theories or ideologies have unduly emphasized other motives. . . . Thus sociologists have shown that factory workers are more sensitive to the attitudes of their fellow workers than to purely economic incentives. . . . It is certainly not my intention to criticize the findings of such studies. My objection is that . . . though sociologists have criticized past efforts to single out one fundamental motive in human conduct, the desire to achieve a favorable self-image by winning approval from others frequently occupies such a position in their own thinking" (1961: 188–189).

To the extent such a conception was prominent in 1961, it resulted in part from Talcott Parsons's attempt, in his landmark book *The Structure of Social Action,* to transcend the problem of order as posed by Thomas Hobbes by emphasizing commonly held societal values (1937: 89–94). Parsons classified Hobbes in what he called the "utilitarian" tradition, which he attacked for treating individual action as atomized, isolated from the influence of others or from any broad cultural or social traditions. Yet a close reading of such utilitarians as Hume, Bentham, and John Stuart Mill does not support such a depiction. Rather, they do show considerable interest in how social institutions, norms, and interaction modify and shape individual action (see Camic 1979).

Most of what Parsons alleged to be the case for the "utilitarian" and "positivistic" tradition does, however, describe classical and twentieth-century neoclassical economics.[11] The orthodox theoretical arguments are reductionist and one might say "undersocialized," disallowing by hypothesis any impact of social structure or relations on production, distribution, or consumption. In competitive markets, no producer or consumer noticeably influences aggregate supply or demand or, therefore, prices or other terms of trade. As Albert Hirschman has noted, such idealized markets, involving as they do "large numbers of price-taking anonymous buyers and sellers supplied with perfect information . . . function without any prolonged human or social contact between the parties. Under perfect competition there is no room for bargaining, negotiation, remonstration or mutual adjustment and the various operators that contract together need not enter into recurrent or continuing relationships as a result of which they would get to know each other well" (1982: 1473).

Classical economists mentioned social relations mainly as a drag on competitive markets. Thus, Adam Smith complained that "people of the same trade seldom meet together, even for merriment and diversion, but the conversation ends in a conspiracy against the public or in some contrivance to raise prices." His laissez-faire politics did not allow him to recommend antitrust measures, but he did urge repeal of regulations requiring all those in the same trade to sign a public register, since "the public existence of such information connects individuals who might never otherwise be known to one another and gives every man of the trade a direction where to find every other man of it" ([1776] 1976: 145). This lame policy proposal is less interesting than Smith's tacit assumption that truly competitive markets *require* social atomization. This position survived into the twentieth century in standard texts like George Stigler's *The Theory of Price*, which observes that "economic relationships are never perfectly competitive if they involve any personal relationships between economic units" (1946, 24).

Though some classical economists like John Stuart Mill and others outside the main line, such as Marx and the German historical school, were interested in the general social conditions of economic action, a more rigorous and quantitative tradition, beginning with David Ricardo, increasingly narrowed the focus in a way that excluded noneconomic matters.[12] This exclusion was extended by the triumph of the neoclassical "marginalists" over the German historical school in the *Methodenstreit* of the late nineteenth and early twentieth centuries. The marginalist approach, especially as codified by Alfred Marshall, "solved" the classical problem of value by reducing it to the determination of market prices by supply and demand, which was to be understood by the mathematics of maximization (see, e.g., Deane 1978, Ch. 7).

But the apparent contrast between oversocialized views and what one might call the undersocialized account of classical and neoclassical economics masks a critical theoretical irony: both share a conception of action by atomized actors. In the undersocialized account, atomization results from narrow pursuit of self-interest; in the oversocialized one, from behavioral patterns having been internalized and thus little affected by ongoing social relations. The social origin of internalized patterns does not differentiate this argument decisively from an economic one, in which the source of utility functions is left open, leaving room for behavior guided, as in the oversocialized conception, entirely by consensually determined norms and values.[13] Under- and oversocialized conceptions thus merge in their atomization of actors from immediate social context. This ironic merger is already visible in Hobbes's *Leviathan,* where the beleaguered residents of the state of nature, overwhelmed by disorder, surrender all their rights to an authoritarian power and then become docile and honorable; by the artifice of a social contract, they lurch directly from an undersocialized to an oversocialized state.

This convergence of under- and oversocialized views helps explain why modern economists can so readily accept oversocialized arguments about the causal force of culture, which are surprisingly consistent with a reductionist view of human action in that once having absorbed the cultural prescriptions, individuals can still be analyzed without further attention to their social location or networks of interaction. Even economic models that take social relationships seriously (e.g., Becker 1976) typically abstract away from the history of relations and their position with respect to other relations. The interpersonal ties they describe are stylized, average, "typical"—devoid of specific content, history, or structural location. Actors are representative agents, whose behavior results from their named role positions and role sets; thus we have arguments about how workers and supervisors, husbands and wives, criminals and law enforcers will interact with one another, but these relations are not assumed to have individualized content beyond that given by the obligations and interests inherent in the named roles. This procedure is exactly what structural sociologists have criticized in the sociology of Talcott Parsons—the relegation of the specifics of individual relations to a minor role in the overall conceptual scheme, epiphenomenal in comparison with enduring structures of normative role prescriptions deriving from ultimate value orientations.

A fruitful analysis of any human action, including economic action, requires us to avoid the atomization implicit in the theoretical extremes of under- and oversocialized views. Actors do not behave or decide as atoms outside a social context, nor do they adhere slavishly to a script written for them by the particular intersection of sociocultural categories they happen to occupy. Their attempts at purposive action are instead embedded in concrete, ongoing systems of social relations. These networks of relations constitute a crucial meso level lying conceptually between individual action and social institutions and cultures, and the way these micro and macro levels are linked through this meso level is a central focus of interest here.

1.5 Social Networks and "Embeddedness"

The "meso" level of social networks is important because it helps avoid the theoretical extremes of under- and over-socialization. More concretely, social networks matter because people's pursuit of both social and economic goals invariably involve known others as a significant element. This argument that networks of known others matter and should be analyzed has come to be identified as the "embeddedness" perspective, in part because of the stream of work that followed my 1985 article on this subject. Much of this work has come to be identified as the "New Economic Sociology" (Granovetter 1985; Swedberg and Granovetter 2011). But while many have identified ideas about "embeddedness" with social network analysis of the economy, an identification that my 1985 paper on "embeddedness" may have furthered, I use the term more broadly here to mean the intersection of economic with noneconomic aspects of society, including not only social networks and their consequences but also cultural, political, religious, and broadly institutional influences. Social networks play a central mediating role between micro and macro levels, and part of my work here is to develop further some of the ways that networks relate to larger themes in the analysis of societies, such as trust, power, norms, and values and the institutional level of analysis. It is precisely because social networks are important in explaining such concepts that they play an important conceptual role.

This book is not the place to spell out technical arguments or details about social network analysis. Numerous excellent guides do so.[14] I assume as general background that the reader has some elementary acquaintance with ideas about social networks. It is helpful, however, to spell out several theoretical arguments or principles about the interaction of social networks with other social outcomes. Here I suggest three, which are not meant to be exhaustive but are useful ideas that I draw on in what follows:

1. Networks and Norms. As I discuss in more detail in Chapter 2, norms— shared ideas about normal or proper behavior in specified situations—are

clearer, more firmly held, and easier to enforce the more dense the social network.[15] The classic argument for this proposition, from social psychology (see, e.g., Festinger, Schachter, and Back 1948), relies on the larger number of unique paths in denser networks along which ideas, information, and influence can travel among nodes. This makes norms more likely to be repeatedly encountered and discussed and also makes it harder to hide deviance, which is thus more likely to be discouraged. A corollary is that, other things equal, larger groups will find it harder to crystallize and enforce norms because their network density is lower. This is because people have cognitive, emotional, spatial, and temporal constraints on the number of social ties they can manage, so that larger networks must fragment into cliques (e.g., Nelson 1966).

2. **The Strength of Weak Ties.** New information is more likely to reach individuals through their weak than their strong ties. Our close friends move in the same circles that we do and thereby learn mostly what we already know. Weak ties, or "acquaintances" as we usually call them, are more likely to know people that we do not and thus receive more novel information. This is partly because close friends are more similar to us than are acquaintances and partly because they spend more time with us. By moving in different circles from our own, acquaintances are our windows on a wider world than our closest friends could reveal. Thus, when we need a new job, a scarce service, or some vital bit of information for an investment or project, they may be a better bet, even though our closer friends have more motivation to help. Social structure may dominate motivation. This is what I have called "the strength of weak ties" (Granovetter 1973, 1983).

At a more macro level of analysis, note that if each person's close friends know one another, they form a clique, and cliques are connected to one another, if at all, through weak rather than strong ties. The configuration and social location of weak ties therefore may be a central determinant of how information diffuses in large social structures. This may be one reason, for example, why high-tech regions with substantial job mobility diffuse cutting-edge technical information more effectively than those with more self-contained, vertically integrated firms (cf. Saxenian 1994; Castilla et al. 2000; Ferrary and Granovetter 2009).

3. **Structural holes.** Individuals with ties into multiple networks that are largely separated from one another may enjoy strategic advantage. When

such individuals are the only route by which resources or information can flow from one part of a network to another, they have the potential to exploit the "structural hole" in the networks that they sit astride (Burt 1992). Individuals in this situation can be effective brokers and thereby enjoy substantial "social capital" (cf. Burt 2005). I discuss in more detail the advantages of brokers as part of a larger treatment of the relation between social networks and power in Chapter 4.

These and other network principles are useful tools in talking about "network embeddedness." Economic action and outcomes, like all social action and outcomes, are affected by actors' social relations to others and also by the structure of the overall network of those relations. As a shorthand, I will refer to these respectively as the *relational* and the *structural* aspects of network embeddedness.

By *relational embeddedness* I mean the nature of relations that individuals have with specific other individuals. This concept is about pairs or, as sociologists like to say, "dyads." Relational embeddedness has typically quite direct effects on individual economic action. How a worker and supervisor interact is determined not only by the meaning of these categories in a technical division of labor but also by their particular personal relationship, which is determined largely by a history of interactions. This is partially captured by economists' use of interdependent utility functions, where the utility of another becomes an argument of your own utility function; in plainer language, their welfare becomes part of your own. But this does not really capture the fact that our behavior toward others depends on a structure of mutual expectations that has become a constitutive part of the relationship and, for strong ties, of the actors' own identity.

Not only particular dyadic relations may affect your behavior but also the aggregated impact of all such relations. The mere fact of attachment to others may modify economic action. Thus, you may want to stay in a certain firm despite economic advantages available elsewhere because you are attached to so many fellow workers. And the noneconomic value of such attachments partly explains the tendency of employers to recruit from among those employees know, even in the absence of purely economic advantages to doing so.

Some economists have emphasized certain elements of relational embeddedness, as when Harvey Leibenstein (1976) or Gary Becker (1976) emphasizes the norms and interests entailed in the roles that pairs of individuals may enact, such as husband and wife or employee and supervisor. This emphasis appears to soften the focus of economics on methodological individualism. But because the behavior of such pairs is abstracted away from their particular personal history and the way that history is embedded in larger networks, I suggest that atomization has not been avoided but merely transferred to a slightly higher level of analysis, the dyad, which is still seen as unaffected by influences broader than that of internalized, prescribed roles. Here we see again the use of an oversocialized conception—people behaving entirely in accord with role prescriptions—to implement what is in effect an atomized and undersocialized view of action.

By *structural embeddedness* I mean the impact of the overall structure of the network that individuals are embedded in. Compared to relational embeddedness, structural embeddedness has typically more subtle and less direct effects on economic action. So, a worker can more easily maintain a good relationship with a supervisor who has good relations with most other workers as well. If the supervisor is at odds with the others, and especially if those others are friendly with one another, they will make life very difficult for the one worker who is close to the supervisor; pressures will be strong to edge away from this closeness. If the other workers do not form a cohesive group, such pressures can be mounted only with difficulty.

In saying this I draw on the principle that to the extent that a pair's mutual contacts are connected to one another, there is more efficient information spread about what members of the pair are doing and thus better ability to shape that behavior. Thus, in this situation of high network density, a worker absorbs norms from the group that would make a close relationship with the supervisor literally unthinkable.

Structural embeddedness also affects the behavior of individuals by its impact on what information is available when decisions are made. Thus, whether you leave your job depends not only on your social attachments but also whether information on alternative opportunities comes to you. Whether you buy a certain brand of soap can be determined in part by the structure of your social network and the information and influences that reach you through it (Katz and Lazarsfeld 1955). Whether workers believe that their wages are fair depends on how they construct their comparison group, a matter that depends not only on their position in a technical division of labor but also in noneconomically determined social networks that cut across workplaces (see Gartrell 1982), such as those of kinship or residential proximity. This is a good example of how economic and noneconomic institutions intersect, with consequences for both, which is the subject of Chapter 6.

At a different level of analysis from relational and structural embeddedness but also exceptionally important is *temporal embeddedness.* This is the opposite of temporal reductionism, which treats relations and structures of relations as if they had no history that shapes the present situation. In ongoing relations, human beings do not start fresh each day but carry the baggage of previous interactions into each new one. Built into human cognitive equipment is a remarkable capacity, depressingly little studied, to file away the details and the emotional tone of past relations for long periods of time, so that even when one has not had dealings with a certain person for years, a reactivation of the relationship does not start from scratch but from some set of previously attained common understandings and feelings. This refers back to the previous discussion of path dependence and extends its purview to the history of social networks.

Structures of relations typically result from processes over time and can rarely be understood otherwise. Thus, talking about strikes in factories with large numbers of rural and "guest workers," such as German automobile plants, Sabel notes that "strikes by peasant workers . . . usually remain episodes, isolated from the rest of the life of the factory and further isolating the peasant workers themselves from other workers. Still, . . . they bring some few peasant workers into contact with the outside society in the person of a union militant, a sympathetic native worker, or a representative of management. . . . To the extent that some of these contacts endure, they can shape the course of later conflict" (1982: 136). By tracing out such relations, Sabel is able to make a new interpretation of the turbulent industrial relations in 1970s Italy (1982, Ch. 4). A good cross-sectional account might notice the importance of these contacts as liaisons between the two groups but would be unable to contribute to any general argument about the circumstances under which such a structure arose. Without such an account, analysts slip into cultural or functionalist explanations, both of which usually make their appearance when historical dynamics have been neglected. This particular case also sheds light on some of the debates on trust that I analyze in Chapter 3, since it displays trust as emerging from a sequence of events rather than as a fixed trait inculcated by families or culture, as in some recent economic arguments.

1.6 A Vocabulary of Individual Motives

To find a viable path between an account based entirely on individual interests and one that presumes those interests always subordinated to some larger social entity requires further discussion of individual motives. I suggest three important distinctions regarding such motives: Behavior may be instrumentally rational or not, it may be ego-oriented or not, and it may be economically or socially oriented.

The first of these distinctions involves whether behavior can be well described as a use of means to achieve specified ends. The issue is sometimes framed as instrumental versus consummatory behavior, the latter being action pursued for its own sake rather than in order to accomplish something else. Such pursuit may range from simple hedonism to the purest of value commitments but is distinctive in not entailing explicit or implicit calculation of *consequences* of an action. Social theory gives short shrift to this kind of action, which is often headlong and thoughtless. One case is what Max Weber calls "value-rational" action: "Examples . . . would be the actions of persons who, regardless of possible cost to themselves, act to put into practice their convictions of what seems to them to be required by duty, honor, the pursuit of beauty, a religious call, personal loyalty, or the importance of some 'cause' no matter in what it consists . . . value-rational action always involves 'commands' or 'demands' which, in the actor's opinion, are binding on him." Such action is not rational in the usual instrumental sense because "the more unconditionally the actor devotes himself to this value for its own sake, to pure sentiment or beauty, to absolute goodness or devotion to duty, the less is he influenced by considerations of the consequences of his action" (Weber [1921] 1968: 25–26). Weber also distinguishes between this and another type of action not oriented to means and ends, namely "affectual" action, driven by the emotions. Some examples he offers are behavior that satisfies a "need for revenge, sensual gratification, devotion, contemplative bliss, or for working off emotional tensions" (25).

In the history of economic thought, the distinction between instrumental and noninstrumental action has sometimes been confused with whether behavior was oriented to economic or other aspects of action—a strange proposition once examined, since rational action for noneconomic goals and nonrational approaches to the economy seem common enough. Albert Hirschman (1977) has traced, for example, over several centuries, the distinction between the "passions" and the "interests," in which the latter, referring to economic motivations, came to be assumed the province of calm, rational, and benevolent behavior. Noneconomic motives were gradually subsumed to the category of "passions" with the accompanying assumption that their pursuit was not a matter of rational action and therefore not suitable for economic analysis. By the time of Adam Smith, this distinction was firmly fixed; it is so clear in the writing of Pareto that his economics and his sociology are separate, so that one could read one without paying attention to the other.[16] Influenced by Pareto, Paul Samuelson thus commented in his *Foundations of Economic Analysis* that "many economists would separate economics from sociology upon the basis of rational or irrational behavior" (1947: 90).[17] One kind of trouble that the equation of economic action with rational and gentlemanly behavior caused for economic argument is that it deflected attention away from the analysis of deception and fraud in the economy.

A second line of demarcation is whether action is "selfish" ("egocentric") or not. Some versions of rational choice theory discount the possibility of altruistic behavior by asserting that any action can be theorized as achieving some personal goal for the actor, whether or not she would agree. Sen (1977 refers to this circular argument as "definitional egoism." The issue for social theory, and in particular for economic theory, which Sen's well-known article addresses, is whether the circularity that forbids altruism is useful. Sen suggests it is not, since there are many important examples where people act contrary to their own interests in order to honor "commitments" that they have to some principle or value or the welfare of some social entity beyond themselves. To make behavior egoistic by definition forecloses the possibility of understanding these important cases. Sen's examples of "commitment," however, remain within an instrumental, means-end framework, as when he distinguishes between the egoistic motive of someone who acts to stop someone from being tortured because it makes him sick and another who stops the torture because he thinks it is wrong, even though such action may be dangerous and reduce his own utility. In both cases, however, there is an end in view (stopping the torture), and the actor is not depicted as pursuing a purely consummatory agenda.

A third distinction is less fundamental from the point of view of human motivation but very important for the discussion of this book, and that is whether an action pursues an economic purpose only, a social (i.e., noneconomic) purpose only, or a mixture of these. For the remainder of this chapter, I home in on this third distinction and its consequences. In Chapter 2, I will assess the second question of how action in the economy is affected by commitments—shared conceptions of what is proper, just, and fair, that transcend the pure pursuit of individual interests. The first question, about whether behavior is best conceived in a means-ends framework or not, is in a way the hardest of all to address and will come up from time to time in specific contexts, especially as I spell out some implications of a pragmatist epistemology.

In addition to economic motives, by which I mean the quest for wanted goods and services, people in all cultures seek, in varying degrees, the noneconomic goals of sociability, approval, status, and power, which are available only in a social context through networks of others. Given the importance of these social motives, people could hardly be expected to seek their economic goals in an arena utterly cut off from the chance to achieve social goals, as would be the case were economic life impersonal and atomized. It is thus common, as we will see in later chapters, for economic relations that begin in a neutral, impersonal way to develop noneconomic content as people try actively to prevent economic and noneconomic aspects of their lives from being separated. This progression was already clear to Emile Durkheim and is a central theme in his *Division of Labor in Society:* "Even where society rests wholly upon the division of labor, it does not resolve itself into a myriad of atoms juxtaposed together, between which only external and transitory contact can be established. The members are linked by ties that extend well beyond the very brief moment when the act of exchange is being accomplished" ([1893] 1984: 173).

I argue in subsequent chapters that many even purely economic goals are most efficiently achieved through contact with known others. But since many people seek economic goals at the same time as sociability, approval, status, and power, it is likely that they will prefer to channel their economic activity through networks of friends and acquaintances, where *all the goals can be simultaneously pursued.* Separating these goals would be not only inefficient but alienating. Especially for those who devote much of their life to economic pursuits, we could hardly expect them to segregate these from the noneconomic needs that so strongly shape human identity. Conversely, the fact that so much economic activity occurs in social networks of known others makes it more difficult for individuals to separate their economic from their noneconomic goals.

That people pursue economic and noneconomic goals simultaneously presents a daunting challenge for economic analysis that focuses only on one and for sociological analysis that focuses only on the other. Current social science theories of action offer little insight as to how individuals mix these goals. It is insufficient to characterize the challenge as one of calculating how individuals trade off the noneconomic for the economic outcomes. This may sometimes be apt, but it is highly misleading to presume that the rational economizing mode can be applied to all sets of motives, since some goals are experienced as incommensurable with others (see Ch. 5) and action is not always instrumentally oriented.

A simple case that illustrates some of these issues is the impact of labor market information flow through social networks. Some sociologists analyze this case by making instrumental arguments about how best to manage one's networks for economic advantage (cf. Boorman 1975 on investment in weak versus strong ties and Burt 1992 on the use of "structural holes"). But despite the value of such arguments, it is difficult to stay within a simple framework of instrumental rationality even in this apparently straightforward case. My empirical study (Granovetter 1995) shows that to imagine job information as always being the result of "investment" in contacts is profoundly misleading. One reason for this is that, as Peter Blau argues in discussing the limits of the concept of "social exchange," positive responses from other people (who are perhaps "investing" in you) are only experienced as rewarding insofar as the recipient does not think that they were *intended* as "rewards" (Blau 1964: 62–63). People want to be liked and admired. Insincere approval is better than none (as sycophants well know) but pales in comparison to approval without ulterior motive. As I have argued elsewhere, "though some 'investors' in social relations may achieve great skill in simulating sincerity, as shown by the success of 'confidence rackets,' the desire of recipients for true approval, and the vigilance of most in ferreting out its opposite, sharply bound the role of calculated instrumentality in social life" (Granovetter 2002: 37).

In the normal course of events, as opposed to the world of social theory, mixtures of motives between economic and social or between instrumental and consummatory activity are routine. For example, people often go to parties with nothing more in mind than having a good time, and yet information about jobs can and does pass among partygoers (Granovetter 1995). Labor markets and weekend socializing are separate institutions whose intersection does not depend only on the action of individuals. The dynamics of such intersections are an important topic to be considered in Chapter 6. How different institutions interpenetrate one another has a big impact on when people carry mixed and multiple motives into their social situations.

As this theme of institutional interpenetration suggests, that economic and noneconomic activity occur together and may be inextricable is of interest not only because it complexifies the explanation of individual behavior but also because it has consequences beyond the level of individuals. In particular, noneconomic activity affects the costs and the techniques available for economic activity. Economists have typically seen only the negative side of this equation. For example, a culture in which corrupt practices are common may impose high economic costs on the normal production of goods and services. Such a case is usually characterized pejoratively as "rent-seeking" (see esp. Krueger 1974). But the other side of the story is that economic costs are often reduced when actors pursue economic goals through noneconomic institutions and practices to whose costs they made little or no contribution. Thus, when employers recruit through social networks, they need not—and probably could not—pay to create the trust and obligations that motivate friends and relatives to help one another find the most suitable employment. This trust and obligation result from how a society patterns its institutions of kinship and friendship, and any economic efficiency gains that result are a typically unintended by-product of action pursued by individuals seeking sociability, approval, and status. By recruiting through networks, employers use their superior position of power to create a situation in which people's economic action and social action are intertwined. So it is misleading to suppose that such mixing of activities is purely the result of individuals' isolated and personal situations (cf. Granovetter and Tilly 1988).

I will revisit these themes in Chapter 2, 5, and 6 and in my sequel volume in my discussion of "corruption."

In the next chapters, I lay out some general principles and arguments about some of the most important conceptual tools, issues, and debates relevant to understanding the economy in its social setting. Chapter 2 develops some arguments about norms, moral economy and culture, and what the vigorous disputes about the role of these in the economy may tell us about analytic strategies. Chapter 3 builds on this discussion and reviews and comments on the voluminous literature on trust in the economy. Chapter 4 considers what place power plays in economic processes, and Chapters 5 and 6 put all these concepts into motion for the important cases where social institutions impinge upon and help to shape economic action. These chapters set the stage for the more detailed empirical chapters in my sequel volume, which try to show how the toolkit of ideas developed here can illuminate a wide range of actual cases.

2

The Impact of Mental Constructs
on Economic Action: Norms, Values,
and Moral Economy

2.1 Introduction

The following three chapters concern the significance for the economy, respectively, of mental concepts such as norms, of trust, and of power. These are deeply interdependent, and there is no obvious order in which they should be treated. Two common interpretations of all these is that they reflect rational action on the part of individuals or are rational in some larger and vaguer sense of resulting from a selective evolutionary process that has produced outcomes more favorable than others to economic efficiency. One thread that runs through these chapters is my profound skepticism that such accounts adequately explain norms, trust, or power and my attempt to develop more nuanced arguments. And I do believe that any understanding of the economy must come to grips with these important social forces, so that a more adequate account is sorely needed.

One thing that sets the discussion of social norms apart from the usual discourse about economic action is that they are difficult to describe fully in terms of people rationally choosing the best course of action from among those available so as to maximize underlying preferences. Instead, an adequate discussion of norms requires us to take seriously that people may have some conception of how things are, ought to be, or must be that supplants, overrides, or at least modifies action that would otherwise follow from self-interest alone. A fierce debate rages about the extent to which mental states matter as a cause of behavior and, if they do, whether these genies can be stuffed back into the rational choice bottle. While I will comment on this latter debate, it is less interesting to me than the more substantive question of what role norms play in economic action and outcomes. I also note that the usual concept of "self-interest" entails the assumption that individuals' goals or ends are well defined, so that "rational" action entails finding means that most efficiently realize them. The epistemology of pragmatism (and its intellectual descendants such as "constructivism") casts doubt on this simple means-ends schema, and I will explore the implications of the coevolution of means and ends in the course of action and problem-solving that these perspectives propose, which is not consistent with the usual paradigms of "rational action" (cf. Dewey 1939; Whitford 2002).

Since norms and values are quintessentially mental concepts that involve individuals' subjective understanding of the meaning and significance of economic situations, to the extent they really matter in the economy, purely behaviorist methods and assumptions become more difficult to defend. Even if we agreed that norms evolved in the service of economic efficiency, we could still not imagine that they would have much effect except insofar as people subjectively believed in their importance and therefore were disposed to follow and enforce them against violation.

I use typical rough distinctions among the concepts. "Norms" are principles people acknowledge, and sometimes follow, about the proper, appropriate, or "moral" way to conduct themselves, and these are socially shared and enforced informally by others. "Values" are broader concepts about what the good life and good society consist of, from which the more specific and situationally oriented norms may, in principle, be inferred. The term "moral economy" was coined by the historian E. P. Thompson (1971) and has since been widely used to mean the set of norms that specifically concern the economy—i.e., conceptions of what is morally appropriate economic behavior. The term "culture" signals, in part, that norms and values are not random across individuals but that groups may develop agreement about what these are as part of a broader consensus about how to view the world. Much of what is usually called "culture" is not necessarily about "norms" in the sense I have used it: a preference to eat with chopsticks is "cultural" but is not the "moral" thing to do. A variant use of "norm" to mean the typical practice in a population would include the use of chopsticks, but most such practices might better be described as "habits," which the pragmatists believed govern much of everyday behavior in a way that strikes actors as unproblematic and not oriented to well-defined goals (see, e.g., Dewey 1939: 33–39).

I explore here broad questions about norms in the economy: What are they? Why do people follow them? How do they interact with other causes of behavior? Where do they come from? What is their content, and is it predictable? How typically are norms economically efficient? How useful is the concept of "moral economy"? In Chapters 5 and 6, I explore the aggregation of norms into higher-level conceptions of action such as cultures, "schemata," "institutional logics," "modes of justification," "varieties of capitalism," and others.

2.2 What Are Economic Norms, and Why Do They Influence Economic Actors?

No one doubts that people have ideas of what is appropriate behavior in economic as well as other contexts. At issue is the extent to which we need to invoke such ideas in order to help explain economic action and outcomes and, secondarily, whether such invocation is consistent or not with rational choice and methodological individualism.

At one time in sociology and, to a lesser extent, anthropology, the distinction between values and norms occupied a prominent place in general theory. Graeber (2001: 4–5) notes that prominent Harvard anthropologist Clyde Kluckhohn strove in the 1940s and 1950s to make variation in values or value "orientations" among societies on central questions of human existence the core of anthropological theory. But he was not able to generate consensus on definitions or dimensions of value and consequently had few followers. In sociology, on the other hand, the immense influence of Talcott Parsons, at least in the United States, from the 1930s to the 1960s gave values and norms a privileged position in sociological theory.

Trying to establish a clear division of labor among economics, political science, and sociology, Parsons argued that political science concerned itself with the use of coercion in society, economics with the rational adaptation of means to ends, and sociology with the study of the ultimate values around which societies cohered. For Parsons, the key to understanding social systems was how a society's most general values were "articulated at successively lower levels, so that norms governing specific actions at the lowest level may be spelled out. Furthermore, all social action is regulated in terms of normative patterns . . ." (1959: 8).

By contrast, economists historically resisted norms and values as causal forces. Although this has changed dramatically in the past twenty-five years (for examples, see Chapter 3 on trust), many would likely still take the position of federal judge and law-and-economics scholar Richard Posner, who doubts that "many people do things because they think they are the right thing to do unless they have first used the plasticity of moral reasoning to align the 'right' with their self interest. I do not think that knowledge of what is morally right is motivational in any serious sense for anyone except a handful of saints" (1998: 560).

When norms *are* important in economic life, why do they influence people who conform to them? A spare rational choice account would be that people conform to norms when and only when the benefits of doing so outweigh the costs. The case against an argument this simple is well stated by Gerald Lynch with regard to formal law: "What society wants from its members . . . is not an intelligent calculation of the costs and benefits of abiding by its basic norms, but more or less unthinking obedience to them. To the extent people are specifically comparing the costs and benefits of breaking criminal laws, the battle is already lost; many . . . must conclude in particular situations that the calculus favors law-breaking" (1997: 46). Or, as Jon Elster more acidly notes, many people "would assent to the proposition that self-interest is the cement of society, until they reflect more closely on the implications. Acting according to self-interest means never telling the truth or keeping one's promise unless it pays to do so; stealing and cheating if one can get away with it . . . ; treating punishment merely as the price of crime, and other people merely as means to one's own satisfaction" (1989a: 263).

But if people conform to norms for reasons *beyond* cost and benefit, what are these reasons? At the most proximate level, it has been argued, especially by Elster (1989a, 1989b, 1990, 1999), that norms bind mainly through their effect on emotions: they are "sustained by the feelings of embarrassment, anxiety, guilt and shame that a person suffers at the prospect of violating them. A person obeying a norm may also be propelled by positive emotions, like anger and indignation" (1989b: 99–100). Social norms, Elster continues, "have a grip on the mind that is due to the strong emotions they can trigger" (100).[1] In later work, Elster shifts emphasis, to say that *one* emotion, shame, is a much more important determinant of conformity than the others: "the emotion of shame is not only a support of social norms, but the support" (1999: 145). Shame is so powerful because it is "triggered by the contemptuous or disgusted disapproval by others of something one has done" (149). It is an "internal, interaction-based emotion" (149).

While rational choice accounts of norm enforcement view sanctions upholding norms as rationally applied by "enforcers," Elster points out an intrinsic fallacy in this view when shame is the sanction: behavior of another that appears *intended* to induce shame is far less effective than the display of recoil that is spontaneous and involuntary. Shame is so devastating because it reflects disapproval of the person rather than the act: "In shame, one thinks of oneself as a bad person, not simply as someone who did a bad thing" (151), whereas guilt attaches to specific actions. The response to guilt is to "make repairs, to undo the bad one has caused. In addition there is often a strong urge to confess, preferably to the person one has harmed" (153), but in response to shame, you want to hide, run away, avoid being seen, and if one cannot run away, "suicide may be the only solution" (153). Elster thinks it is "generally agreed that the burning feeling of shame is more intensely painful than the pang of guilt. . . . Hence we often do everything we can to avoid the feeing of shame. . . . In contrast to guilt, we cannot easily avoid shame by self-deceptive maneuvers" (154), and this is why guilt is less important than shame in the regulation of behavior.

But whether shame or guilt is more significant in conformity is surely arguable. Elster's view that guilt is more easily assuaged than shame may not be shared by members of religions and cultures that make an industry of guilt, and one can imagine Catholics and Jews the world over raising eyebrows in unison at his downplaying of its pain. In the mid-twentieth century, the "culture and personality" school of anthropology was strongly influenced by Ruth Benedict's distinction between societies mainly regulated by shame and those by guilt, developed in her wartime account of Japan, *The Chrysanthemum and the Sword* (1946). And while her sweeping characterization of entire cultures would rarely be endorsed by twenty-first-century scholars (see the interesting account in Hendry 1996 of how Benedict's work on Japan was received), it is hard to imagine that cultures do not vary systematically, in ways that have yet to be well charted, in the relationships between social control and human emotion.

I note also that Elster's focus on the importance of emotions as supports for norms maps onto more recent work in "moral psychology" that documents, in part with brain scans (such as fMRIs), that two separate processes seem to be activated in the course of moral decision-making: one is automatic, unconscious, and emotion-based and the other slower, more conscious, and based on consideration of alternate outcomes. These can be associated with what moral philosophers denote as "deontological" (i.e., absolute, unconditional) moral principles as opposed to "consequentialist" behavior (i.e., moral decisions based on expected outcomes). (For a nuanced account, see Cushman, Young, and Greene 2010; a less balanced account arguing that the fast, emotional process is overwhelmingly dominant is Haidt and Kesebir 2010. Kahneman 2011 provides a popularized narrative, and Vaisey 2009 attempts a translation of these concepts into sociological language and argument. The distinction in moral philosophy between deontological and consequentialist views is summarized by Pettit 2001.

Adherence to norms so as to avoid shame or guilt is a negative motivation. Elster suggests, as noted above, that some are also motivated by "positive" emotions like anger and indignation. But these do not strike me as tipping the positive side of the emotional scale very far, if at all. It seems likely that some norms are pursued because of even more positive commitments to principles deeply and passionately held, as is visible during mass protests against the alleged affects of globalization on the conditions of labor and the distribution of income and in many other historical circumstances, as I discuss further below in considering "moral economy."

One reason emotions are important in explaining the force of norms is that people often do not experience norms as external injunctions but rather have "internalized" and follow them more or less automatically, without calculation of costs and benefits. In this case, social norms are "non-outcome oriented" (Elster 1989b: 100); they are simply injunctions to act a certain way that are to some extent followed unreflectively, as in the "fast" responses noted by moral psychology experiments, where norms appear deontological.

One might think this would remove norms from the circuit of rational choice argument, but some law and economics theorists such as Cooter (2000) argue that people internalize certain economic norms, such as those disposing them to be trustworthy, in order to create more opportunities to engage cooperatively with others in the future. Since a conscious effort to internalize norms would seem a contradiction in terms, a crucial question has to be by what mechanism this could be accomplished. Cooter acknowledges that changing ourselves, in the way that following a new norm would require, "is a difficult technical problem, and I will not offer a theory to solve it. . . . Instead, I assume the existence of a technology for preference change without explaining it. In other words, I assume that people can change their preferences at some cost" (2000: 1593). As if to underline the wishful-thinking aspect of this proposal, Cooter continues: "The dependence of opportunities on preferences gives a person an incentive to change his preferences. If a dishonest youth wants more opportunities for employment, for example, he might become honest" (1594). I would suggest that a more persuasive argument than this will be needed before internalized norms, driven by emotion, can be thought to have been subsumed to a rational choice argument.

If we accept the importance of emotions in the understanding of norms, we have only come part of the way. For while the psychology of emotions is an important part of fuller explanation of norms at the level of individuals, we need to move up in a more macro direction to understand better why some social situations *elicit* the strong emotional responses that they do. Experiments in moral psychology pose moral dilemmas to subjects that are designed to elicit responses indicating either automatic or conscious processes in making a decision, but there is no social component or background to these experiments (see, e.g., Cushman et al. 2010). In many natural situations, however, it is less the nature of a moral dilemma than the reactions of others who observe what we have done that causes us embarrassment, regret, shame, or guilt. For this to matter, we have to *care* what those particular people think. The disapproval or contempt of strangers is sometimes worrisome and upsetting but likely has far less impact than that of people who know us personally and to whom we have some social tie.

This means that to understand the force of norms requires us to consider what sets of people provide feedback or examples that one is sensitive to. In mid-twentieth-century sociology, this question came under the heading of "reference group" theory (see esp. Merton 1957, Chs. 8, 9), one of whose main conclusions was that it was far from straightforward which sets of people constituted such groups and that this depended on a variety of sometimes complex circumstances. One of Robert K. Merton's main points was that individuals were responsive not only to the norms articulated in their own primary, small, close-knit group but also to those in groups of which they were *not* members but aspired to join.

This is one of several reasons to be skeptical about the reduction of reference groups to close-knit groups in local communities. For example, Cook and Hardin argue that "norms work best for smaller groups or communities with long-standing relationships" (2001: 327) and go on to say that the small community "commonly works through norms that are quasi-universal for the community and that cover virtually all aspects of potential cooperativeness. The urban society works through networks of ongoing relationships . . . so that we are each involved in many quite different networks" (334). Law-and-economics scholar Robert Ellickson similarly proposes that increasing urbanization, among other forces, weakens the informal control system (by which he means the force of norms) and expands the domain of law (1991: 284).

But while it is reasonable to argue, as I do also in Chapter 1 (and in Granovetter 2005), that the enforcement of norms is more effective the more cohesive or close-knit the network, it does not follow that such networks in a complex society must be locally defined. Studies of the spatial aspect of people's social lives have long noted that the social networks that provide guidance and support are increasingly spatially dispersed (see, e.g., Wellman 1979). In economic life, as Durkheim (1893) pointed out, there are what we might now call "communities of practice" in societies with substantial division of labor that are defined not by spatial proximity but by common activities. Of these, he argued that occupations were the most important and that they played a vital role in ensuring societal solidarity in the face of the centrifugal tendencies inherent in a highly differentiated economy. Recent studies (e.g., Grusky and Sorensen 1998) provide modern statistical power for the claim that occupations have some coherence as communities.

Modern studies of the professions correspondingly note the universality of codes of ethics created by professional societies (see esp. Abbott 1983).

While these are more formal than social norms, they do not have the binding force of legislation. Yet they do establish general understandings within a professional community as to what standards of behavior should be met, and while these standards may sometimes be violated with impunity, their clear statement still impacts daily practice. (For a more general treatment of the history of "business ethics" in the United States, see Abend 2014). Geographic dispersion of business executives with common identities and loyalties may, as with professions, be mediated by organizational arrangements. In Japanese *keiretsu*, for example, geographically scattered affiliated companies in a group such as Mitsubishi feel bound by norms of reciprocity that are energized periodically by meetings of company presidents and various rituals and symbols that reinforce group identity, despite its lack of legal standing (cf. Gerlach 1992; Lincoln and Gerlach 2004). The general argument would be that to understand the force of norms requires us to chart the contours of social solidarities and networks within which such force operates, often a nontrivial effort that cannot be confined to small, local settings and certainly not reduced to value questions on national surveys.

If norms do impact economic behavior, a natural question is how they interact with non-normative forces like self-interest. Perhaps the central issue is whether norms and their force are somehow reducible to some other determinant of behavior or, instead, operate independently. Elster suggests that actions "typically are influenced both by rationality and by norms. Sometimes the outcome is a compromise between what the norm prescribes and what rationality dictates" (1989b: 102). Or, in his geometric metaphor, "Often, norms and rationality coexist in a parallelogram of forces that jointly determine behavior" (1990: 866).

The mechanism by which norms and rationality interact is a major theoretical issue. The simplest resolution is to grant the independent force of norms but reduce that force to a "shift parameter" as Williamson calls it, changing the cost of alternatives (1991). Similar proposals appear in the burgeoning law and economics literature on norms. Thus, Cooter proposes to measure the strength of an internalized norm by how much someone will pay in order to conform to it (2000: 1586), and Sunstein suggests that norms are "taxes on or subsidies to action" (1996: 912). This assumes that norms enter the chain of causation in a linear, additive way. Aside from the complexities of understanding the determinants of such cost parameters, there are reasons to question whether simple additive models capture the influence of norms. Insofar as they reflect the impact of emotions, this reduction of their force to cost-benefit analysis may be worrisomely oversimplified and unlikely to be consistent with recently dominant dual-process models of moral action in psychology. Elster comments (in his mild-mannered way) that the idea of "modeling emotions as psychic costs and benefits is jejune and superficial. The fact that emotion can cloud thinking to the detriment of an agent's interests is enough to refute this idea" (2000: 692).

The role of emotions in underpinning values that are deontological rather than based on consequences is a major theme in recent experimental and neural moral psychology, and this is precisely the point also of scholars of conflicts involving "sacred values." So Atran and Axelrod (2008), focusing on conflict in the Middle East, make a strong case that negotiators who conceive such values in terms of cost-benefit trade-offs badly misunderstand combatants and are highly unlikely to succeed in their negotiations. They observe that "sacred values" "differ from material or instrumental values in that they incorporate moral beliefs that drive action in ways that seem dissociated from prospects for success" (2008: 222) and that "offering to provide material benefits in exchange for giving up a sacred value actually makes settlement more difficult because people see the offering as an insult rather than a compromise" (2008: 223). See also Gladwell (2014), who attributes the Waco, Texas, Branch Davidian disaster to a similar misunderstanding on the part of FBI negotiators.

2.3 The Origin, Content, and Efficiency of Norms

If we agree that norms affect economic action, we would like to know where they come from and whether they improve "economic efficiency." How economic or other norms arise is a question that has not always been asked. Most discourse on the economy takes norms as a cultural given and a starting point for further analysis. There has long, however, been discussion of the origins of certain noneconomic norms, such as the "incest taboo," which appears to be universal.[2] Much of that discussion, which prefigures that of economic norms, concerns whether there is a functional explanation for this norm, some way it makes human society more stable or successful than it would be in its absence. A subsidiary question is whether, if functional, this norm results from biological, cultural, or social evolution in the usual sense of emerging from variation, selection, and retention.

Because few if any *economic* norms are as universal as the incest taboo, long-term macro-social evolutionary discussion of norms is less common. A recent exception emerges from an experimental study of fifteen small-scale societies in which several game protocols were administered in order to determine whether results would vary from those obtained in industrialized settings.[3] All the experiments concern instances of cooperation beyond that dictated by rational self-interest—a typical experimental finding as I will discuss in Chapter 3 on trust. Following Henrich et al. (2005), I discuss mainly results from the "Ultimatum Game," or UG. In this two-person game, the first player, A, is given some endowment and instructed to offer some of it to player B, who may then accept or reject the offer; if he accepts, the allocation is final, but if he rejects, then neither player gets *anything*. A rational player A should offer some very small amount, which a rational B should accept, as it is better than nothing. But, in fact, most experimental evidence shows that A's typically offer considerably more than a minimum and B's often reject offers less than 50 percent. Among student populations in various industrialized countries, modal offers have hovered around 50 percent (Henrich et al. 2005: 799). I find it hard to escape the conclusion that players B hold some normative conception of a proper or fair division, with sufficient strength that they would rather forego any resources than allow its violation, and that A's either share this norm or are at least sufficiently aware of it to know better than to make a low offer.[4]

These results have been highly consistent across the industrialized societies where the UG has been played, but the authors found much more variation across their fifteen societies, with mean offers from A ranging from 26 to 58 percent, though the "selfishness axiom was violated in some way in every society we studied" (802). This variation suggested taking the societies themselves as units of analysis, using multivariate statistics, where societal characteristics are the independent and offer and rejection percentages the dependent variables. It turns out that about half the variance in outcomes is explained by the extent of market exchange, settlement size, "socio-political complexity" (a measure of how much decision-making occurs beyond the household), and the extent to which the society's economic system rewards cooperation (measured by the presence of extrafamilial cooperative institutions). The authors interpret this result with "culture-gene coevolutionary theory"—which "predicts that humans should be equipped with learning mechanisms designed to accurately and efficiently acquire the motivations and preferences applicable to the local set of culturally evolved social equilibria (institutions)" (812). This assumes that individuals in experiments "bring the preferences and beliefs that they have acquired in the real world into the decision-making situation" (813) and that these result from experience over time in the society. For example, extensive "market interactions may accustom individuals to the idea that strangers can be trusted (i.e., expected to cooperate). This idea is consistent with the fact that UG offers and the degree of market integration are strongly correlated across our groups" (813).

How should we evaluate these claims? Certainly, the impressive correlations between some independent measures of economic organization and game responses are of interest. But taken at face value, the authors' interpretation of these results implies that societies always and necessarily get the economic norms and institutions they need. The idea that market interactions accustom individuals to cooperate with strangers sweeps blithely past centuries of debate on interpersonal and group conflict and sometime turmoil resulting from the introduction of market processes. It is strongly reminiscent of the seventeenth-century idea that the market is invariably a civilizing force, represented as "doux commerce" in Montesquieu, and chronicled by Albert Hirschman in *The Passions and the Interests* (1977). Logically pursued, this leads to the dubious claim that there have been no failed or failing economies, or at least none where inappropriate norms or institutions were implicated. This claim can hardly be defended once stated, so where do the problems lie?

First, the experiments all concern the norms of distribution and the cooperative tendencies of individuals. And while it is interesting to get hard evidence that these vary among societies (there was already substantial ethnographic evidence of such variation—for some details, see Granovetter 1992), in most cases we have little clear way of connecting the norms apparent in experiments to actual economic practice. As critics note, "the intuitive and experimental simplicity of the UG, which is probably responsible in part for its popularity among experimental economists, may make it difficult to relate to real-world phenomena" (Grace and Kemp 2005: 825). The actual guidance actors require in real economic situations is far more complex and detailed than what can be inferred from the norms that operate in games like the UG.

Moreover, and perhaps even more critically, *no single economic norm is isolated from other norms,* and each evolves in a larger cultural and economic context as part of a complex of norms that only *taken together* can be seen as exerting a significant influence. Norms about fairness of distribution, for example, may be important in many contexts, but what their actual role in a real economic system is depends heavily on what other institutions and norms provide their context. Thus, norms of reciprocity, as I will discuss in my sequel volume in a chapter on corruption (and see also Granovetter 2007), may specify a fair return to another that is, however, widely condemned as "corrupt" in groups outside that which a pair of actors refers itself to. Evidence on a single norm, in the absence of reference group detail about how groups are defined and intersect, may be suggestive but hardly conclusive.

Finally, the evolutionary or coevolutionary argument offered here is historical speculation, derived from suggestive cross-sectional contemporary data. As such, it suffers from all the difficulties identified by Gould and Lewontin (1979) in their strictures against Panglossian theorizing. Evolutionary game theory has at times also been used as a framework to investigate the emergence of norms. One example is Bendor and Swistak 2001, whose model suggests that that in the long run, dynamics tend toward more efficient norms but that some non-Pareto-efficient norms are evolutionarily stable (1497–1498). This model, however, depends on small groups or even dyads being the primary locus of interaction, and so the authors concede that such a model works best for small communities.

Empirical and theoretical work in law and economics has focused on more specific contexts and norms. Much of the recent wave of interest in norms was sparked by Ellickson's 1991 study of how disputes are resolved in Shasta County, California, between cattle ranchers and other residents. Ellickson chose his setting in part because a famous contribution to the law and economics literature by Ronald Coase (1960) used such a conflict as its main example. Coase's argument concerned the implications of a shift in legal liability between parties, but he assumed in either case that the parties would settle a dispute through litigation. Ellickson was thus surprised to find that Shasta County residents "apply informal norms, rather than formal legal rules, to resolve most of the issues that arise among them" (1991: 1). Though this finding exactly paralleled Macaulay's earlier study of business disputes (1963), Ellickson's discussion was more influential because unlike Macaulay, he provided an interpretation congenial to those whose study of law is rooted in neoclassical economic theory.

His central hypothesis is that "members of a close-knit group develop and maintain norms whose content serves to maximize the aggregate welfare that members obtain in their workaday affairs with one another" (Ellickson 1991: 167). To be more (but perhaps still not sufficiently) exact, this means that they want to minimize the sum of "deadweight losses" (those losses that arise from failure to cooperate) and transaction costs. "Workaday affairs" are defined as "ordinary matters conducted on the stage that the ground rules have set" (176). A group is "close-knit" when "informal power is broadly dis-tributed among group members and the information pertinent to informal control circulates easily among them" (177–178).[5] In effect, Ellickson treats close-knit groups as the locus of repeated games, and such a group is a "social network whose members have credible and reciprocal prospects for the appli-cation of power against one another and a good supply of information on past and present internal events" (181). To the extent any of these conditions is not met, this is a "social imperfection" analogous to market imperfections.

Ellickson ties the efficiency of norms to their origins because he sees norms as emerging in order to solve problems. But this conclusion follows too easily from the selection bias that begins with problems and inquires what, if any, norms arise to solve them. The efficiency conclusion is reinforced because in his main case, disputes over cattle in Shasta County are known to have been resolved. Had he begun with a case of internecine warfare over the intrusions of cattle into farmland, a different conclusion might have emerged.

Moreover, Elster notes a number of norms, some of which are clearly about "workaday matters," that are inefficient not only in some weak sense of Pareto optimality but in the stronger sense that they make everyone worse off—e.g., norms of etiquette (which require substantial expenditures of time and energy to get things "right")—and, in the economic sphere, norms against the use of money in situations where it would create Pareto improvements—e.g., buying a better place in a bus queue or charging a neighbor money to mow his lawn (Elster 1989b: 109–110). Codes of honor and norms of revenge, commonly invoked in some societies upon provocations little more serious than animal trespass, typically lead to escalation rather than the amicable settling of disputes (see, e.g., Elster 1990).

Among the serious difficulties with the idea that functional norms generally emerge in close-knit groups is the absence of a mechanism. In work subsequent to the Shasta County study, Ellickson tries to fill this gap and make the emergence of norms endogenous to a rational, economic process by proposing the importance of a "market for norms," where the supply side consists of "change agents" who are "norm entrepreneurs" and the demand side is the social group in need of new norms, the "audience," which can "compensate worthy suppliers of new norms by conferring esteem or trading opportunities upon them" (Ellickson 2001: 37) If there are such entrepreneurs, why would they be successful? To complete the mechanism proposed requires that we understand why people comply with old or new norms and why anyone is willing to impose the social sanctions necessary for norms to have any force. In the law and economics literature, a number of answers have been offered to these questions. The argument of McAdams (1997) depends on people's need for "esteem": norms arise "because people seek the esteem of others"—i.e., their 'good opinion or respect'" (355) and conform to norms in order to receive it. McAdams addresses the problem of why anyone would go to the trouble of enforcing a norm by assuming that a "key feature of esteem is that individuals do not always bear a cost by granting different levels of esteem to others," as this means that esteem sanctions are "not necessarily subject to the second-order collective action problem [i.e., free riding among potential norm enforcers] that makes the explanation of norms difficult" (365).

But it is implausible that it can be costless to express approval or disapproval of others, and I find prima facie validity in Elster's contrary argument that "expressing disapproval is always costly. . . . At the very least it requires energy and attention that might be used for other purposes. One may alienate or provoke the target individual, at some cost or risk to oneself" (Elster 1989a: 133).[6] A different view of what rewards those who obey or enforce norms is suggested by E. Posner, who proposes that people do so because of their interest in signaling to all who observe their action that they are "desirable partners in cooperative endeavors. . . . People who care about future payoffs not only resist the temptation to cheat in a relationship; they signal their ability to resist the temptation to cheat by conforming to styles of dress, speech, conduct and discrimination. The resulting behavioral regulari-ties . . . I describe as 'social norms' . . ." (2000: 5). In effect, Posner reduces all adherence and enforcement of social norms to a desire to enhance one's rep-utation in order to secure future cooperative interaction. This rather spartan view of norms and their force seems too austere for the real world we inhabit, and indeed, Posner notes the "recurrent objection" to this theory that norma-tive behavior also entails the impact of "instincts, passions, and deeply ingrained cultural attitudes," but he responds that while cognition and emo-tion are not irrelevant, they are "just not well enough understood by psychol-ogists to support a theory of social norms, and repeated but puzzled acknowl-edgements of their importance would muddy the exposition . . . without providing any offsetting benefits" (2000: 46).

This pragmatic view of theory might be reasonable if we were setting aside minor causal factors, but insofar as cognition, emotion, and other social factors are central determinants of norms, as suggested by Elster and by most recent literature in "moral psychology," it is an invitation to settle for a dra-matically inadequate explanation because it is so hard to do better. This does not seem a good recipe for scientific progress. To give just one example, Posner comments on the important (but neglected) topic of when consumers judge a merchant to be "price gouging": "sometimes prices do reflect confor-mity to social norms. A business might keep prices for kerosene down after a hurricane, even though this would result in a shortage, because it fears that customers would infer from a high price that the business is an opportunist, a bad type, which cannot be trusted even under ordinary circumstances, when it makes representations about the quality of its products" (2000: 26).

Now this signaling argument (cf. Spence 1974) is reasonable up to a point but gives a highly misleading view of the state of mind of those reeling from a hurricane, who desperately need fuel for light and heat. Such individ-uals will object to a rise in prices to accommodate the new equilibrium resulting from huge demand increases in the face of fixed supply, not only because of their cool judgment that this reflects badly on the likely ordinary behavior and credibility of the merchant but more importantly because of anger ignited by principles they hold about the moral responsibilities of economic actors. A typical such principle is that in times of natural calamity, the community should pull together, and no member should profit from the misery of others. Merchants who hold the line on prices may well be motivated by fear of consumer anger, but they may also subscribe to the norm cited. I will say more about this below under the heading of "moral economy" and suggest some systematic theoretical arguments on the subject.

The weakness of arguments about mechanisms that lead to following or enforcing norms also weakens the case that norms result from a market process. Further assumptions in Ellickson's argument may also give pause, especially the idea that participants in the "market for norms" have a "utilitarian bias"—i.e., they will support a norm change if it meets the Kaldor-Hicks efficiency criterion, even weaker than Pareto superiority. (A change is Kaldor-Hicks efficient if it is better for the group in aggregate, even though detrimental to some, provided that those who gain become sufficiently better off that they could compensate losers in such a way that all would gain. Because of the obvious objection that gainers may feel no incentive to provide such compensation, this has been at best a controversial criterion in welfare economics.)

Ellickson does qualify in significant ways his proposal that norms emerge efficiently. He notes that it is costly to displace norms already internalized (2001: 56) and that high transaction costs may slow the process or result in "inefficient" norms (2001: 54). In fact, most analysts who study norms stipulate that harmful or inefficient norms are possible. Elster, as noted above, mentions a variety of such norms. E. Posner (1996) notes a number of different reasons why norms that are inefficient may develop. One is that norms often have a strong emotional valence, so that, as in the case of dueling norms, they might last long after they cease to be efficient (1738).

McAdams, whose argument is that norms are supported by the need for esteem by others, suggests that this implies some norms will be inefficient. This is because the reasons people give or get esteem do not necessarily relate to economic efficiency or the solution to collective action problems. So norms may arise that reward conspicuous consumption, and these may lead to wasteful escalation of consumption so that people can keep their relative status (McAdams 1997: 413; this argument was first made by Thorstein Veblen in his 1899 *The Theory of the Leisure Class* and greatly elaborated by Frank 1985). Esteem may be more scarce for minority members of a group, leading to situations in which majorities impose exclusionary norms against them. McAdams uses the example of interracial dating (415), but the same logic would apply to racially integrated workplaces or service establishments.

In an observation similar to that I made in discussing explanations of cross-societal variation in Ultimatum Game outcomes, E. Posner notes that whether a norm is inefficient "cannot be determined in isolation; the norm must be analyzed in connection with related norms." Suppose, for example, that there is a norm of honor. It may well be related to other norms, such as one that favors self-help over cooperation and another against government interference. So there may be a network of norms, and it may be hard to identify "the" inefficient norm or the best entry point to such a discussion (1996: 1727). Eggertsson offers an interesting example, noting that over many generations in Iceland, strongly held norms of cooperation and sharing discouraged farmers from storing hay; instead, any surplus was shared with other farmers, leading to livestock starving in lean years. Yet farmers resisted many attempts over the centuries by government to impose storage (2001: 89–92). Eggertsson explains this inefficiency by noting that the norm of sharing hay was part of a more general norm of sharing. This norm, he suggests, "which supported the country's system of social security and made possible the sharing of food and housing for the human population, could not be truncated to exclude the sharing of animal fodder. Sharing of hay may have been inefficient, but human psychology excludes segmentation of closely related values" (90).

Insofar as evolutionary reasoning applies at all to norms, this example points to the danger of isolating a single element from a complex that has evolved over a long period. Evolutionary biologists speak of *pleiotropy*, situations where a single gene affects the phenotype of an organism in a variety of different ways. In such a case, the reason the gene has been selected may not be easily inferred from some of the visible outcomes, leading to incorrect "adaptive stories." Gould and Lewontin comment that when the "form of the part is a correlated consequence of selection directed elsewhere," we come "face to face with organisms as integrated wholes, fundamentally not decomposable into independent and separately optimized parts" (1979: 591; and see related comments by Elster 1989a: 149).

In complex social structures, the most important observation on the "efficiency" of norms has to do with where in social networks norms originate and for whom they are beneficial. It is a general theme in the literature on norms that they are most easily created in small, cohesive networks. Ellickson, who in general believes that norms are adaptive, notes that even he worries that "the norm-making process may go wrong when the members of a group are not closely knit" (1998: 550). But he and others also note that there are certain ways norm-making can go wrong even when, or perhaps especially when, they are generated within a cohesive network, and the most important of these is that of "externalities"—i.e., producing good results for the group that has generated the norm at the expense of others outside the group. So for example, Ellickson describes norms among whalers and argues for the efficiency of these norms but then concedes that perhaps they were so efficient that they encouraged overfishing—which harmed the community in general, countries not yet active in whaling, and also future whalers from currently active locations. Though a quota system would have reduced this problem, he notes that this would unlikely be adopted through informal social control but only through centralized authority (Ellickson 1991: 206). E. Posner points to a variety of norms that support activities harmful to outside groups, such as criminal activity, aristocratic exclusion, and cartels, and comments that groups "have a stronger incentive to adopt or develop norms that externalize costs than those that merely maximize joint welfare without producing negative externalities. Therefore, one should be wary about assuming that group norms are efficient" (1996: 1723). And as I will note in my sequel volume, many groups develop internal norms of loyalty that disadvantage other groups, which refer to this situation as "corruption" (see also Granovetter 2007).

But I also note that the opposite may occur—that group norms may have *positive* externalities while harming the group itself. An example is Burawoy's observation, in *Manufacturing Consent* (1979), that machine tool workers in the shop where he did his research had a culture where the masculine virtue of high skill on the machines was the main status currency, which led to competition along this skill dimension; but this ultimately was of more help to the company than to the workers themselves, who, in his account, were in effect helping the company to exploit themselves.

Thus, to the extent relatively cohesive networks produce norms whose enactment entails externalities, we will not understand the consequences of these norms until we know how the connections of these networks to other groups determines the nature and direction of those externalities—which is a matter of structural, not only relational, embeddedness. When professional groups enact norms that limit entry, externalities affect their clientele (see, e.g., Collins 1980). Whalers' norms, like those of any cartel, affect the welfare of consumers as well as potential competitors. How norms affect overall welfare then depends on the contours of social networks and the distribution of conflicts of interest in a population. This is a far cry from the assumption that a straightforward dimension of economic efficiency controls the evolution of norms.

2.4 How Do We Know That Norms Matter?: The Problem of "Moral Economy"

Skeptics often ask how we can actually know that norms significantly impact economic action and pose self-interested behavior as a more parsimonious account of why people acted as they did. This critique becomes more plausible when proponents of the causal significance of norms offer as evidence situations in which actors behave in ways that self-interest would also have prescribed. Because their null hypothesis is that humans are social and thus oriented to social norms, these proponents consider this situation to support their argument. But those for whom rational action is the null hypothesis consider it more "parsimonious" and thus supported in this same case. If we distance ourselves from both of these null hypotheses and also have independent confirmation that individuals indeed subscribed to values and norms that would predict the behavior we have seen, then such a case does not really offer persuasive evidence for either argument. For this we need cases where predictions differ.

Experimental methods may help with this impasse. Consider the finding of Fehr and Gaechter (2000) that experimental subjects are more positive in response to friendly reciprocal actions, and more negative in response to unfriendly ones, than self-interest alone would prescribe. This appears to be evidence for a norm of reciprocity, but while Fehr and Gaechter do indeed cite the "normative power of reciprocity" (2000: 161) and argue in general that "the large majority of interactions in peoples' lives . . . are not regulated by explicit contracts but by informal social norms" (166–167), they do not actually ask experimental subjects what they believe about reciprocity; instead, they take a behaviorist view, referring to people who reciprocate in kind as "reciprocal types." Conversely, interesting survey data that tease out the principles people hold about what behavior is or is not morally appropriate in the economy (e.g., Kahneman, Knetsch, and Thaler, 1986a, 1986b) do not go on to investigate whether the individuals who hold these ideas actually put them into practice.

We can see the importance of these issues in the literature that has arisen in economic history and political science under the rubric of "moral economy," a phrase coined, as I note above, by English historian E. P. Thompson in his 1971 article on collective action among poor eighteenth-century villagers. By moral economy Thompson meant collective, shared understandings as to what minimum moral standards economic action must meet to avoid being condemned and opposed, sometimes by force. We might call this "ethno-political-philosophy," the folk version of principles that political philosophers debate, as to what constitutes the good society and what is the duty of citizens.

Economics textbooks sometimes convey the impression that such judgments have disappeared in the modern economy, because supply and demand have supplanted such medieval ideas as "just price," but there is ample evidence to the contrary. Behavioral economics has produced survey data on what kinds of price changes people consider fair. Kahneman et al. (1986a) suggest from their data that a key concept is the "reference transaction"—a price that market participants have come to consider typical. Thus, survey respondents express resistance on fairness grounds to changing the *prevailing* price or wage. They consider it unfair to reduce someone's wage because of slack demand in the labor market but not to hire a *new* person at a lower wage. People think firms are entitled to their "reference profit"—thus you can pass on increases in costs. But they consider it unfair to take advantage of an increase in monopoly power or to price discriminate when possible, and consumers may punish firms they consider unfair, whether or not it is in their interest to do so. Kahneman et al. note that the "absence of considerations of fairness and loyalty from standard economic theory is one of the most striking contrasts between this body of theory and other social sciences. . . . Actions in many domains commonly conform to standards of decency that are more restricting than the legal ones" (1986b: 285). They also note that retailers "will have a substantial incentive to behave fairly if a large number of customers are prepared to drive an extra five minutes to avoid doing business with an unfair firm" (1986a: 736), but it is also the case that "unenforced compliance to the rules of fairness is common" (1986a: 737).

Survey respondents' emphasis on reference transactions finds many echoes in empirical studies. For example, economist Truman Bewley's study of why employers rarely cut wages during a recession, as economic theory prescribes (and which would greatly mitigate the rise in unemployment that recessions typically cause), found that employers explain their inaction by arguing that it would be inappropriate to reduce their workers' living standard. One said that everybody "gets used to a standard of living. If you cut pay by 5% everyone would feel they had worked last year for nothing" (Bewley 1999: 176). They also stressed that resentment at a wage cut would show itself in reduced effort: "If morale is low, they get so that all they want to do is beat the system. In this case, they need lots of supervision. People would not recognize that the market for their services was down" (178); another told Bewley that pay cuts "would be regarded as unfair and would affect morale for a long time. Employees would never forget it" (180). A car dealer, citing possibly special circumstances, believed that this resentment would lead to emotional and perhaps irrational responses: "If I cut pay, people would leave out of rage, even though they have no place to go. They would feel they had to. . . . The body shop people would certainly leave. They are crazy. They smell too many fumes" (179).

The idea of "reference transactions" finds resonance in E. P. Thompson's analysis of eighteenth-century crowd actions that forced sellers to reduce prices. He notes that "riots were triggered off by soaring prices, by malpractices among dealers, or by hunger. But these grievances operated within a popular consensus as to what were legitimate and what were illegitimate practices in marketing, milling, baking, etc." (1971: 78). He goes on to say that this consensus was "grounded upon a consistent traditional view of social norms and obligations" (79) and explains the idea of "legitimation" by saying that the "men and women in the crowd were informed by the belief that they were defending traditional rights and customs" (78). They looked to a "paternalist model" in which the authorities were supposed to enforce traditional concepts of what was fair, including reasonable prices, kinds of bread supplied, and many other market details (1971: 88).

But it would be a mistake to assume that concepts of fairness and moral economy are merely inertial, resting solely on reference transactions to which people have become accustomed. Such judgments are also infused with emotional reactions that result from judgments about what is right and wrong. The pure reference-transaction model is expressed by Kahneman et al. (1986a) when they suggest that people object to stores' raising the price of snow shovels after a blizzard because "such an action would violate the customer's entitlement to the reference price" (734). But surely this understates the case, as part of the resentment must come from a moral principle forbidding economic actors to take undue advantage of the troubles of others that are no fault of their own, as in natural disasters (as I argued above in response to E. Posner's analysis of price increases for kerosene after hurricanes). That is to say there are general moral principles, not merely inertia, that operate in conceptions of what is appropriate in the economy. When these principles are violated, people respond in emotional and not necessarily self-interested ways.

In this connection, Bewley notes that workers "have so many opportunities to take advantage of employers that it is not wise to depend on coercion and financial incentives alone as motivators. Employers want workers to operate autonomously, show initiative, use their imagination, and take on extra tasks not required by management; workers who are scared or dejected do not do these things" (1999: 431). Perhaps surprisingly, a "theme recurring frequently in interviews was that businesspeople and labor leaders were preoccupied with the defense of civilized values, which they depend on to hold their organizations together. . . . the majority believe that success required decency and trust, a belief that contrasts sharply with the standard model of man in economics" (436). What is missing from the neoclassical theory of the firm, Bewley suggests, is

> an appropriate theory of the firm as a community. . . . Leaders strive to inspire enthusiasm and trust, so that subordinates do the right thing of their own volition. . . . Many businesspeople believe that moral commitment is all that stands between them and chaos. The society within a firm is brittle and constantly threatened by waves of suspicion, many caused by individual managers' abuse of authority. This fragility is one reason employers are sensitive to morale, and the main drawback of pay cuts is that they fill the air with disappointment and an impression of breached promise, which dissolves the glue holding the organization together. (436–437)

E. P. Thompson also notes that the eighteenth century English "traditional" view of proper behavior was not merely inertial but was deeply infused with moral judgments. Millers and bakers were "considered as servants of the community, working not for a profit but for a fair allowance" (1971: 83). There was a "deeply-felt conviction that prices *ought* in times of dearth, to be regulated, and that the profiteer put himself outside of society" (1971: 112). Innocent of supply and demand curves, villagers were nonetheless well aware that shortages might result from holding prices below the market level. Yet Thompson notes that it appeared to them "unnatural" that "any man should profit from the necessities of others," and "it was assumed that, in time of dearth, prices of 'necessities' should remain at a customary level, even though there might be less all round" (131–132). The anger that greeted violations of these moral precepts led to retaliation often contrary to the crowd's own interests, as when "men and women near to starvation nevertheless attacked mills and granaries, not to steal the food, but to punish the proprietors," dumping flour or grain into the river and damaging machinery (1971: 114), and this behavior recalls the subjects of Fehr and Gaechter, whose punishment of those violating norms of reciprocity exceeded what rational actors would impose.

But it is not enough to show that moral principles sometimes animate emotional economic action contrary to self-interest. For this to be a usable

theoretical insight requires systematic theoretical purchase on the circumstances under which this occurs. To move toward such insight I find it useful
to analyze and comment upon a debate in the 1970s between two political
scientists on the existence and significance of "moral economy" among
Southeast Asian peasants.

In his 1976 book *The Moral Economy of the Peasant: Rebellion and Subsistence in Southeast Asia,* James Scott argued that in pre-market peasant societies, there was a moral economy in the form of a subsistence ethic—that
everyone had the right to a minimum standard of living. It was

> above all within the village—in the patterns of social control and
> reciprocity that structure daily conduct—where the subsistence
> ethic finds social expression. The principle which appears to unify a
> wide array of behavior is this: 'All village families will be guaranteed
> a minimal subsistence niche insofar as the resources controlled by
> villagers make this possible'. . . . Few village studies of Southeast
> Asia fail to remark on the informal social controls which act to pro-
> vide for the minimal needs of the village poor. The position of the
> better-off appears to be legitimized only to the extent that their
> resources are employed in ways which meet the broadly defined wel-
> fare needs of villagers. Most studies repeatedly emphasize the
> informal social controls which tend either to redistribute the wealth
> or to impose specific obligations on its owners. (40–41)

An important part of Scott's argument is that the norms composing the
"moral economy" were binding on local elites as well as poor villagers, and
they violated these at their peril: ". . . many of the assassinations and pillages
seemed directly motivated by the belief that the wealthy and those in
authority had an obligation to share their resources with the poor in times of
dearth—and failing that the poor then had the right to take what they needed
by force. Thus, a good many assassinations [in early 1930s Vietnam] were
traceable directly to the failure of the local official/notable to respect the
redistributive norms of village life" (1976: 145). The bottom line is that the
"moral principle of reciprocity permeates peasant life, and perhaps social life
in general" (167), and there is "strong evidence that along with reciprocity,

the right to subsistence is an active moral principle in the little tradition of the village" (176).

Samuel Popkin's 1979 book *The Rational Peasant* opposed this argument from a rational choice perspective, asserting that peasants are "continuously striving not merely to protect but to raise their subsistence level through long- and short-term investments, both public and private. Their investment logic applies not only to market exchanges but to nonmarket exchanges as well" (4). The village institutions stressed by moral economy theorists "work less well than they maintain, in large part because of conflicts between individual and group interests, and . . . far more attention must be paid to motivations for personal gain among the peasantry" (17). While Popkin does not deny the existence of norms, he prefigures later law and economics scholars in using "the concepts of individual choice and decision making" to "discuss how and why groups of individuals *decide* [emphasis supplied] to adopt some sets of norms while rejecting others" (18). Norms, he suggests, are not independent forces but are "malleable, renegotiated, and shifting in accord with considerations of power and strategic interaction among individuals" (22).

He views investment logic as ubiquitous: "That children (in addition to everything else) are an investment is clear. . . . As a family firm . . . peasant couples will make tradeoffs between children and property that have a long-run focus. . . . In an earlier age, European peasant couples not infrequently practiced infanticide rather than sell property, because children were easier to replace than oxen, tools or land" (Popkin 1979: 19–20). Contributions to "the village, participation in insurance and welfare schemes, and exchanges between patron and client are all guided by investment logic." It follows that in hard times, villages will function worse rather than better as "individuals become more cautious about contributing to insurance and welfare schemes . . . and use the money for themselves. . . . I predict that peasants will rely on private, family investments for their long-run security and that they will be interested in short-term gain vis-à-vis the village" (23). Free-rider problems make communal village institutions fragile, so that "whenever there is coordinated action to produce collective goods, individuals may calculate they are better off not contributing" (24). And thus Popkin expects to find "few insurance schemes that require peasants to contribute money to a common fund—since someone can always abscond with the money—and more schemes that are . . . based on strict reciprocity and require labor (not so easily stolen), such as a plan whereby everyone helps victims to rebuild after a fire" (47).

As Talcott Parsons observed in his 1937 discussion of Thomas Hobbes, a "purely utilitarian society is chaotic and unstable" (93–94), which led Hobbes to propose that only a strong central power could overcome this chaos. Popkin's conception of village life is neo-Hobbesian, and it is then not surprising that he explains the rise of powerful leaders by their ability to control the excesses of individual selfish motives. Hence the success of "political and religious movements that reorganized villages even in precapitalist society. These movements could improve peasant life and bring profit to the leaders by offering better local leadership and therefore less risky and more profitable collective goods" (Popkin 1979: 27). In this regard, Popkin's view of the origins of political leadership and Oliver Williamson's on the conditions for superiority of authoritative hierarchies over chaotic market relations (to be discussed in my sequel volume) are similar proposals from a similar perspective.

I highlight Scott's and Popkin's baldest statements, but more detailed textual analysis shows that neither actually adheres strictly to such views. Scott repeatedly notes self-interested motives for behavior that he means to describe as mainly driven by moral economy, and Popkin lapses into explaining behavior in terms of normative commitment. These inconsistencies are less interesting in themselves than as demonstrations of how difficult it is to sustain either extreme position.

What we need is a more nuanced and detailed account of the circumstances under which moral economy norms are, in fact, felt and practiced by peasants and landlords alike. Because Scott and Popkin are preoccupied with showing that they always or never are, they do not notice that in both their accounts lie the beginnings of an argument about such variation. Such an argument lies at a meso level.

Thus, Scott notes that the strength of the moral economy ethic "varied from village to village and from region to region. It was . . . strongest in areas where traditional village forms were well developed and not shattered by colonialism—Tonkin, Annam, Java, Upper Burma—and weakest in more recently settled pioneer areas like Lower Burma and Cochinchina" (1976: 40–41). This variation is instructive, however, for it is in precisely those areas where the village is most autonomous and cohesive that subsistence guarantees, part of the moral economy, are strongest. To cohesion and autonomy, Scott adds the matter of social distance: "a man cannot count with as much certainty or for as much help from fellow villagers as he can from near relatives and close neighbors. Patron-client ties, a ubiquitous form of social insurance among Southeast Asian peasants, represents yet another large step in social and often moral distance, particularly if the patron is not a villager" (27), and tenants "could count more on such protection where landlord and cultivator were linked by kinship or lived in the same village . . ." (48). To this, Popkin adds that many precapitalist villages, however cohesive, had a stratum of residents without full citizenship rights—outsiders not included in the "rights and benefits of insiders" (1979: 43).

The picture that emerges is that cohesive villages with few outsiders, whose poorer members are tied to personally known patrons and elite members who depend on local support and are oriented to local prestige, are the settings most likely to display shared standards of moral behavior, especially a sense of moral obligation between landlords and peasants. Like all cohesive groups, cohesive peasant villages are more able to generate and enforce a clear-cut set of norms. Thus, Popkin comments on the older sharecropping system in Tonkin that "landlord and tenant shared production expenses and risks. In a bad year, the landlord would take a share of the crop smaller than his usual 50 percent. . . . Sharecropping required trust and a long-standing relationship between landlord and tenant; it was only for relatives, friends, or people to whom the landlord felt personally obligated" (1979: 156)

But when economic and demographic circumstances reduced the proportion of individuals with personal ties to landlords, moral economy fell away. Thus, in Tonkin (Vietnam), by the early part of the twentieth century, population increases, the blockage of migration by the French, and the consolidation of landholdings by landlords led to the introduction of intermediary agents between owners and tenants, which ended many traditional paternalistic practices. "These agents, remembered to this day with hatred throughout Vietnam, became an additional source of hardship to the tenants as they used their position to profit at the expense of both tenant and landlord" (Popkin 1979: 157). Similar developments occurred in Cochinchina, as large landowners began moving to Saigon or provincial cities and acting through agents (Scott 1976: 80). Although we need more information about who these agents were, it seems clear from both accounts that they were outside the social networks that previously sustained a clear sense of moral obligation across social classes and had no moral scruples against milking their position for all it was worth.

This dramatic shift in the geography and ultimately the prevalence of moral standards shared across social classes was a by-product of a series of economic and demographic changes resulting from macropolitical and macroeconomic forces that were not primarily or even incidentally motivated by a "market for norms" or an attempt to modify peoples' sense of how one ought to behave. These macro-level forces operated on norms through an intervening mechanism of social structural impacts on local behavior. If the large-scale changes were some kind of evolutionary adaptation to global political economy, we would point to pleiotropy, as do Gould and Lewontin (see discussion above), and note that such macro-level changes have many consequences, some of which are not part of the selection regime. But the same point remains even if we are skeptical that the larger patterns result from adaptation and suspect that they have more to do with struggles for political and economic dominance. Yet the forces that disrupt moral economy, even though they are far removed from any intention to change the normative framework of peasant society, still do contribute in a serious way to political instability by creating moral resentment on the part of those disadvantaged by the failure of the old understandings. Such resentment is only a necessary condition for peasant rebellions and revolutions, which require other causes to operate before they ignite. This does not make them any the less important: we would discount a theory of forest fires that did not implicate tinder.

2.5 A Preface to the Study of Culture and Institutions

Two critical points I have argued thus far are that it is misleading (1) to analyze the origin or functioning of single norms in isolation, since they are typically closely related to other norms, as I explore in detail in Chapters 5 and 6; and (2) to suppose that norms operate effectively only in small, localized social networks. These points lead us to analyzing norms as elements in larger conceptual constructions that occur in a larger social framework. How to understand the way these constructions influence behavioral patterns in the macroeconomy may be the most difficult analytical problem we face, and I note here and in the chapters on trust and on power the hazards of simple extrapolation of small-scale regularities to large-scale patterns without a careful analysis of mediating mechanisms.

A purely logical flow of argument would lead me now to discuss the aggregation of norms into larger conceptual and mental structures, which go by such names as culture, institutional logic, and institutions, including such special cases as "varieties of capitalism" and which may entail more than simply a collection of norms, including distinctive ways of thinking and perceiving, different aesthetic standards and conceptions, specific ways of organizing activity, and different conceptions of man's place in the world. But before I can offer a reasonable account of these meso or macro-level phenomena, there are two sets of issues that I would like to discuss that have a serious impact on what kinds of institutional phenomena emerge in the economy or other social realms. One is the sources and contours of trust between individuals or between individuals and larger, collective social entities; and the other is the meaning, origins, and consequences of power that individuals and collectivities wield over one another in the economy. These are the subject of the next two chapters, after which I once more pick up the thread of institutions to round out the arguments of this book.

3

Trust in the Economy

3.1 Introduction: The Concept of Trust

The concept of trust, mentioned briefly in the previous chapter on norms, is important enough to deserve its own separate treatment. Trust and trustworthy behavior are critical assets for any economy, principally because they lead people to cooperate and otherwise act more benignly toward one another than the pure logic of self-interest would predict. This is one reason why I consider purely self-interest-based explanations for trust perverse. Trust matters because, as economists have often noted, the resulting cooperation saves substantial costs of precaution and monitoring that would be expended in its absence. Kenneth Arrow observed that trust "is an important lubricant of a social system. It is extremely efficient; it saves a lot of trouble to have a fair degree of reliance on other people's word" (1974: 23), and Arthur Okun suggested that "enormous resource costs could be saved in a perfectly honest and open world that would permit do-it-yourself cash registers and communal lawn mowers" (1980: 86).

But historically, economists paid trust little attention, perhaps because, as Albert Hirschman noted in his remarkable book *The Passions and the Interests* (1977), from the seventeenth century on, philosophers argued that economic action was a species of calm, rational, and benevolent behavior and thus economic interests were pursued only by gentlemanly means (Hirschman 1977; and see Fourcade and Healy 2007). This assumption came to be widely accepted by classical and neoclassical economists (though not by those of socialist and other heterodox persuasions—see Hirschman 1982), and the Hobbesian question of how society contained the perils of force and fraud—which highlights the problem of trust—thus faded from the analysis of economic life.

Two related mid-twentieth-century developments stimulated a resurgence of economists' interest in trust. One was the advent of an economics of information, which noted the difficulties that asymmetric information causes. This was first of special interest in insurance markets, which face the dual problems of "moral hazard" (insurance reduces the motivation to avoid dangers insured against, but insurers cannot know, without large search costs, which claims result from such negligence) and "adverse selection" (those at higher risk are more likely to buy insurance but do not fully disclose this risk to insurers).

The interest in asymmetric information and uncertainty accompanied and was compatible with increasing attention to the limitations of human rationality. One manifestation of this attention was closer analysis of the micro-level details of imperfectly competitive markets, peopled by small numbers of traders with sunk costs and "specific human capital" investments. In his 1975 book *Markets and Hierarchies,* Oliver Williamson noted that any complex contingent contract that specifies that obligations of each party depend on what has occurred faces difficulties when the parties differ, as they often do, in knowledge of relevant occurrences (31–37). This led Williamson to search for organizational devices that mitigate the tendency for actors to pursue their interests with "guile," and in general, he and other "new institutional" economists have stressed organizational and institutional solutions and downplayed the significance of "trust" as being confined mainly to families and close personal relationships in "noncalculative" situations of minor economic significance (see esp. Williamson 1993). Williamson here implicitly makes the Hobbesian assumption that one can normally expect others to deceive and betray unless restrained by organizations and institutions and thus interprets "trust" to mean belief that this will not happen even in the absence of such restraint, which he thinks justified only in close relations unlikely in most economic transactions.

Yet many social scientists have focused heavily on the role of trust in social and economic life, largely because there are so many real-life situations in which individuals do cooperate more readily and to a greater extent than pure instrumental rationality predicts. Even those whom real-world evidence does not persuade have been impressed that experimental results on "deci-sion dilemmas" consistently lead to outcomes that are perplexing if we try to avoid the concept of trust.[1] As Elinor Ostrom pointed out, the some-times-technical discussions of these outcomes, when broadly considered, really raise the Hobbesian question: "How do communities of individuals sustain agreements that counteract individual temptations to select short-term, hedonistic actions when all parties would be better off if each party selected actions leading to higher group and individual returns? In other words, how do groups of individuals gain trust?" (2003:19). The issue in the large experimental literature on social dilemmas is that for a Pareto optimal outcome,[2] players must cooperate by selecting "strategies other than those prescribed by a subgame-perfect equilibrium solution" (23). Most relevant experimental studies have found levels of cooperation well above the pre-dicted level of zero, and while these levels sometimes decline when experi-ments are repeated, face-to-face communication substantially increases these levels again, even without changes in incentives. This Ostrom links to the building of trust (34). I have reviewed some of this experimental literature in Chapter 2 with reference to the norm of reciprocity.

What then should we mean by "trust"? There are many explicit and implicit disagreements in the voluminous literature on trust, but most stu-dents of the subject agree broadly that trust is the belief that another person with whom you might interact will not cause you harm even though he or she is in a position to do so. Such a belief on the part of a "trustor" may lead to "trusting behavior"—predicated on the assumption that the "trustee" (a term that I will use in what follows to refer to the person who is trusted) will act in a "trustworthy" way. So a trustor puts herself at some risk because of her trusting belief and action, and the existence of such risk is a central element in nearly all definitions (cf. Gambetta 1988: 219), of which the following three are typical: (1) in the literature on trust in organizations, a widely cited defi-nition is that trust is a "psychological state comprising the intention to accept vulnerability based upon positive expectations of the intentions or behaviors of another" (Rousseau et al. 1998: 395); (2) Foddy and Yamagishi (2009: 17) propose that trust is "an expectation of beneficent reciprocity from others in uncertain or risky situations"; and (3) Walker and Ostrom (2003: 382) simi-larly define trust as the "willingness to take some risk in relation to other individuals on the expectation that the others will reciprocate." Despite the convergence in definitions, there is little agreement on measurement (see, e.g., McEvily and Tortoriello 2011).[3]

One reason for the lack of consensus on measures is that the broad definition is compatible with many different *reasons* one may trust another, but most scholars focus narrowly on some single such reason, which leads to a single corresponding measure. It is therefore useful in setting out a systematic account of trust in the economy to talk about the main such reasons, the implications of each, and how they relate to one another. A major theme of this chapter is my resistance to the argument of many scholars that only trust caused by their favorite reason should be called "trust" at all.

3.2 The Sources of Trust

1. **Trust based on knowledge or calculation of interests of the other (rational choice accounts).** Perhaps the simplest possible argument about trust and trustworthy behavior is that a potential trustor assesses whether the interests of the trustee would lead her to be trustworthy, considers the benefits and risks to herself of the other's possible actions, and then acts in a trusting way only if it is to her benefit to do so. Thus, James Coleman presents an expected utility maximization model in which a rational actor engages in trusting behavior towards another if the "ratio of the chance of gain [from trusting behavior] to the chance of loss is greater than the ratio of the amount of the potential loss to the amount of the potential gain (1990: 99). Note that this is equivalent to assuming that the expected gain to the trustor if the trustee acts in a trustworthy way is greater than the expected loss if the trustee betrays her.

There is an obvious danger of circularity in such an assumption if we observe trust only after the fact. To avoid this requires us to assume that individuals are able to make calculations of this kind—which involves questions of cognitive capacity and information acquisition—and also that the gain or loss from possible behaviors of the other can be clearly quantified. But even when all these conditions are met, as they may often not be, the trustor's assessment of costs and benefits and the likelihood of betrayal need not assume that the behavior of the *other* is based on rational choice. If, for example, one knows that one's friend will not betray because of her group membership, her normative commitments, her emotional attachments, or other nonrational causes, then only one of the two actors involved in this trust decision is in fact a rational actor, and this is troubling for any claim that this is a "rational choice" theory of trust.

While it might appear that trusting another because of their attachment to you would transcend rational choice, Russell Hardin's account of trust attempts to re-position such an argument squarely into a rational choice framework (e.g., Hardin 2001, 2002). In order to do so, Hardin argues that the concept of trust should mainly be confined to others you know, since you can trust them if and only if you know that they have an interest in continuing your relationship. This he refers to as the idea of "encapsulated interest," where the interests of another include (or "encapsulate") your own. He justifies this argument by noting that if in fact trust always required *more* than the

> rational expectations grounded in the likely interests of the trusted . . . then we are at a very early stage in the development of any theory to account for trust or even to characterize it in many contexts. If an account from interests is largely correct for a large and important fraction of our trusting relationships, however, we already have the elements of a theory of trust that merely wants careful articulation and application. . . . The sense that trust inherently requires more than reliance on the self-interest of the trusted may depend on particular kinds of interaction that, while interesting and even important, are not always of greatest import in social theory or social life—although some of them are, as is the trust a child can have in a parent. (Hardin 2002: 6–7; cf. Williamson 1993)

This account relies on a claim of parsimony but also displays an element of wishful thinking. Closer examination suggests complexities that muddy the alleged parsimony. In particular, if trust is based on the assumed interest of another in continuing our relationship, then a savvy actor would need to know more about the nature of that interest. This varies in ways that Hardin places along a dimension that he calls "richness" but does not define:

> At a minimum, you may want our relationship to continue because
> it is economically beneficial to you. . . . In richer cases, you may
> want our relationship to continue and not be damaged by your
> failure to fulfill my trust because you value the relationship for many
> reasons, including nonmaterial reasons. For example, you may enjoy
> doing various things with me, or you might value my friendship or
> my love, and your desire to keep my friendship or love will motivate
> you to be careful of my trust. (2002: 4)

I would describe this dimension as ranging from instrumental to consummatory, as I discussed above in Chapter 1, referring to whether a goal (here,
maintaining a relationship) is desired as a means to another end or only for
its own sake. *Which is the case makes a big difference in talking about trust.*
This is because when deciding whether to trust another, one would like to
know whether she will be *unconditionally* trustworthy (as in the purely consummatory case) or whether she may perhaps look for subtle and undetect-
able ways to betray the trust placed in her (as in the purely instrumental case).
If the latter, trust must be very guarded indeed, as the human mind and
complex economic institutions present a multitude of opportunities to the
devious.

The problem is that only in the purely consummatory case do another's
interests *truly* encapsulate yours. Here, no trustee will betray because if she
harms the trustor's interests, *even undetectably,* then she harms her own as
well—as follows from how Hardin defines "encapsulation." But in the many
cases that Hardin discusses, where the trustee wants a continuing relationship because of *benefits* derived from it—such as money, prestige, position,
reputation, resources, or contacts—there is no true encapsulation, and in fact
a rational other should want to extract the maximum benefit from the relationship *regardless* of harm to the trustor, provided only that she not be dis-
covered doing so and that this extraction not reduce the trustor's ability to
benefit her.

In deciding whether to trust another, one must then assess whether the
other seeks continuation of the relationship for its own sake—as in love or
close friendship—or for something to be gained outside the relationship. In

the latter case, where instrumentality blocks a true encapsulation of interests, one must be appropriately wary. The rational choice account is muddied because in real life, these ideal types are hard to distinguish and there is typically a mixture of motives. The decision on how much to trust must depend on understanding the relationship sufficiently to know the balance of motives and how this affects the other's behavior.

When true encapsulation of interests results from love or deep friendship, there is a certain irony in construing this to ratify some rational choice model, based, as it ultimately is, on the least understood and most subtle emotions and passions of humankind. Whether we really want to understand this situation by referring to "interests" depends in part on what that means. With a sufficiently broad concept of "interests" we might feel more comfortable. Swedberg defines "interests," for example, as anything that "drive[s] the actions of individuals at some fundamental level" (2003: 293–295). In this conception, "interests" seem equivalent to "motivation," and if "rational choice" then means acting in accord with "interests" so defined, then all motivated behavior is rational choice by definition. Hardin, on the other hand, construes "interests" more narrowly but notes that interests are typically not the "whole story of a person's motivations" because one may have "an interest in having more resources, such as money, only because they enable me to consume or experience various things. . . . The whole story is one of well being through the use of resources. Interests are merely a proxy for this whole story" (2002: 23). But this synecdoche misleads, since that piece of the story beyond "interests" requires a different theoretical argument.

2. **Trust based on personal relationships.** Hardin's "encapsulated interest" argument is a special case of trust based on one's personal relationship to another, in that it tries to assimilate such trust to a matter of interests and rational choice. A different argument about trust and personal relations is made by Zucker (1986), who proposes that industrial society has gradually shifted the grounds for trust from more personal to more institutionalized ones. For Zucker, in the early period (which she identifies for the United States as occurring before the late nineteenth century), she refers to personal sources of trust as being "process-based," by which she means that trust is "tied to past or expected exchange such as in reputation or gift-exchange" (1986: 60). So this kind of trust depends on having exchanged previously with

the potential trustee or at least knowing the reputation of that person or firm for making satisfactory exchanges. Here one might think of the way that physical markets, such as bazaars, sometimes produce stable relationships among particular buyers and sellers, of the kind that anthropologist Clifford Geertz referred to as "clientelization" (1978) because exchange partners have built up trust in one another in situations where quality of goods is very hard to assess before purchase. As anthropologists and social exchange theorists have often noted, potential exchange partners typically work their way up from minor to more major exchanges in order to test the other's reliability in reciprocating properly (see, e.g., Blau 1964: 94 ff.).

Although this exchange-based trust and that based on "encapsulated interest" are compatible with a rational choice argument, that argument is neither a necessary nor a sufficient condition for supposing that trust depends on personal relations. Whether based on instrumental or consummatory motives, that trustworthy behavior may be a regular part of a relationship reflects one of the typically direct effects of relational embeddedness (see Ch. 1) and explains the widespread preference of many economic actors to deal repeatedly with the same others. Our information about such partners is cheap, richly detailed, and typically accurate. But assessing the balance of instrumental and consummatory motives in others is not always easy, and the trust engendered by personal relations presents, by its very existence, enhanced opportunity for malfeasance, which we must note to avoid a simplistic functionalism. In personal relations an old song reminds us that "you always hurt the one you love"[4]—which is possible because someone who loves you is far more vulnerable than a stranger. In the Prisoners' Dilemma, knowledge that one's co-conspirator is certain to deny the crime (because, e.g., she loves you) presents all the more rational motive to gain by confessing, and personal relations that abrogate this dilemma may be less intense and symmetrical than imagined by the party to be deceived. This elementary fact of social life is the bread and butter of "confidence" rackets that simulate close personal relationships, sometimes for long periods. The greater the trust, the more to be gained from malfeasance. That this occurs infrequently is a tribute to the force of personal relations and their capacity to transcend simple rational choice; that betrayals do occur shows the limits of this capacity.

Correspondingly, in her random sample of files from the Securities and Exchange Commission over the period 1948–1972, Shapiro "found the degree of intimacy of prior victim-offender relationships surprising. There are indeed more cases in the sample in which at least some of the victims and offenders were acquainted . . . than those in which they were strangers. . . . This . . . conflicts with stereotypes of white-collar crime in which a chasm of interpersonal distance, disembodied transactions, cover-up techniques, middlemen, records, papers, documents and computerization are thought to permanently separate victim and offender" (1984: 35). So individuals have reason to continuously scan relationships to determine the balance of motives behind them. One reason this is difficult, aside from instances of clever deception, is that even relationships that begin for obviously instrumental purposes may develop an overlay of social content of the kind I call consummatory— where part of the reason for maintaining the relationship becomes the value of the interaction itself.[5]

When personal relationships do lead to trust and trustworthy behavior, one may ask what kind of argument might best explain this outcome. In instrumental cases, it seems reasonable to suppose that the trustee is indeed protecting his interests by acting in a trustworthy way, though, as I noted above, this case calls for wariness on the part of the trustor, since, by hypothesis, there is incentive for the trustee to deceive. As I also noted, the consummatory case, where the relationship is valued for its own sake, is an uncomfortable fit for the usual rational choice paradigm. But then what does drive it? One argument might be that in this case trustworthy behavior is driven by emotions that lead to love or other varieties of attachment to another. Behavior driven by affect is one of Max Weber's four fundamental types of social action (Weber [1921] 1968: 24–25; cf. Elster 1999).

A different way to think about how trust and personal connections are related is to consider the idea that people act in certain ways because of their conceptions of who they are, what kind of person they want to be, and what kind of obligations they have to other individuals and groups; such arguments usually fall under the heading of "identity." A core element of philosophical and sociological arguments about identity and the constitution of the self is that these emerge out of the interactions we have with others. As argued by classic figures such as Charles Cooley and George Herbert Mead in the early twentieth century, we have little way of judging what we are like and what our characteristics are except insofar as we learn what others think of us and how they view us (cf. Blumer 1969). A natural extension of this is to say that the specific relationships we have with others, and their contents, are building blocks of our identity or conception of self. Individuals in close relationships with others arrive at clear expectations of their behavior toward one another, that are on each person's side, to the extent the relationship is serious and long-lasting, part of their sense of self. So, for example, I may deal fairly with you not only because it is in my interest or because I have assimilated your interest to my own but because we have been close for so long that we *expect* this of one another, and I would be mortified and distressed to have cheated you even if you did not find out—it would be inconsistent with how I think about myself. This would explain the severe sense of becoming partially unmoored and losing part of one's self when one loses a loved one as the result of death, the ending of a relationship, and perhaps worst of all by unexpected betrayal.

This way of thinking is different from saying that I will be trustworthy because I encapsulate your interests in my own, although that may be true as well. But to act in a way that is consistent with your personal identity is action caused by something about yourself rather than something about the relationship between your interests and those of another. And it is also different from acting according to a moral code, though that may also be involved. It is more about acting in a way that reflects the person, or kind of person, you have decided you are or want to be.

3. **Trust based on membership in groups and networks.** The discussion of how trust and trustworthiness are impacted by personal relationships is at a rather micro level and depends, as I have suggested, on a concept of relational embeddedness. But pairwise relationships are nested in more complex structures of social relations, which correspond to what I have called (Ch. 1) "structural embeddedness." The simplest argument associated with social structures beyond dyads is that trust is more likely among those who consider themselves members of the same group, however "groupness" may be defined.

Cook, Levi, and Hardin comment that in the research on trust that they coordinated, funded by the Russell Sage Foundation, a major emphasis is on "situations in which ethnic, racial or other markers facilitate certain kinds of trust relationships while inhibiting others and when they do not" (2009: 2). Foddy and Yamagishi suggest that shared group membership is particularly critical in understanding how the previously unacquainted may trust one another. They suggest two possible reasons to trust a fellow group member: (1) stereotype-based trust, where you think that your own group members are more generous, trustworthy, and fair; and (2) the "group heuristic hypothesis," where we expect altruistic behavior from ingroup members toward one another (2009: 19). Their experiments suggest that the second mechanism is the critical one. Other experimental work confirms that strangers of the same race and nationality are more trustworthy toward one another (e.g., Glaeser et al. 2000: 814). But this empirical finding does not provide an argument for why this should be so. The dictator experiments of Habyarimana et al. (Cook et al. 2009) suggest that the ingroup effect comes from ingroup norms of reciprocity. Walker and Ostrom (2009: 105) note abundant evidence that "individuals sanction those who engage in selfish activities at the expense of other group members," and that, moreover, norms of "fairness and reciprocity appear to shape the expectations of . . . group members beyond purely strategic responses" (2009: 107).

Here I note that although I write separate sections on particular causes for trusting and trustworthy behavior, most real situations where someone has to decide whether to trust another entail more than one of these causes, so the separation is artificial. In this particular case, part of the impact of common group membership on trust derives from commonly held norms about what group members owe to one another. The most seriously misleading arguments about trust arise from the attempt of scholars to limit explanations of trust to their own single, favorite factor, which typically leads to simplistic and irreproducible conclusions.

Zucker (1986) refers to "characteristic based trust," which depends on characteristics such as family and ethnicity (60), which is ascriptive and cannot be invested in or purchased. She proposes that in the United States, this became more critical with economic development because the labor force became more culturally heterogeneous, and you had to interact with strangers, but you could at least assume that people with similar characteristics to your own would provide satisfactory outcomes, as in ethnic enclaves. Zucker's take on why this works is not based on norms but on cultural familiarity with co-group members: "Many background understandings will be held in common, smoothing or eliminating the negotiation over terms of exchange and making it more likely that the outcome of the exchange will be satisfactory to both parties" (61). Broadly speaking, this is an argument about commonly held "cultures."

Another argument about how common group membership leads to trust that is distinct from rational choice, norms, or culture is provided by "social identity" theory. Tyler (2001) notes that social exchange theory is based on the assumption that "people want resources from others and engage in orga-nized life in order to exchange resources" and that they are "motivated by the desire to maximize their gain of resources and minimize their losses. . . . To do so they need to have an estimate of what others will do in response to their own behavior" (287). Though this is obviously sometimes the case, Tyler argues that it is "not a complete model of the psychology of trust" because people may also have feelings of obligation to a group that are "distinct from calculations about anticipated personal gain or loss owing to the actions of others" (288). He cites experimental evidence that "identification with the group to which one belongs decreases one's propensity to engage in noncoop-erative behavior that removes resources from a common pool," and this is so even without expectation of future reciprocity or current rewards or punish-ments or reputational consequences. Instead, people "feel an obligation to the group that develops out of identification with the group and group values. That identification shapes their behavior, leading to cooperation that is dis-tinct from that based on expectations about the behavior of others" (288). This Tyler calls "social trust," and he proposes that in groups where people have social connections, their trust judgments "become more strongly linked to identity concerns, and less strongly linked to resource exchange" (289).

These varying accounts show mainly that common group membership engenders trust and trustworthy behavior. Institutional economists have made similarly positive arguments. So, Ben-Porath, for example, in discussing the importance of trust in the exchange of valuable commodities, noted that "continuity of relationships can generate behavior on the part of shrewd, self-seeking, or even unscrupulous individuals that could otherwise be inter-preted as foolish or purely altruistic. Valuable diamonds change hands on the diamond exchange, and the deals are sealed by a handshake" (1980: 6). His emphasis is mainly on personal relations between traders, but it seems clear as well that such transactions are possible also because they are not atomized from other transactions but embedded in a close-knit community of diamond merchants who monitor one another's behavior closely and generate clearly defined standards of behavior easily policed by the quick spread of information about instances of malfeasance. The temptations posed by this level of trust are considerable, however, and the emergence of *separate* cohesive groups may bound the reach of trust, identity, and moral action.[6]

Frauds as well as legitimate business enterprises attempt to tap into existing membership networks in the hope of wide diffusion, more difficult if attempted through impersonal channels. In Shapiro's study of SEC fraud investigations, she found, as I reported earlier, that victims and perpetrators typically knew one another. But the fraud usually was not just a dyadic matter but was structurally embedded: "Offenses touch victim populations containing groups of associates or portions of various social networks. The sample contains cases with victim pools composed of members of particular church congregations or ethnic associations, officers at several military bases, members of political or social clubs or recreational associations, members of a professional athletic team, a textbook editor and a network of social science professors, members of investment clubs, and networks of political conservatives" (1984: 36). Some such networks are brought into the fraud by "bird dogs"—enthusiastic investors aware of the fraud who convince others to invest; the use of celebrities or community leaders, usually innocent of the fraudulent nature of the scheme, is common as an incentive for others to participate (1984: 36–37). And, indeed, the vast Ponzi scheme of Bernard Madoff, uncovered in 2008, depended almost entirely on recruitment of investors through networks of trust, especially among wealthy members of the Jewish community.

4. Institutional sources of trust. A common theme in the literature on trust is that there are cases where one trusts another because of institutional arrangements that make deception or betrayal less likely. One of the main reasons people are at risk in such situations is that the other with whom they might deal is a stranger or at least not well known to them. To be sure, there are theorists who want to reserve the term "trust" for only those who know one another well, e.g., Hardin, who considers trust to depend upon

"encapsulated interest." In a later section, where I discuss the most reasonable scope for the concept of "trust," I will reject this as well as other arguments for a narrow application of the term.

Arguments about the importance of institutional sources of trust sometimes make the evolutionary assumption that trust is originally personal and small-scale but that the increasing growth, complexity, and differentiation of societies make it impossible for all trust in the economy to be so derived, so that to the extent a society is economically successful, it will develop institutional supports that make it possible to take risks in relation to those about whom one knows less than they would in a much smaller-scale social situation. Cook, Levi, and Hardin suggest, for example, that as far back as Madison and Hume, it was argued that institutions like government were important in enabling cooperation and trust. If the state is reliable and neutral, it facilitates trustworthiness by "allowing individuals to begin relationships with relatively small risks as they learn about each other, and by providing insurance against failed trust" (2009: 4).

Zucker suggests that as societies progress economically, trust based on personal relations and exchange history or on group membership becomes insufficient, and institutions such as escrow accounts and credit ratings take up the slack (1986: 64–65; see also Carruthers 2013 on the history of credit ratings in the United States. But note that the history of the 2008 financial meltdown shows the severe limitations of credit ratings as a source of trust—cf. Lewis 2010). Zucker argues that between 1840 and 1920, institutionally based trust came to predominate in the United States (1986: 99) but does not actually suggest how one could measure the different kinds of trust in order to confirm this assertion. It is a common argument that a well-developed legal system that renders verdicts with some degree of impartiality in disputes is congenial to risk-taking in situations where exchanging parties might otherwise fail to reach agreement on terms. Even in situations where parties reach agreement without the use of formal institutions, the existence of these may provide a backdrop that overcomes distrust that might otherwise make this infeasible. An example is the oft-cited work of Mnookin and Kornhauser (1979) on how private negotiations on the terms of divorce amount to "bargaining in the shadow of the law," since without legal guarantees of promises made, the "inability to make an enforceable promise may inhibit dispute settlement" (957)

So many institutional sources of trust are familiar in everyday life that it is not necessary to inventory many of them to make this point. But acknowledging their significance does not require accepting evolutionary arguments about how such sources "displace" mechanisms that assured trust in earlier periods or in less advanced societies. I consider these claims in more detail below.

5. **Trust based on norms.** It is fairly straightforward that one might think another trustworthy because she adheres to norms that prescribe such behavior. The scope for such trust depends on the nature of the norm. If it is a norm of reciprocity, trust another who owes you a favor. If the norm prescribes reciprocity based on group membership, trust others in your own group. If it is a norm that one should act in a trustworthy manner in general, then one might be justified in extending trust beyond merely reciprocative situations. Given that arguments about the importance of norms sound sociological, it is curious that most authors presenting this argument for trust are economists. These arguments divide into two broad streams. One is culturalist (as described in Ch. 1) and conceives of "norms" as pertaining not to individuals but rather to collectivities that formulate, enforce, and embody them. Like most culturalist views, this idea meshes uncomfortably with the usual methodological individualism of economics. Economists taking this view typically cite data provided by a single question asked in the World Values Survey (henceforth WVS: see http://www.worldvaluessurvey.org/): "Generally speaking, would you say that most people can be trusted or that you need to be very careful in dealing with people?" and respondents are asked to choose between two alternatives: "Most people can be trusted" or "You can never be too careful when dealing with others." Countries vary dramatically from one another in the levels of trust, with the highest scores found in Scandinavia and the lowest in Latin America. (See, e.g., http://www .jdsurvey.net/jds/jdsurveyMaps.jsp?Idioma=I&SeccionTexto=0404 &NOID=104).

Although standard economics is incurious about where preferences come from—treating utility functions, for example, as given rather than a dependent variable to be investigated—economists who study trust sometimes suggest that its presence is an element of the norms and "culture" of a nation, region, or ethnic, religious, or other social group, and this foray into culturalism is said to explain differences. They (e.g., LaPorta et al. 1997; Guiso, Sapienza, and Zingales 2006) cite approvingly works of non-economists who elaborate this view such as Fukuyama (1995) and Putnam (1993) (who casts trust as resulting from "social capital," which leads some economists, such as Glaeser et al. 2000, to consider trust as a *measure* of social capital). But this view also leaves open the question of how the belief that others are trustworthy arises and how it may relate to other norms that may yield trustworthy behavior. (We know more about trusting behavior than about when and why people are trustworthy in part because surveys of values ask about trust but seldom if ever ask respondents whether and when they think it appropriate to cheat or deceive others, for the obvious reason that few would admit to ever thinking this appropriate.)

Economists address the question of how people come to be trustworthy by a stream of related argument that casts the passing down to children of trustworthy and cooperative or untrustworthy behavior as a *decision* that families or groups make, thus addressing the issue of how such norms arise. All such arguments encounter the difficulties noted in Chapter 2 in arguing that internalized norms are chosen rationally to gain advantage. So, for example, Aghion et al. (2010) define trust as "beliefs resulting from decisions about civicness made in families" (1015). Families, in this account, have two choices. They can teach their children how to behave in a "civic" way—"learning tolerance, mutual respect and independence"—or to "behave uncivicly outside the family" (1023). Uncivic children who grow up to be entrepreneurs can be expected to pollute, offer inferior risky goods, and cheat others. Societies that attain an equilibrium where everyone is civic naturally become "high-trust" societies and otherwise low-trust ones (1027–1028). Guiso et al. (2011) argue that we should focus on "investment in civic capital," which is the "amount of resources that parents spend to teach more cooperative values to their children," where "civic capital" is the "values and beliefs that *help a group overcome the free rider problem in the pursuit of socially valuable activities*" (423, emphasis in original). There is thus an "intergenerationally transmitted prior" that "affects each individual decision regarding whether to trust other members of the society and participate in an anonymous exchange" (424). If this trust is not well founded, then the individual could suffer a major loss. Thus, to "protect children from costly mistakes,

parents transmit conservative priors to them" which can lead to an "equilibrium of mistrust" (425). People do, however, "adapt their norms and beliefs in
response to the social pressure of the community they live in" (426) but dif-
ferentially in relation to how strongly the norms are held: "If civic values are
completely embedded in preferences, they should not be modified by socialization. If, however, civic values are supported, at least in part, by the desire to
conform to others, then socialization can lead to changes" (426).

3.3 More on the Definition of Trust and the Scope Conditions for the Concept

Before continuing to discuss the causes and dynamics of trust, it is useful to
consider some issues about the scope conditions for use of the concept of
"trust" that are closely related to the discussion of causes. Scholars of trust
often argue for limiting the term to some specific circumstances. Here I argue
against such limits and for construing the idea of trust very broadly, creating
distinctions instead around differences in the circumstances under which
trust is present and/or relevant and the different causes of trust and trustworthy behavior attaching to those different circumstances. This shifts the
discussion away from what I think pointless disputes about whether a particular situation "really" involves trust to the more interesting, complex, and
critical problem of how to understand under what circumstances economic
actors do in fact trust one another—i.e., act in ways that make them vulnerable to others, assuming that these others will not take the opportunity to
harm them or their interests.

One common argument is that because trusting someone requires the
trustor to take a risk about the trustworthiness of the potential trustee, we
should not apply the term "trust" to situations in which there is no such risk.
This argument appears in various forms. Appealing to parsimony, Russell
Hardin argues that if it is in another's interest to avoid harming ours, our
belief that they will not do so should not be called "trust" because to define
trust as "nothing more than incentive compatibility or rational expectations
of the behavior of the trusted" would make the term "otiose . . . because it
would add nothing to the somewhat simpler assumption of compatible interests" (2002: 5). Foddy and Yamagishi similarly argue that trust is "not required

when others' interests are totally allied with our own," and they refer to such situations as "the domain of assurance"; we only need to *trust* others when our interests are *not* allied, as this is when they can gain at our expense. Trust, they add, is most important in "uncertain, not certain relationships" (2009: 17). In their excellent study of taxi drivers, Gambetta and Hamill propose that "it is not enough to predict . . . that people will behave in a trustworthy manner if doing so is in their self-interest. This removes the problem of trust altogether" (2005: 4). Even broader is Farrell's assertion that when "actors have good reason to be *certain* that others will cooperate, these expectations are better described as confidence than as trust" (2009: 25). The reason for this is that when I "know that another will behave honestly in a predetermined and well-anticipated situation," there is not any real risk of unanticipated behavior (26).

The key assertion in all these statements that I want to contest is that there are circumstances where the behavior of the other whose trustworthiness we assess is *completely predictable,* without uncertainty. This is equivalent to saying that there are situations where actors have no agency whatsoever, though so rephrasing the assertion makes it seem more problematic. In the first two citations above, this certainty derives from knowing actors' interests. But this assumes an implicit null hypothesis of the sort that I discussed in Chapter 1, that we should *by default* expect others whose behavior concerns us to act according to their interests. Insofar as this is not a tautology, i.e., if agents can act counter-preferentially—against their own interests—as Sen 1977 suggests, we may have uncertainty and therefore the possibility of trust *even in the case where interests are aligned.* Sen analyzes the example of someone acting so as to prevent or stop torture. Let us pursue this case: it may be in my colleague's best interest to be complicit in my torture of prisoners under my care, so by the argument from interests, my expectation of his doing so should not be called "trust," as his behavior is automatic and entirely predictable.

But this is so only if interests perfectly predict behavior. Sen's argument suggests, however, that the other's commitment to moral principles may intervene and cause my undoubting expectation of his silence to be misplaced. If we take counter-preferential behavior seriously, this is not simply a matter of how the balance of incentives plays out and cannot be reduced to a simple incentive-based account. My expectation of his complicit silence may indeed be a matter of trust, if there is some chance that he will pursue overriding normative principles and report my torture, even at possibly high cost to himself. To address fully the likelihood that this will take place requires a treatment of the role of norms of the sort that I undertook in Chapter 2. The point is that whether expectations of another's behavior should be described as "trust" may depend not *only* on the other's interests but also on any *other* factors that may cause her to support or harm my interests. So the assumption that behavior is driven by interests alone is an implicit null hypothesis that may often be plausible but at critical times can dramatically mislead, as I noted in my discussion of "sacred values" in Chapter 2.

Frequent accounts of "whistleblowers," many of whom experience serious losses from their exposure of wrongdoing, exemplify the power of norms or identity to override self-interest. For this to matter it need not be the common or typical case, only a possibility, which can lead to serious consequences, as it did in such famous cases as the Enron frauds. I know of no systematic study of the balance of consequences for those who whistleblow, but I think it plausible from the fact that government agencies offer considerable rewards to those who flag wrongdoing that there is some presumption that without such rewards, the likely consequences for those who do so are negative on balance.

More generally, the fact that there are numerous causes to trust or distrust another besides their interests casts doubt on any argument that there are situations when another's behavior is easily and completely predictable. This is not to say that judgments of trust are random or not plausibly based on information available to us about the likelihood of another being trustworthy, nor does it follow that new information will not reasonably give us more or less confidence in that likelihood. Indeed, one of the most important research agendas on trust should be to understand better how people make such judgments and to what extent they are accurate. Here I only mean to suggest wariness of oversocialized views of human action that depict others as acting in ways entirely determined by factors that we understand without doubt, as this discourages the detailed and subtle investigations of actual trusting behavior that are needed.

Another aspect of when it is appropriate to speak of "trust" concerns the level of social structure where the term well describes how we might assess the likely future behavior of others. While some theorists propose that we can only properly speak of trust in cases where people know each other well, others suggest quite the opposite—that the concept is helpful almost entirely in relation to how we deal with strangers. I argue against both propositions and against restricting the idea of "trust" in such ways.

As noted above, Russell Hardin has proposed that we can trust others mainly when their interests encapsulate ours, so they benefit from continuing our relationship. On this argument, trust is fundamentally a small-scale interpersonal phenomenon and cannot be of much importance in the more macro-level structures of a large industrial society. This position is elaborated by Cook, Hardin, and Levi (2005) (CHL), who assert that as societies become more complex, *"the actual role of trusting relations has declined relatively"* so that trust is "no longer the central pillar of social order, and it may not even be very important in most of our cooperative exchanges which we manage quite effectively even in the absence of interpersonal trust" (1). They argue that that for complex societies to work well requires institutions, such as third-party enforcement of obligations, that make exchange and other kinds of cooperation possible even when interpersonal trust is absent (2). The argument construes trust in Hardin's sense of "encapsulated interest," and by this definition it is "impossible . . . to trust strangers and even many of our acquaintances, and . . . virtually impossible . . . to trust institutions, governments or other large collectivities" (4–5). This being the case, "trust plays a relatively small role on the grand scale in producing and maintaining social order. We usually rely on and cooperate with each other, not because we have come to trust each other, but because of the incentives in place that make cooperation safe and productive for us" (14–15). The reach of trust cannot extend very far because it is "only beneficial for us to trust those who are trustworthy in our interactions with us, and these people constitute nowhere near all of the society" (68).

This argument is similar to that of Zucker (1986) who, however, refers to such cases as instances of trust based on institutional sources. I would take this position as well, since I believe that the fundamental dependent variable here, whether at a small scale of interpersonal relations or a larger scale where people consider the impact of institutions on the actions of others, is still whether people behave as if those in a position to cause them harm will in fact do so, and the broad question should be about what independent variables cause one assessment or another.

I believe that views of where trust is relevant turn on how scholars think about the impact on trust of interests as compared to that of norms. CHL, following Hardin's concept of trust as based on encapsulated interpersonal interests, want to separate trust from the confidence you might have in others' behavior based on the power you think norms have over them. Thus, they assert that in small-scale communities, "trust is generally not at issue [i.e., a relevant concept]" because in small, dense networks, "reliability can be enforced by norms that are backed by the sanctions the community would apply" (2005: 92). Thus in small towns, helping behavior is not, as one might think, caused by interpersonal reciprocity but rather by "helping or communal norms" unlike seemingly similar behavior in urban areas which really is "a matter of reciprocity" given their assumed absence of communal norms (92). This argument borrows a page from Durkheim's (1893) concept of "mechanical solidarity" in assuming that people in small towns lack individuality or strong dyadic relations that are not completely subsumed by the "community ethos." I suggest that this idea implicitly reflects an "oversocialized" conception of human action, as it strips away agency from actors in "communal" settings. CHL extend Durkheim's evolutionary account by suggesting that over the course of "social evolutionary time" we may think of trust as "rising to displace control by social norms and then . . . fading to be displaced by regulation by modern social institutions" (195). Thus the "massive institutionalization of most of life makes modern society possible when mere [sic] trust could not have done so" (197).

This argument, and its separation of the influence of norms from the concept of trust, depends on conceiving of norms as pertaining not to individuals but rather to collectivities that formulate, enforce, and embody them. Such a concept has a family resemblance to the sociological exceptionalism promoted by Durkheim and others, that mental concepts are not the properties of individuals, and that society is an entity *sui generis* rather than a mere collection of separate persons. If norms have this effect on an entire group, then it is plausible to suppose that one can expect another to act in a trustworthy way not because of any characteristics of the other and not because of the relationship you have to her but because of your common membership in a group whose norms guarantee that behavior and eliminate all risk from the situation. Here, the criterion for not applying the concept of trust is a mixture of the imagined certainty of the situation and the fact that whether to act in a trusting manner has been stripped of any connection to assessing anything about the other as an individual (rather than as a group member) or about your relationship to him or her, which is a central part of what "trust" usually means.

If, however, you think of norms as possessed not by groups but by individuals, as a null hypothesis of methodological individualism implies, then the relationship of norms to trust can be quite different from and even opposite to the CHL proposal. This description fits well the way that economists and their sympathizers have talked about trust in the past twenty years, from which they conclude that norms are in fact a major source of trust, and that, moreover, trust is relevant mainly in one's relations to *strangers* rather than between those who know one another well.

So, for example, LaPorta, Lopez-de-Silanes, Shleifer, and Vishny (henceforth LLSV) (1997) propose that trust is "more essential for ensuring cooperation between strangers, or people who encounter each other infrequently, than for supporting cooperation among people who interact frequently and repeatedly." In order to assert this, these economists must have a very different idea about how cooperation comes about within small communal groups than the CHL idea that shared norms create unfailingly reliable behavior, and indeed, they argue that in such small and close-knit social clusters, as in families or partnerships, automatic and invariable cooperation, without deception or malfeasance, is supported by reputations and the likelihood of transgressions being punished even if levels of trust are low (333)—in other words, cooperation results from interests. That both CHL and LLSV agree on the unproblematic nature of cooperation in such small settings, though for quite different reasons, corresponds to what I have flagged in an earlier work (Granovetter 1985) as the convergence of oversocialized and undersocialized accounts, in this case to agreement that individuals in small communal settings lack agency, which makes trust irrelevant. But the views diverge because the economists conclude that trust is most needed in large organizations since you interact a lot with people you *don't* know well, so that the power of reputations and the likelihood of punishment for deviations are reduced.

As I described in the previous section, it is in these circumstances that economists often appeal to the power of norms in driving trustworthy behavior, drawing on empirical data such as those provided by the World Values Survey. They often code such norms and values as being part of the "culture" of geographic units, typically nations. In so arguing, they cite scholars such as Fukuyama (1995), who believes that national culture determines the distribution of trust and, in particular, that societies vary in the extent to which people are able to trust others beyond their family circle, and that societies can be broadly dichotomized into those characterized by "low trust," where people trust principally family members, and 'high trust," where it is more common to trust those outside the family. The reason this matters, he argues, is that in "low trust" societies, family bonds tower over other social loyalties, with the consequence that collections of economic actors based on mutual trust must be small. Family businesses dominate, and such societies are unable to develop large, professionally managed corporations. This implies difficulty adopting efficient, modern management practices and inability to "move into certain sectors of the global economy that require larger scale" (110). Large firms, if they exist in such societies, will not be private but can only be state-owned and managed, so there will be very large state-owned firms and small family firms without much in between. On the other hand, high-trust countries, whose cultures allow and encourage trust outside the family, make it much easier to form large firms. While legal forms like the joint-stock company allow unrelated people without trust to collaborate, nevertheless, "how easily they do so depends on their cooperativeness when dealing with nonkin" (150). Countries with well-developed patterns of association with nonkin have an emphasis on community and communitarian institutions, often referred to as "social capital," and this eases the transition from family business to professional management.

LLSV (1997) cite this argument with approval because it is compatible with their assertion that trust in strangers is critical for large-scale organizations and economic activities to thrive, and they note that measures of the level of trust in families in survey data are negatively correlated with the significance of large firms in the economy (336).

If one thinks that differences in trust across nations or other geographic units depend largely on cultural differences, some way is needed to link such an argument to methodological individualist theory. In the previous section I reported that economists such as Aghion et al. (2010) and Guiso et al. (2011) propose that trustworthy behavior results from family decisions to teach their children to be "civic." The link of this argument to culture lies in the assumption that cultures condition and affect the decisions of families to transmit the tendency to be trustworthy to their children, and this transmission, when aggregated up to a macro level, has a major impact on economic action. For example, the proportion of individuals who become "civic" (read: trustworthy) in the model of Aghion et al. (2010) is a major determinant of the extent of regulation of the economy, and high-trust societies "exhibit low levels of government regulation and low-trust societies exhibit high levels" because "distrust drives the demand for regulation. In low-trust societies, individuals correctly do not trust business because business is dishonest"; even government corruption is less bad than this dishonesty (1028). Note that this is an account "in which beliefs and regulations jointly influence one another" but where there is virtually no study of the behavior or sequence of events that intervenes between individual beliefs and larger-scale economic patterns. Another way to say this is that there is little interest in the mechanisms that lead from beliefs to institutions (for more on mechanisms in social theory, see Hedstrom 2005 and the essays in Hedstrom and Swedberg 1998).

Similar arguments are presented by Guiso, Sapienza, and Zingales in a series of papers on culture, trust, and economic outcomes. So they note that trust beliefs affect the probability of someone becoming an entrepreneur (where the measure is self-employment—2006: 36) and that, using the WVS measure of trust in Holland, "trusting individuals are significantly more likely to buy stocks and risky assets . . ." (2008: 2558). They conclude this implies that companies will "find it more difficult to float their stock in countries characterized by low levels of trust" (2559). In their 2011 account they extend the argument about trust to incorporate ideas about "civic capital," which they characterize as the "missing ingredient in explaining the persistence of economic development" so that "communities/countries that, for an historic accident, are rich in civic capital enjoy a comparative advantage for extended periods" (420).

In this account, civic capital is the result of investment. It is the "amount of resources that parents spend to teach more cooperative values to their

children" (423), and lest they fall victim to the usual criticism of "social capital" that one might learn to cooperate in criminal, racist or other socially
undesirable activity, they define this away by stating that the definition of
civic capital "purposefully excludes . . . those values that favor cooperation in
socially deviant activities, such as gangs" (423). (The authors seem confident
of universal agreement on what is "socially deviant," uncomfortably reminiscent of Talcott Parsons's mid-twentieth-century focus on social consensus,
which sociologists have long since abandoned.) So the argument proceeds as
one in which parents "decide how much trust to transmit to their children"
and this "intergenerationally transmitted prior affects each individual decision regarding whether to trust other members of the society and participate
in an anonymous exchange" (424). From a theoretical point of view, they
note, we could talk about trust in family or neighbors or more generalized trust, but they argue that the latter is the right measure because for
"institutions and markets to work properly, people need to trust strangers"
(442). As in the work of Aghion et al., behavior and events intervening
between beliefs and larger-scale outcomes are glossed over or attributed to
"historic accident."

     To summarize my discussion of what is the proper scope for the concept
of trust, I think it counterproductive to confine it to small-scale situations
where individuals know one another well or to argue that it should only apply
to large-scale situations where people interact mainly with acquaintances or
strangers. To me it is more fruitful to theorize at both small- and large-scale
levels under what circumstances people assume that others in a position to
hurt their interests will not do so. But while saying this opens up the issue of
trust to more general arguments, it does not yet clarify what, if any, relation
there is between trust at a small-scale level and that in large, complex organizations that define the macro shape of an economy. If we think of trust as
being at issue at both levels, then this relation becomes especially important
to theorize, and I suggest a high level of caution about arguments that link
individual decisions to large-scale outcomes without a detailed or plausible
account of how this aggregation takes place.

3.4 The Aggregation of Trust from Interpersonal to More Macro Levels

The arguments on trust that I have reviewed and critiqued focused either on very small-scale instances of trust or on accounts of trust at a larger social and institutional scale that either derived such trust from historical and political developments or assumed aggregation from individual beliefs without providing theoretically detailed or coherent arguments and behavioral mechanisms to explain such developments. A fuller treatment of trust would explore this aggregation more thoroughly, and part of this discussion would concern how political, historical, macroeconomic, and other institutional contexts are critical in explaining trust at higher levels. Here I set myself the more limited goal of setting out some social network ideas that may provide an important piece of the puzzle as to when trust does or does not aggregate up from micro to macro levels.

First note, as I suggested in Chapter 1, that relational embeddedness bears heavily on trust. Consider whether I cheat a business associate with whom I have friendly personal relations. Whether I do depends in part on the nature of my relation with him. It also depends on the configuration of incentives and on those moral principles I apply to the situation, and both of these are in turn affected by this relation. But incentives and moral principles are also determined by structural embeddedness—the structure of ties within which my relation with my friend is located.[7] My mortification at cheating a friend of long standing may be substantial even when undiscovered. It may increase when the friend becomes aware of it. But it may become even more unbearable when our mutual friends uncover the deceit and tell one another. Whether they do will depend on the structure of the network of relations— roughly speaking, on the extent to which the mutual friends of the dyad in question are connected to one another. When these connections are many— the situation of "high network density"—the news will spread quickly; when they are isolated from one another, much less so, as I argued in Chapter 1. So we can expect greater pressure against such cheating in the denser network; such pressures are an important part of incentives and relate directly to economic and social costs of developing a bad reputation.

But the pressure against cheating arises not only because of direct sanctions that group members would apply to me or because of reputation, both matters of interests and rational choice, but also because cohesive groups are more efficient than those with sparse relational networks at generating normative, symbolic, or cultural structures that affect our behavior. Thus, in such a group, it may never even *occur* to me to cheat my friend since I have absorbed a set of standards from the group that literally makes it unthinkable, at least in the group setting. So at relatively small-scale and communal levels, both interests *and* norms bear on trust. It is a commonplace from studies of intergroup relations, however, that the most scrupulously adhered-to norms within a well-defined group may be considered irrelevant when dealing with those outside its pale. Closely related yet importantly distinct from arguments either about information spread and sanctions or about norms is "social identity" theory, as discussed by Tyler (2001), which I noted above in my discussion of how group membership impacts interpersonal trust. The situational aspect of normative influences on behavior results from the structural embeddedness of social action and its impact on social norms as mediated by group identity. As I have noted, the power of these identities can also be harnessed on behalf of frauds that exploit the trust within identity groups or lead to conflict when such groups become fragmented.

The discussion thus far assumes that trust depends on preexisting relational and structural embeddedness and group identities but does not inquire how these arise. To assume that the situation of embeddedness is fixed and unalterable implies that the configurations of possible trust depends entirely on structure and cannot be impacted by conscious action of agents. This fatalistic view is sometimes drawn upon to show why regional differences in "social capital" are intractable, deriving as they do from many centuries of civic disengagement, "amoral familism" (Banfield 1958), or other afflictions closely related to trust or its absence. But it is important to keep in mind that social networks are themselves embedded in an economic and political institutional context that may have important impact on who comes into contact with whom and with what result.

Sabel, for example, suggests that the boundaries between trust and mistrust are blurred in practice, and that the absence of trust does not preclude discussions of conditions under which it might exist or be created. Both he

(Sabel 1993) and Locke (2001) suggest that industrial policy carried out by government at various levels, with the assistance of private groups, may have the consequence of forcing actors to work together who previously had only thought of themselves as having opposed interests that made trust impossible. For Sabel's Pennsylvania case, he notes that, in effect, the different groups he studied redefined their situation as the result of having to interact with one another. Locke's cases come from areas often written off as culturally incapable of forming trusting economic relationships—southern Italy and northeastern Brazil; here, private associations with broad membership were the locus for generation of trust, but public policy was crucial because without its support and its encouragement for inclusiveness in association membership, the key actors would not have come together in the first place in such associations, and the suboptimal outcomes of a typical social dilemma—in this case, individual producers of cheese or melons producing adulterated or inferior products so as to free-ride on the reputation of the larger region—would have dominated, sinking local economic development (Locke 2001).

Relational ties and structural networks are embedded not only in contemporary institutions but also in a particular moment in time and space. How trust varies with these has attracted a great deal of attention, and in the empirical chapters of the sequel volume, I will develop some specific arguments about this. Here I would like to review and comment on the major positions that have been staked out.

Though much contemporary writing on trust treats the subject as if unrelated to cultural, institutional, or historical variations, there are accounts that explore this connection. Allan Silver, for example, argues that the eighteenth-century Scottish moralists, most famously Adam Smith and David Hume, considered personal relations to have been considerably changed by the increasing dominance of markets. But unlike later critics of both left and right, from socialists to Burkean conservatives, who bemoaned the deleterious effects of markets on intimate personal relations, they proposed that a vigorous market actually carved out a new and important place in society for friendships unencumbered by the calculations of social exchange (Silver 1990). Indeed, they "celebrate the liberation of friendship from instrumental concerns made possible by the advent of commercial society" (1480), arguing

that such friendships are instead based on "sympathy," an emotional tie innocent of interest calculations.

Before the market, they proposed, personal relations were necessary in
order to ward off enemies or to acquire needed resources. This necessity in
war, economy, or politics introduced an element of calculation into personal
relations and made them "susceptible to damaging betrayal" (1487). The
dominance of the market and associated legal institutions of contract as ways
to provide goods and services and resolve disputes had the effect of "puri-
fying" personal relations by "clearly distinguishing friendship from interest
and founding friendship on sympathy and affection" (1487). So this was new,
in the sense that only with "impersonal markets in products and services
does a parallel system of personal relations emerge whose ethic excludes
exchange and utility" (1494) and plays an important role in creating a "mor-
alized civil society." In the modern, ideal conception of friendship that flows
from this argument, personal trust "achieves a moral elevation, lacking in
contractual or other engagements enforced by third parties" (Silver 1989:
276). And such trust is explicitly non-calculative because commitments
"based on an understanding of others' interests fall outside the moral ideal of
modern friendship" (277). So this conception of trust between friends is in
fact the polar opposite of trust as "encapsulated interest."

In later chapters I will assess how far this conception carries us. The
sharp distinction between market relationships and the non-market relations
of friendship that Silver attributes to the Scots is hard to maintain, as the
empirical evidence will show, so we will need to reconsider this entire issue.
The Scottish argument provides, however, an excellent reference point. But
the idea that the nature of trust relations changes as institutions and culture
do goes beyond the pre-market–commercial society distinction. One way
this idea has been pursued has been to argue that different societies and cultures vary systematically in how much and in what way they facilitate trust
among their members. Consider the argument of Fukuyama (1995), described
earlier, that the existence and significance of trust at a large scale result from
how it plays out at a small scale. Fukuyama argues for the crucial importance
of a society's particular culture, since he believes it determines whether people
are able to trust those outside their family circle. In "low trust" societies where
they cannot, collections of economic actors based on mutual trust must be

small, family businesses dominate, and it is difficult to develop large, professionally managed corporations, which, however, form easily in "high trust" countries.

The most obvious criticism of this argument concerns Fukuyama's particular classification of societies into the "low trust" or "familistic" category (China, France, and Italy being his main cases) and the "high trust" category (Japan, Germany, and the United States). Aside from whether countries in each grouping properly fit the description or belong together in such an argument, there are countries whose characteristics belie the main hypothesis—such as South Korea with its tight Confucian family system in an economy dominated by large, professionally managed and highly successful, yet typically family-based, business groups such as Samsung, LG, and Hyundai.

But I consider the more serious issue here to be the omission of inquiry into how the nature of trust at a small scale might translate into the capacity to structure larger-scale economic organizations one way or another and in particular whether it is true that societies that place a strong emphasis on family become thereby unable to construct large, private, professionally managed firms. The issue is whether and how the details of trust in small face-to-face groups provide the foundation for understanding the significance and extent of trust at more macro social levels. This issue arises as well in the work of economists who attribute trust at the macro level to culturally influenced family decisions whether to inculcate "civic" behavior into their children. I suggest that such conceptions overly privilege the micro level of analysis and that we need more detail to explain how trust at a small-scale level may aggregate up to a larger-scale level of analysis. That is, we need to understand the relationship between trust relations among individuals and in small communities and those in larger-scale networks of interaction. This question has attracted little attention.

In a related argument, commenting on community mobilization against the threat of urban "renewal" in mid-twentieth-century Boston, I proposed that local social network structure could make a big difference in whether leaders emerged whom people trusted at a larger scale. "Trust" in this context meant being willing to commit one's time and resources to an organization run by people whose efforts one assumed would not be self-regarding but rather who would look out for community welfare. This seems consistent with the idea of trust as acting on the premise that another will not harm your interests in a situation where he could. In particular, I argued that communities with predominantly strong ties would tend to generate networks that were fragmented into closed cliques, and that the resulting problem for community organization is that

> whether a person trusts a given leader depends heavily on whether there exist intermediary personal contacts who can, from their own knowledge, assure him that the leader is trustworthy, and who can, if necessary, intercede with the leader or his lieutenants on his behalf. Trust in leaders is integrally related to the *capacity to predict and affect their behavior.* Leaders, for their part, have little motivation to be responsive or even trustworthy toward those with whom they have no direct or indirect connection. Thus, network fragmentation, by reducing drastically the number of paths from any leader to his potential followers, would inhibit trust in such leaders. (Granovetter 1973: 1374)

This discussion of whether we can trust leaders whom we do not know personally could not be conducted at all if we defined trust as "encapsulated interest" in which one can only trust another whom one knows personally very well. But my discussion of trust in organizational leaders suggests that it is meaningful to talk about whether one trusts even individuals one does not know personally, since such individuals are entirely capable of harming your interests, whether they are aware of you or not. So my argument here is that you may trust that potential leader if there is a link or short chain of personal links to that person that conveys enough information to afford you some confidence that she will act in a trustworthy manner—e.g., will really have the interests of the community at heart and will not simply use the organization as a springboard for higher political office or as a source of funds for her country club membership or luxurious vacation. Because you have to decide whether to commit your own energies and resources to such an organization, you need to know this and can make reasonable decisions about it even though you do not know whether the prospective leader has encapsulated your own individual, personal interests—which may be impossible if there is no personal relationship to her.

The critical point here is that *a little trust goes a long way:* if people can trust those who are vouchsafed *indirectly,* then the size of structures in which trust matters expands far beyond what would be possible if only *direct* ties could be effective. This is why Fukuyama's observation that some societies' cultures are more family-oriented than others is not decisive for the structure of industrial organization. Indeed, one of the great surprises in the recent economic literature on the ownership and control of firms around the world is that the role of families has not declined nearly as significantly as mid-twentieth-century modernization theory led us to expect. It turns out that in much of the world, even most *large* firms are controlled by families (see LaPorta et al. 1999), and more than one-third even of the Standard and Poor's 500 leading American industrials are "family firms" and are, by some accounts, better performers than the nonfamily firms on this list (Anderson and Reeb 2003).[8]

One way that families can succeed in dominating large economic networks is when they understand the need to locate trust relations *strategically* in a network of economic relations that may be large and complex. We see this especially clearly in the organization of large business groups (see the chapter on this subject in my sequel volume for more details). A particularly interesting case, given Fukuyama's depiction of Chinese culture as incapable of supporting large, professionally managed firms, are Chinese business groups or "conglomerates" (as they are often called). The expansion of small family firms into large conglomerates seems common to Taiwan, Hong Kong (before 1997), various East Asian countries where ethnic Chinese business is important, and even the heartland of mainland China itself (see Keister 2000).

A representative account is offered by Kiong (1991) for Singapore, which is ethnically about three-quarters Chinese. While early Chinese entrepreneurs were in the traditional small-firm sectors of service, retail, and import/export, they gradually expanded into manufacturing, banking, and extractive industries such as rubber. The typical evolution was that an original family firm expanded not by getting larger but by setting up branches as independent companies or by buying already-established businesses. Authority, however, remained highly centralized across the component companies. Reputation and personal trustworthiness are crucial, contracts unimportant (182). Complex strategies are used to ensure the family's control over larger numbers of legally separate firms. Nominee and trustee companies are set up to hold the family's interests, and the structure of cross-stock-holding can be very complicated. Although the number of outsiders employed exceeds that of family members, "family member and kin are put in charge of subsidiary companies" (188). Generally, family members sit on all the boards. Professional management is achieved in part by educating family members in such skills, often abroad, and also by hiring nonfamily professionals who, however, do not exercise broad control comparable to that of family members. These business groups can be very large and diversified, but control is maintained through pyramids—family firms that control other firms that control still other firms, etc.—and dense interlocking directorates.

Thus, family members who have strong trust relations with the central family group are strategically sprinkled through the many holdings in such a way as to knit the entire structure together. Employees who are not in direct touch with the core family members may nevertheless trust the motives of that group through their direct ties to the local family representatives and work harder and more effectively than if they had no commitment to the central group, and conversely, local family members can assure the central family group of the loyalty of top subsidiary employees who are nonkin. Sometimes friends of the families are called upon as investors to help accumulate the capital necessary for expansion, but the resulting networks of cooperation do not dilute the control of the families, as it is generally understood that the outside investors will be more or less "silent partners" (cf. Hamilton 2000 whose data are drawn mainly from Taiwan, Hong Kong, and Thailand). (For a detailed argument about the different types and levels of trust activated in expanding concentric circles of Chinese management, see Luo 2011).

Chung (2000) provides a detailed analysis of Taiwanese business groups. He shows that, contrary to arguments about Chinese culture inhibiting substantial-sized economic structures, the size of Taiwanese groups grew linearly during the period of study, from the 1970s to the 1990s, and by 1996 the top 113 groups contributed 45 percent of the GNP, nearly double the proportion in the 1970s (14). Closely analyzing the structure of ownership, stockholding, and leadership using social network data analysis techniques, Chung found that cohesion in these groups resulted from the same set of core leaders, typically family members such as the sons, brothers, and nephews of a founder, occupying duplicate leadership positions in various group firms. Decisions are based on the "social relationships existing among members of the inner circle. The composition of the core leaders and the way that they relate to each other are the keys to understand the management practices within Taiwan's business groups" (82). While the proportion of key employees with professional training increased, this did not imply dilution of the importance of families. On the contrary, in 1994, 42 percent of sons had graduate degrees, a higher proportion than that of long-term employees. "In other words, sons, who are expected to succeed the founders' enterprises, are the most 'professionalized' among all patrilineal core leaders" (92)

Placing trusted family members strategically across the firms in family-dominated business groups provides a way to leverage dyadic trust in such a way as to create large and viable economic structures. Do ties with relations of trust integrate even larger structures and perhaps entire national economies? This could not be plausible if very large numbers of ties that connect cohesive clique-like structures were required to create overall connectivity. But as Watts and Strogatz showed in a highly influential 1998 paper in *Nature*, a surprisingly small number of such connecting ties, even when inserted into a network at random, may dramatically decrease path length in the network of economic units; arguably, when such ties are placed strategically rather than randomly, the effect may be even greater. These arguments about "small worlds" are taken up more systematically in Chapter 4 on power.

3.5 Trust, Norms, and Power

I have proposed that ties featuring trust may be scattered across a large social structure in ways that make them more important than if we thought of trust as mattering only at a small-scale and localized level. The weak point of this argument is that the ties I have described, important as they might be, are more than ties of trust. In fact, the empirical accounts on which I draw are mostly not oriented to discussions of trust and emphasize other aspects such as power differentials, norms and values, the search for strategic leverage, or just information exchange. A drawback in my organization of this book into

separate chapters on trust, norms, and power is that most real economic phenomena encompass more than one of these features in important ways that
must be combined for fuller understanding. The ties that integrate large economic structures are good examples of this, and for that reason I return to
them in subsequent chapters. In the sequel volume, organized around particular economic settings and cases, I will feel freer to pull together all the relevant theoretical arguments at one time.

Nevertheless, I argue that this discussion still properly belongs in a
chapter on trust because trust is a critical feature of the ties in question, which
cannot be well understood without taking it into account. It is not an accident
that so many of the ties that integrate large economic structures around the
world are those of kinship and that people go to considerable lengths to preserve the family business form against the typical judgment of economists
and the business press, drawing on neoclassical economic arguments and
mid-twentieth-century modernization theory, that families are a drag on economic development and efficiency (for a dissenting voice, see historian
Harold James [2006]). Certainly part of what drives this persistence is the
larger element of trust found in families than among unrelated individuals.
This is not to romanticize family ties, which are often fraught with difficulty.
The literature on the Chinese family, for example, often features discussions
of normative obligation and power relations. Hamilton (2000), among other
observers, stresses the great importance of patriarchal authority as a force in
holding together large structures of Chinese economic organization and
emphasizes the importance of power relations within the family. Despite this,
it is hard to imagine that trust is not a necessary part of this story, and in
Chapter 4, I will talk more about how trust and power are related.[9]

4

Power in the Economy

4.1 Introduction: The Varieties of Power in the Economy

The picture of the economy I have assembled thus far considers individual incentives and actions, social networks, norms, and trust, all of which may be strongly shaped by, and in turn shape, macro-level institutions. Before turning more systematically to institutions, the subject of Chapters 5 and 6, it remains to discuss power, an object of sharp disagreement between those who think it by far the most important determinant of economic outcomes and others who view it as largely irrelevant or tautological as a cause.

I argue that we cannot neglect power if we hope to construct persuasive explanations of the economy. But few concepts have created more confusion. A standard definition of power from Max Weber is still helpful in fixing ideas: power is the "probability that one actor within a social relationship will be in a position to carry out his own will despite resistance, regardless of the basis on which this probability rests" (Weber [1921] 1968: 53). Every definition has liabilities, and this widely cited one elides important questions such as what is an actor's "will," what it means to "carry it out," whether all power is exercised in the conscious way the statement implies, and what is meant by a "social relationship." For critiques and alternative definitions, see Lukes 1974 and Wrong 1995. But Weber's conception has the virtue of corresponding to common intuitive ideas of what power means and provides a good starting point. Weber also observes that this concept of power is "sociologically amorphous. All conceivable qualities of a person and all conceivable combinations of circumstances may put him in a position to impose his will in a given situation" ([1921] 1968: 53).

He goes on to note a special case of power that he calls "domination," the "probability that a command with a given specific content will be obeyed by a given group of persons" (53). This term, a translation of the German *Herrschaft,* is often rendered as "authority," and the reference to "given" content and groups typically involves formally constituted organizations such as corporations or political structures in which occupants of formally defined positions are authorized to give orders of defined kinds to specified subordinates.[1] "Domination," Weber adds, may be "based on the most diverse motives of compliance: all the way from simple habituation to the most purely rational calculation of advantage" (212).

In his main concept of "power" and his subtype of "domination," Weber emphasizes that his definitions abstract away from the *source* of power and the *motives* for compliance. But to emerge from the usual conceptual muddle, it is first vital to appreciate that power in the economy, as elsewhere, does have several distinct sources. In what follows, I distinguish three—power based on dependence, power based on legitimacy, and power based on influencing actors' definitions of the situation—ranging from simple control of the agenda to impact on cultural understandings of the economy.

4.1.1 Economic Power Based on Dependence

The conception of power that recurs most commonly among scholars of many persuasions is *dependence:* someone who controls resources that you value has power over you—can cause you to modify your behavior in an attempt to obtain more of those resources than otherwise. Theorists of otherwise apparently dramatically different schools of thought share this conception. Marxists attribute power to ownership of the means of production, which creates dependence and exploitation of workers who have only their labor to offer. In many ways, Marx elaborated on classical economics, so it should not surprise that his underlying conception of power bears a family resemblance to the standard economic conception of "market power": the theory of "imperfect competition" stipulates that some firms, as a result of barriers to entry that prevent others from producing a good, may raise prices to levels that competitive markets would not allow. They can do so because they have cornered the market for resources or products that others depend upon and cannot adequately replace. Thus, like the Marxist conception, this interpretation of power rests on dependence, though exerted over consumers rather than workers.

But the dependence created by market power is more limited than that created by class power because monopolists and oligopolists are still partially captive to consumers: the typical nonzero price elasticity of demand for any product predicts declining consumption as prices rise. Given limited incomes and other needs, even consumers faced with firms' market power can call some shots since their consumption of a given product is a choice and not mandated unconditionally by others with total power over their action. As in all dependence definitions of power, a key issue is availability of *alternatives* that undercut the power of those controlling a product or resource. It is the assumed lack of alternatives for the proletariat that makes class power so stringent and prompts the Marxist conclusion that only a revolution can bring change.

In discussing dependency-based power, which he described as being due to a particular "constellation of interests," Max Weber emphasized this element of choice, noting that even in a market monopoly, influence is "derived exclusively from the possession of goods or marketable skills guaranteed in some way and acting upon the conduct of those dominated, who remain, however, formally free and are motivated simply by the pursuit of their own interests" ([1921] 1968: 943). He offers the example of a bank that "can impose upon its potential creditors conditions for the granting of credit. . . . [I]f they really need the credit, [they] must in their own interest submit to these conditions." But the banks do not "claim 'submission' on the part of the dominated without regard to the latters' own interests; they simply pursue their own interests and realize them best when the dominated persons, acting with formal freedom, rationally pursue their own interests as they are forced upon them by objective circumstances" (943).

This formal equality of power can be mocked as meaningless for those with few choices, as when novelist Anatole France observed that the "law, in its majestic equality, forbids the rich as well as the poor to sleep under bridges, to beg in the streets, and to steal bread" (1894: Ch 7). But his contemporary, German sociologist Georg Simmel, insisted on the theoretical significance of formal freedom, noting that even in what appear to be much more stringent relationships of subordination than in the market, the

> exclusion of all spontaneity is actually rarer than is suggested by such widely used popular expressions as "coercion," "having no choice," "absolute necessity," etc. Even in the most oppressive and cruel cases of subordination, there is still a considerable measure of personal freedom. We merely do not become aware of it because its manifestation would entail sacrifices which we usually never think of taking upon ourselves . . . the super-subordination relationship destroys the subordinate's freedom only in the case of direct physical violation. In every other case, this relationship only demands a price for the realization of freedom—a price, to be sure, which we are not willing to pay. ([1908] 1950: 182)

Simmel's observation challenges a distinction often made between positive and negative dependence. Positive dependence emphasizes the rewards of gaining valued resources from those who control them. Negative dependence focuses on punishment and the search for ways to avoid it. The latter case suggests that coercive power is a separate type, as those who achieve compliance by withholding physical punishment that they might otherwise inflict are surely doing something different from those who secure compliance with positive rewards. This distinction seems strongest in the case of what Simmel calls "direct physical violation," which presumably includes beatings, torture, and similar actions. In behavioral psychology (e.g., Solomon 1964) as well as sociological exchange theory, coercion and punishment have been treated separately from more positive dependence. For our purposes, however, it seems simpler to note that whether positive and negative, both are forms of dependence, much as one may need to keep in mind differences in their manifestations.[2]

That power in the economy can derive from dependency arising from some particular distribution of resources has been a persistent social science theme at least since the mid-nineteenth century. In twentieth-century sociology and social psychology, a tradition of experimental work on social exchange was initiated by Richard Emerson's 1960s formulations of power as based on dependency. Emerson noted that the "power to control or influence the other resides in control over the things he values, which may range all the way from oil resources to ego-support," and thus an analysis of power has to revolve around the concept of dependence (1962: 32). Emerson's arguments concerned how dependence and power affected social exchange, and while his conception of resources was open-ended and included such items as "ego-support," in practice, the experimental tradition that he initiated has focused on the exchange of actual or putative economic resources, beginning with the work of Cook and Emerson 1978 (for a review of the experimental exchange literature, see Cook and Rice 2003). Dependence, in this tradition, forces the less powerful to exchange at a ratio less favorable than they might otherwise achieve. Emerson does note that power imbalances can be reduced in two possible ways. One is to find alternate exchange partners, which means a change in the structure of networks. Another is to reduce the value one places on the resources on which one has become dependent (see Cook and Rice 2001: 706). Thus the usual conception and experiments hold networks and preferences constant.

An interesting variation on the themes of dependency and subordination comes from Blau (1964), who focuses on organizational situations where those who need advice and expertise have nothing tangible to trade for it but can offer deference. He notes that willingness to "comply with another's demands is a generic social reward, since the power it gives him is a generalized means, parallel to money, which can be used to attain a variety of ends. The power to command compliance is equivalent to credit, which a man can draw on in the future" (22). A consequence of this is the emergence of a status hierarchy. There is no reason why deference could not be exchanged for economic goods rather than expert advice, and it seems likely that this is an important part of the equation in the functioning of feudal or sharecropping arrangements, though economic analysis has typically abstracted away from these elements. These ideas draw a causal relationship between power based on dependency and status differentials, an important general theme that has been neglected in the literature on the economy but emphasized in the political science and political sociology literature on patron-client relationships (e.g., Eisenstadt and Roniger 1984).

Dependency thus far in this discussion focuses on resource imbalances between individuals. But organizations are the unit of analysis in the work of "resource dependence" theorists. In their seminal book, Pfeffer and Salancik

(1978) argue that resources vary in how critical they are to an organization's operations, and some are harder to obtain than others. Thus, external organizations that control needed resources gain power, as do those individuals or subunits within the organization "that can provide the most critical and difficult to obtain resources," which include, in addition to the obvious material ones, "money, prestige, legitimacy, rewards and sanctions, and expertise, or the ability to deal with uncertainty" (Pfeffer 1981: 101).

But Pfeffer emphasizes, as does also Emerson (1962), that *what* resources matter and therefore confer power is not merely given by objective circumstances, as supposed by Marx and Weber and at times by economists (as in the economic concept of "natural monopoly"). Pfeffer suggests instead the value of a "social constructionist" view that there are "few, if any, unchangeable, immutable requirements for organizational survival. Organizations can change domains, constituencies, or technologies, and by so doing, can change the pattern of resource transactions that are required. Moreover, survival or failure occurs only in the long run, and in the present, what is or is not appropriate for organizational success is problematic. Therefore, what comes to be considered a critical resource, or an important contingency or uncertainty in the organization "is a matter of social definition" (Pfeffer 1981: 125). Thus, organizations or social actors who possess a resource can "increase the value of that resource and their own power by claiming scarcity and behaving as if the resource were scarce" (82). Thus, dependence and its converse, power, may result from strategic action. Pfeffer gives as an example the rise of finance as the most important unit in General Motors by the 1960s (127–129).

Gulati and Sytch (2007) point out that the usual conception of power based on dependence assumes that dependence is both substantial and asymmetric. But in situations where dependence is substantial but symmetric, they argue that while asymmetric dependence is properly treated with the "logic of power," symmetric dependence is better understood with the "logic of embeddedness" for two reasons: one is that mutually dependent relationships get infused with sentiment, "leading them to become less instrumental" (2007: 33). This leads to more joint action, more trust, and better information. Partners identify more with one another and develop mutual empathy and a "focus on joint success, embracing a long-term horizon for the relationship" (39). One might then expect companies to show better performance, problem solution, and technological innovation where the high level of mutual dependence encourages trust and commitment—a "culture of trust" (41) that counters moral hazard and thus reduces the need for contractual safeguards. Behavioral norms emerge that would lead to better information exchange, which in turn leads to more efficiency. This argument nicely ties together considerations of power, norms, and trust and illustrates how closely they intertwine in real-world situations. Research on such questions is still sparse, however, and requires data of a kind typically difficult to find. Gulati and Sytch had fieldwork and survey data from lead buyers of components for Ford and Chrysler autos and found partial confirmation of their arguments.

4.1.2 Economic Power Based on Legitimacy

Although power as dependence dominates most discussions and is treated by many writers as the only possible conception of power, it is very important to emphasize that power in the economy (as well as in other social institutions like the polity) derives only in part from resource dependencies. A different type of power is closely related to our discussion of norms in Chapter 2: in many important circumstances, individuals comply with what others require *not* because they depend on them for resources but because these others occupy some position of authority that compliers believe *entitles* them to issue commands that should be obeyed. These others possess "legitimate authority," which receives its classic exposition from Max Weber. In fact, Weber discusses power based on dependence almost in passing and implies that it is less interesting than power based on legitimacy.[3] He posits two "diametrically contrasting types of domination, viz., domination by virtue of a constellation of interests (in particular: by virtue of a position of monopoly) and domination by virtue of authority, i.e., power to command and duty to obey" ([1921] 1968: 943).[4]

Talcott Parsons highlighted the importance of legitimacy when he analogized power to money, and argued that both could be used expansively or narrowly, depending on the degree of confidence and legitimacy they inspired. He noted that just as a "monetary system resting entirely on gold as the actual medium of exchange is a very primitive one which simply cannot mediate a complex system of market exchange, so a power system in which the only negative sanction is the threat of force is a very primitive one which cannot function to mediate a complex system of organizational coordination" (1963: 240). For money to work well it must be "institutionalized as a symbol; it must be legitimized and must inspire 'confidence' within the system" (240). Similarly, for power to be the "generalized medium of mobilizing resources for effective collective action . . . it too must be both symbolically generalized and legitimized" (240). One can reject Parsons's idea that legitimate power functions mainly to support collective action but take his point that coercion is a highly limiting basis for the exercise of power compared to the force of legitimate authority.

Compliance based on a belief that commands are legitimate occurs at many levels. In traditional families the world over, parental authority is a given that (at least young) children rarely question. Some part of children's obedience no doubt results from dependency, but were this the only reason, obedience would be much harder to obtain than it is. The norm that parents are *entitled* to command is inculcated in many cultures. As I will discuss further in the sequel volume's discussion of business groups and family firms, this authority, usually paternal, is a strong cohesive force in the economy, for better or for worse. Beyond the family, employees are enjoined by their firms' rules, organization chart, and everyday procedures to follow instructions they are given. In political units such as states, provinces, countries, and supra-national units (such as the European Union), individuals and firms follow legal requirements that have been set by established procedures, in part because they acknowledge the legitimacy of these procedures.

Of course, the impact of formal rules also results in part from dependency—the control over needed resources and possible punishments by those who enforce them. *But rules at all levels are obeyed in situations where they could be avoided,* and individuals rarely use all available means to avoid them. One reason is that actors in most situations acknowledge some normative obligation to follow rules that have been appropriately set and commands issued by those whose position entitles them to do so. This is what is meant by the force of legitimate authority.

That people obey laws and defer to government because they consider their authority legitimate is also increasingly supported by a body of empirical research devoted precisely to sorting out what part of obedience is due to dependence and consequent rational self-seeking and calculation of benefits as compared to the force of norms and legitimacy. Thus, Tyler (2006) summarizes a series of studies devoted to contrasting the "instrumental and normative perspectives on why people follow the law" (3). He notes that while most literature on crime stresses the instrumental issue of how deterrence and the fear of being caught impacts rates of violations, voluntary compliance "costs much less and is, as a result, especially valued by legal authorities" (4). Voluntary compliance based on normative factors falls into two categories: obeying the law because of personal moral views that coincide with the law's prescription of what behavior is appropriate and obeying because of a belief that the police, courts, and other law enforcers use appropriate, fair, and rational procedures in establishing and enforcing the law. Of these, Tyler's review suggests that the more important of these is belief in procedural justice, which is an important determinant of legitimacy for the authorities, and that, by comparison, the avoidance of punishment as a motive for potential law violators is small (269).

The emphasis on procedural justice corresponds to Max Weber's category of legitimation based on "legal-rational" grounds (as Tyler notes, 2006: 273). Speaking mainly about political order but making an argument that applies equally well to economic rules, Weber argued that there are only three general principles by which authorities legitimate and ordinary citizens understand the validity of rules, laws, and commands. One is "rational-legal" grounds, which correspond to what I have argued thus far. These grounds are broadly impersonal. The other two principles refer to personal authority. Of these, the first is "traditional grounds"—the idea that the person or persons exercising authority are entitled to do so because of the "sanctity of immemorial traditions" (Weber [1921] 1968: 215), and the second is "charismatic grounds," "resting on devotion to the exceptional sanctity, heroism or exemplary character of an individual person and of the normative patterns or order revealed or ordained by him" (215). While most of our discussions will concern the impact of laws and regulations, this does not exhaust the sources of legitimate authority in the modern economy, as I will discuss further under the heading of familial and paternal authority, which falls more under Weber's concept of "traditional authority."

A category of power and resulting obedience that is related to legitimacy but involves a different emphasis derives from a consideration of the importance of group identity. Tyler in particular has distinguished this source from legitimate authority and the pursuit of interests in a situation of dependency. He notes that an "important aspect of people's interaction with others involves the creation of social identity. . . . people both define themselves through their association with groups and organizations and use their membership in groups to judge their social status and through it their self-worth." (2001: 289). In groups where people have social connections, their trust judgments "become more strongly linked to identity concerns, and less strongly linked to resource exchange" (289), as I noted in Chapter 3 on trust. Identity concerns are "distinct from concerns over resource exchange" (289). Those who feel "respected and valued by the group respond by following group rules and acting on behalf of the group, that is, by deferring to authorities" (290).

I do not distinguish obedience resulting from group identity as a separate type of power, since in the Weberian conception of obedience to what is perceived as legitimate authority, an implicit necessary condition for such legitimacy to be in place is that a group of people feel enough common identity to be part of a unit where authoritative positions would be relevant. But it is certainly useful to note this as part of a discussion of the conditions under which legitimacy would lead to power and compliance.

4.1.3 Economic Power Based on Control of Agenda and Discourse

A third type of power cannot be reduced to dependence or legitimacy: that based on shaping the agenda or discourse on economic issues. This type of power was first clearly delineated as the result of mid-twentieth-century debates in political science. These were initially framed as a dispute between the "elitist" view that an identifiable "power elite" made the important decisions in large American cities and the "pluralist" view that different groups exercise power over different issues, a view more promising for democratic process. (The details of this debate are nicely summarized in Lukes 1974). Both positions were criticized by scholars who pointed out that the emphasis on control over decisions and issues took these as given, whereas those who could determine what people thought the issues *were* could be even more powerful since they might prevent important decisions from even reaching the public agenda (cf. esp. Bachrach and Baratz 1962). For the case of power in organizations, Pfeffer similarly notes that one of the "best and least obtrusive ways of exercising power is to prevent the decision issue from surfacing in the first place. This strategy is particularly applicable to those interests within the organization which favor the present condition. . . . Thus the exercise of power frequently involves controlling the agenda of what is considered for decision" (1981: 146).

Matthew Crenson, for example, showed that air pollution became a political issue with much higher probability in some mid-twentieth-century American cities than in others, net of the actual pollution level. So air pollution was an important issue that led to regulation in East Chicago, Indiana, by 1949, while similarly (and heavily) polluted neighboring Gary, Indiana did not take action until 1962. Crenson shows that the dominance of Gary by U.S. Steel was the most important factor in this delay. It was well understood what the corporation's position was, even though it took little part in the political process. In fact, U.S. Steel was typically sympathetic but evasive on the issue and carefully avoided taking a strong position (1971: Ch. 2). As Padgett and Ansell (1993) note in discussing the enormous power of Cosimo de Medici in medieval Florence, quite contrary to the advice and description of Machiavelli, one way to control a situation is to avoid taking action that will define your interests clearly and thereby provoke opposition. Thus Cosimo was known to be "sphinxlike" and "multivocal" (1262–1264). While it was no doubt clearer than with Cosimo what the interests of U.S. Steel were with regard to air pollution, its careful avoidance of clear action made it more difficult for potential activists to find a target or even define what needed to be done.

Controlling the agenda is closely related to a broader conception that we might call control of the *ideas* that generate the social and political agenda that people pursue.[5] In their account of the 2007–2009 financial crisis, Johnson and Kwak (2010) argue that an oligarchy of officials from six banks of enormous size—"too big to fail"—ultimately determine American fiscal and monetary policy. I return to this assertion below in discussing the existence and impact of elites. But here I note their argument that a necessary condition for this to occur was that the general public and policymakers alike came to hold the view that the financial sector had special status and should be shown deference and protection. They note that what they refer to as the "Wall Street banks" were, in 2009, one of the wealthiest industries in the history of America and "one of the most powerful political forces in Washington." But beyond this, investment bankers and their allies had for more than a decade "assumed top positions in the White House and Treasury Department," and the "ideology of Wall Street—that unfettered innovation and unregulated financial markets were good for America and the world— became the consensus position in Washington on both sides of the political aisle" (2011: Ch. 4). Whether one concurs with the causal argument here, it is clear that economic policymakers in the Clinton, Bush, and Obama administrations were predominantly bankers with Wall Street origins or connections or economists closely tied to those banks and bankers, so that their perspectives had a privileged position in discourse on remedies and reforms for the emerging crisis.

The importance of agenda control may be related to Foucault's argument that there is a secular trend in modern history for economic and political power, at least outside the orbit of despotic regimes, to become less and less visible. Under feudalism, pomp and ceremony, aided by elaborate costume and sumptuary rules to prevent the lower orders from wearing garb reserved for the elite, clearly signaled who were powerful actors. Graeber notes that Europe's elite gradually became less interested in elaborate personal adornment and male dress became much less colorful. In the Renaissance, wealthy men wore "bright ornamental clothing, makeup, jewelry, etc.—[but by the eighteenth century] all of this came to be regarded as appropriate only for women" (2001: 95), and the formal male costume that would become the modern business suit was already more or less in place by 1750. Formal male dress "seems intended to efface not only a man's physical form but his very individuality, rendering him abstract and, in a certain sense, invisible" (96). In the modern setting, the power in question, e.g., in the Johnson and Kwak argument, takes the form of technocratic expertise, subtle and behind the scenes, and critics are depicted as unable to comprehend the complex technical issues and therefore a threat to financial stability. Insofar as this is successful, it is a very distinct and effective use of power.

4.1.4 Relations among Types of Power

It is useful for clarity to distinguish analytically power as dependence, legitimacy, and discourse/agenda control. But powerful actors typically combine these types, and the more seamlessly they do, the more powerful they will be. So the inaction and apparent neutrality of U.S. Steel in Gary, Indiana, may have inhibited the perception of air pollution as a serious policy issue, but it also appears that policymakers feared that effective pollution control would lead the company to divert some production to other sites less burdened by regulation (cf. Crenson 1971: 78), so here Gary's dependence on the company for employment confers considerable power. There are also sequences in which power of one type facilitates the development of another, and this is one way that power positions sustain and reproduce themselves. Max Weber offers the simple example where domination by a constellation of interests (i.e., dependence based on a monopoly position) may gradually morph into domination based on legitimate authority. For example, when a bank has leverage over a corporation because of the latter's dependence on it for capital and then demands that a member of its board be put on the board of a debtor corporation, then this leads to the possibility that the interlocked board will "give decisive orders to management by virtue of the latter's obligation to obey" ([1921] 1968: 944). Conversely, a position of legitimate authority can be exploited in such a way as to lead to economic dependence on the part of subordinates and control of the agenda through influence on what ideas, news, and discourse are permitted to circulate. Authoritarian and totalitarian political authorities use all of these tools to reinforce their grip on power.

4.2 Power and Social Structure

Classifying the sources or types of power can get us only so far and must be followed by discussion of under what circumstances which actors or types of actors are able to wield the different types of power and combinations thereof.

4.2.1 Power Based on Individual Characteristics

The methodological individualist might begin by supposing that some individuals are bound to be powerful because they have characteristics or resources that make it highly likely they will create dependence, engender compliance by conveying legitimacy, or persuasively shape the economic agenda. But all such circumstances are embedded in social settings that define what resources matter and how they are allocated, how people conceive of legitimacy, and by what process agendas are set and followed. Without under-standing the relevant settings, individual characteristics tell us all too little about how economic power can be exerted.

In fact, it is extraordinary that the quest to explain power differentials through the characteristics of individuals alone fails even for subhuman spe-cies where one might think them obviously sufficient. Chase, for example (1974, 1980: 908–909; Lindquist and Chase 2009), shows that to predict the transitive dominance hierarchies typical of animals from individual charac-teristics or even from success in isolated pairwise encounters would require correlations between individual traits and competitive outcomes consider-ably higher than those actually observed. He goes on to show through exper-iments with chickens and other animals that even in relatively simple species, complex interaction processes account for the substantial gap between the hierarchies found empirically and those that might have resulted from indi-vidual characteristics alone.

4.2.2 Power and Social Network Position

The next level of analysis up from a pure focus on individuals is that of the social networks in which they are embedded. A large but diffuse literature suggests that an actor's network position predicts his or her power over other actors, net of the actors' own characteristics (which, in the sociological exper-imental tradition, are controlled). Most of this literature defines the power derived from such positions in terms of dependence, typically enacted in social exchange.

Before summarizing efforts to find simple relationships between an actor's social network position and power over others, I note that the findings turn out ultimately to depend heavily on the details of exchange and depen-dence and on the kind of resources exchanged. This is so even abstracting away from historical, cultural, and institutional context, important as I will later argue those to be in making such assertions.

Mid-twentieth-century work on group decision-making found that cen-tral actors in small and simple networks are more powerful (for a review, see Mizruchi and Potts 1998, and for details of the various ways to measure net-work "centrality," see Scott 2013). But later work in sociological exchange theory showed that this simple relationship was misleading because whether a node's centrality confers power depends in part upon whether a network of exchange is connected negatively or positively: in the former, exchange with one partner *precludes* exchange with others, whereas in the latter, exchange in one relationship *facilitates* that in others. Centrality in negatively connected networks is less relevant for power than is access to actors who are highly dependent and have few alternatives (see Molm 2001: 264). In fact, since more central actors tend to be connected to others who are also central, and therefore also well connected, this cuts against their ability to gain advantage in exchange, the usual measure of power in this literature. On the other hand, in positively connected networks, central actors *are* more powerful because they can serve as brokers in cooperative relations, as was first suggested by Cook, Emerson, and Gillmore (1983).[6]

Most experimental social psychology has dealt with negatively connected networks, which have, by definition, a zero-sum aspect. Such exchange is similar to that analyzed in microeconomics, and power consists of having a relative monopoly position in terms of the resources you possess and the relatively poor alternatives available to others who need them. The bulk of such research concerns exchanges that are negotiated ahead of time, before exchanges take place, rather than those in which an actor makes an offering and waits to see what she will get in return, denoted in this literature as "reciprocal exchange."[7] I argue that the emphasis on negotiated exchange in negatively connected networks lends itself to a focus on small-scale competitive interaction but is less likely to shed light on the way localized or small-scale social structures develop into larger entities. Molm formulates this issue as involving a distinction between the "cooperative and competitive faces of exchange" (2003: 14), arguing that the study of negotiated exchange leads to an emphasis on power and inequality, whereas that of reciprocal exchange leads to an emphasis on attraction, sentiments, cohesion, group formation" i.e., the "cooperative aspects of social exchange relations" (2003: 15).

I think this is partially correct but differ in arguing that the use of power is not irrelevant to and may in fact be crucially important to the study of trust, cooperation, cohesion, and group formation. Certainly, social aggregations of any substantial size are unlikely to be assembled in the absence of concerted efforts by powerful actors, as has often been noted by students of empires (see especially the classic work of Eisenstadt 1963).

4.3 Brokerage

One way to bridge the conceptual distance between small-scale exchange and the emergence of larger economic structures where power matters is to look more closely at brokerage, whose importance in exchange studies has been noted for positively connected networks, where actors are typically engaged in positive-sum activities. The idea that under some circumstances central positions create power by facilitating brokerage leads me to analyze more closely what brokerage means and how it can lead us to more general arguments about power in the economy. In the experimental sociology exchange theory literature, "brokerage" means that the broker, B, obtains resources from A and exchanges them with C, in situations where A and C are not directly connected. A different conception of brokerage entails B *creating* a connection between A and C, who then transact directly with one another, a particularly strong example of which would be brokering a marriage ("match-making"). Obstfeld (2005) elaborates on the consequences of this distinction and contrasts the classic observations of Simmel on the *tertius gaudens* (literally, the "third who enjoys"—i.e., benefits from playing off two other actors against one another—see Simmel [1908] 1950: 154–162) to what he calls the *tertius iungens*—the third who joins, i.e., an actor whose brokerage consists of bringing others together. (And his contribution stimulates the further reflections of Stovel et al. 2011, Stovel and Shaw 2012, and Obstfeld et al. 2014.) The difference between these two conceptions is highly consequential for the way groups are structured and for whether brokers are able to maintain their power over substantial periods.

In addition to sociological exchange theory, Ronald Burt's work on "structural holes" elaborates the former of these conceptions of brokerage and was the first to develop systematically the relation of brokerage to power, influence, and economic gain (1992). Burt built on earlier work of mine (1973, 1983) proposing that dense clusters in social networks may be connected to one another by a small number of ties that "bridge" them and thus make information flow more likely across the entire network. I noted that individuals whose ties provided these bridges were in a better position to gain information about jobs or other valuable opportunities, and the overall network would benefit from increased information flow in such activities as science. My emphasis in this work was on the likelihood that the ties bridging clusters are weak, which I called the "strength of weak ties."

Burt shifted the emphasis away from the quality of ties to the strategic advantage of having ties that provided the only route through which information or resources could travel between network segments otherwise disconnected from one another. He called such disconnections "structural holes" and emphasized that those whose contacts were "nonredundant" (i.e., each connecting you to different network segments) enjoy the *tertius gaudens* advantage emphasized by Georg Simmel: they may play the unconnected actors off against one another (Burt 1992: 33), in effect brokering the relationship between them and generating profit by being between others—the literal meaning of the term "entrepreneur" (34). He developed the corresponding concept of "structural autonomy"—the extent to which a "player" (the term Burt uses to emphasize the active agency that he attributes to the actors he analyzes) has a network "rich in structural holes . . . and thus rich in information and control benefits" (44). The converse, "network constraint" on a person, is high if "he or she has few contacts . . . the contacts are closely connected with one another . . . or they share information indirectly via a central contact" (2005: 27). In his 2005 account, Burt emphasizes the concept of "social capital," a term he uses to describe the advantages of an actor high in network autonomy and low in constraint.

Burt's empirical studies typically use measures of autonomy or constraint to predict such outcomes as having better ideas, higher promotion likelihood, higher salaries, and more favorable evaluations for individuals or greater profit for firms and industries. These measures of individual nodes' success in relational networks are similar to the conception of power in sociological exchange theory, as the ability to gain a more favorable exchange ratio than others in transactions. As a conception of power, this is only a subset of outcomes that might exemplify the Weberian conception that power is the ability to carry out your own will in a social relationship.

4.3.1 Brokerage beyond Small Groups

One way to consider power more generally is to note that the networks studied in experimental exchange or structural hole studies are typically homogeneous with regard to social affiliations or identities. This reflects in part an implicit conception of brokerage as operating at a rather small-scale level where homogeneity of identity may be a reasonable assumption. But in even modestly larger settings, brokers are often thought of as mediating between groups that have differing social identities that matter to members and that in fact are what make communication and transaction across group boundaries difficult without a broker.

Reagans and Zuckerman (2008) point out that gaining power from a potential brokerage position is not an automatic consequence of structure, since the broker who has contacts into many separated cliques gains power from this in exchange *only* insofar as individuals within each clique want and need what those in other cliques have to trade. If for whatever reason individuals prefer to exchange within their *own* group, then those whose networks are highly nonredundant—with a high level of structural autonomy, in Burt's terminology—can gain little if any advantage from this and would have done better to "invest" in redundant contacts within their own group. Those with nonredundant contacts will be highly knowledgeable because of their diverse connections, but as the title of the Reagans and Zuckerman article notes, this would be a case where "knowledge does not equal power." This leads me to ask why individuals would prefer resources that are near them in social network terms. Reagans and Zuckerman interpret this as a taste for the local as opposed to the exotic, a kind of provincialism, a preference for the familiar that they refer to as "homophilic tastes" (2008: 907, 919). Such preferences could plausibly result from strong group identities.

But there are other reasons why individuals might have preferences to trade only with locals or only with "foreigners" that do not mainly concern their level of cosmopolitan taste or group identity. One obvious case would be where local production is simply inadequate to meet all consumer demand, and there are variations among groups in what is produced such that there are advantages to intergroup trade, like those suggested by the classic economic theory of comparative advantage. This case is a simple matter of economic rationality and perhaps should be regarded as the null hypothesis when we encounter preferences for distant goods.

Strong group identities produce deviations from this null. One situation is where there is a preference to trade with one's own group so as not to confer advantage on another group with which yours has cultural or political differences. Carruthers (1996), for example, shows that in early eighteenth-century England, the trading of stock in the East India Company followed not anonymous economic logic but rather that of political affiliation, as Whigs and Tories traded shares almost exclusively with members of their own party rather than facilitate increasing control over that entity by their opponents. In such a situation someone who could plausibly broker between Whigs and Tories would not gain, since neither group's members sought or desired such trades.

Brokers could gain advantage when opposing political interests needed to deal with one another to reach political agreement about issues, many of which are economic, but have difficulty doing so without mediation. Roger Gould analyzed situations like this in an effort to develop arguments about brokerage and power. He studied political conflict in two cities, one of which had a stable structure of political cliques, defined mainly by party affiliation[8]. Many of the political differences between groups revolved around economic issues. What Gould found is that individuals with good network contacts into both groups might be influential but actually became less so to the extent that they also possessed traditional influence resources such as money, official authority, or control over jobs or land (1989: 545). He points out that this is contrary to what one might expect from a more typical sociological exchange theoretic argument in which the "ability to control other individuals' exchange opportunities would enhance the value of one's resources" (545). The problem is that the "mobilization of influence resources erodes the image of impartiality which is crucial to the brokerage role" (546), and this "militates against current theoretical work rooted in an exchange perspective, which tends to predict a positive interaction between resource-based and position-based power" (548).

This argument is interesting because it breaks out of the more or less behaviorist mold of much exchange theorizing by calling on the importance of social identity (what group people conceive themselves as being affiliated with), norms about how a "broker" should behave, and feelings of trust that would be evoked if the broker is thought to be acting without regard to his own interest. This trust would be eroded by his use of traditional resources in a setting where he was supposedly above the fray. We should also note that the conception of power or influence that Gould invokes is quite different from the one normally used in exchange theory, which is that you exchange at a more favorable ratio than others. Here, the concept means that people have more influence than others over the outcomes of issues in economics or politics, and the two conceptions of power are somewhat at odds, since in Gould's case, those who make their interests clear or use resources to achieve them lose their broader ability to shape issue outcomes.

Gould and Fernandez (1989) formalize arguments for the case of two identifiable groups by developing a five-way typology about brokerage based on whether a broker operates within a single group, coordinating its members; coordinates members of another group—as where a stockbroker brings investors together; brings members of another group together with members of his own ("gatekeeper" role); brings members of his own group together with members of another ("representative" role); or brings together people from two different groups, neither of which he is a member ("arbitrator" role) (92–93).

In a later empirical study of the health care domain, where network nodes are organizations, Fernandez and Gould showed that those governmental organizations or bodies occupying a gatekeeper or representative role were considered influential only insofar as they refrained from expressing their own policy views and could thus be seen as impartial brokers. They refer to this as the "paradox of state power" (1994: 1483) and a special case of the general principle that "actors whose structural position bridges 'synapses' in a social network derive an advantage from this position only as long as they do not openly try to use this advantage" (1483).

The word "openly" in this sentence suggests an ambiguity closely related to the concept of "robust action" articulated originally by Leifer (1991) and developed further by Padgett and Ansell (1993) with regard to Cosimo de Medici and his enormous political and economic power in medieval Florence. Leifer (1991) argued that ideas about strategic action are typically simplistic and that the most effective players in a game like chess (whose tournaments he studied in great detail) are by no means those who plan far ahead and lay out elaborate branching diagrams for strategy, as game theory might prescribe, but rather those who keep their intentions unclear and preserve maximum flexibility for their own action while maneuvering opponents into showing their own strategies. This conception of optimum strategy was adapted by Padgett and Ansell in their study of the Medicis, in particular the surprising 1434 seizure of the reins of Florentine power by Cosimo de Medici.

They note that in any structure of authority, there is a contradiction between the role of "boss" and that of "judge." For the latter, legitimacy requires others to believe that "judges and rules are not motivated by self-interest" (1993: 1260). This is quite similar in spirit to the earlier arguments of Gould and Fernandez. Padgett and Ansell invoke contemporary evidence that vividly describes Cosimo de Medici as "sphinxlike," rarely answering questions or requests directly and being extraordinarily difficult to read as to what, if anything, he meant to accomplish in any particular activity. One aspect of this is that Cosimo had a variety of interests within particular institutional contexts that were well known—financial interests, family interests, and political interests. But these did not align clearly with one another, and this made it possible for it to be obscure in any given situation, which involved more than one such interest, which one he was in fact pursuing.

The variety of institutional realms in which they were active also meant that Cosimo and his fellow Medicis could assemble a number of different sets of followers—those to whom they were tied by kinship, others by neighborhood, some by political patronage, and still others by financial and business dealings. These various cliques of Medici followers were not connected to one another and so owed their influence and importance only to the Medicis to whom they were therefore loyal. So Cosimo de Medici sat astride a structural hole of high magnitude.

This leads us to a critical issue: if a broker's power arises from occupying the central position in a structural hole—i.e., he or she is the kind of broker who profits from keeping people apart rather than from bringing them together—what is to prevent erosion of that power by members of the various spokes allying with one another to overcome the broker's advantage? In the Florentine case, what made this so unlikely was that each spoke was an identity group that had strong negative feelings toward other groups of equal status and utter social contempt for those of lower rank. So, as Padgett and Ansell note, the Medicis had a kinship network of patrician families into which they had married and an economic network of "new men"—from recently upwardly mobile families. There was no danger that these two separate networks of individuals would coalesce and present a united front against the Medicis since they "despised one another" (Padgett and Ansell 1993: 1281) and could neither marry nor do business with one another given overwhelming status norms of the period.

4.3.2 Brokerage, Entrepreneurship, and Spheres of Exchange

We can get further insight into actors at crucial social structural intersections by looking at a line of argument on this subject that emerged separately and without mutual awareness in economics and in anthropology and made virtually no subsequent contact with sociology or social psychology, despite their great relevance to work in those fields. The economic argument begins from the simple idea of arbitrage, the act of buying a good cheaper in one market and selling it dearer in another, capturing the profit available from the separation of the markets. The arbitrageur exploits a structural hole, having one foot (the invisible foot?) in both markets and exploiting the fact that he is the only one who clearly sees and thus can profit from the price differential. This simple idea was seized upon by economists of the Austrian persuasion as the foundation of a theory of entrepreneurship. Israel Kirzner (1973) took the lead, defining an "entrepreneur" precisely as someone who connects previously isolated markets by arbitrage. Typical of Austrian economics, he emphasizes not so much rational calculation as alertness to information and opportunity. The entrepreneur, in his view, needs to "discover where buyers have been paying too much and where sellers have been receiving too little and to bridge the gap by offering to buy for a little more and to sell for a little less. To discover these unexploited opportunities requires alertness. Calculation will not help, and economizing and optimizing will not of themselves yield this knowledge" (41).

Meanwhile, Norwegian anthropologist Frederick Barth was developing a related but somewhat more complex line of argument. He built on the idea of economic anthropologists that, especially in non-capitalist societies, there are well-defined and distinct "spheres" or "circuits" of exchange. The basic idea is that in any given society people do not define all items as goods, and even among those so defined, some may not be commensurable with one another. Those goods and services that are mutually commensurable can be traded only with one another, and this leads to distinct spheres of exchange in which every item within a sphere may be exchanged for every other but not with those in other spheres (see Bohannan and Dalton 1962; cf. Espeland and Stevens 1998 and Zelizer 2005). Firth's classic account, for example, of the Tikopia describes three distinct spheres of exchange, and he notes that "objects and services in these three series cannot be completely expressed in terms of one another, since normally they are never brought to the bar of exchange together. It is impossible, for example, to express the value of a bonito-hook in terms of a quantity of food, since no such exchange is ever made and would be regarded by the Tikopia as fantastic" (1975 [1939]: 340). Barth's idea is that whatever the cognitive, moral, or practical forces may be that keep these spheres of exchange separate, there may be individuals who for whatever reason may transcend them, and the reason to do so is that if one can commensurate by some yardstick items in one sphere with those in another, it is likely that one item can be bought or produced cheaply in one sphere and then sold at a higher price in another, yielding profit from the differential. He refers to the individual who carries out this activity as an entrepreneur, and it is clear that as in the examples above, this is again someone who stands *between* social structural units, which, in this case, however, are separated spheres of exchange rather than networks of individuals (see Barth 1967).

As a case study, Barth (1967) describes the Sudanese Fur, a tribe in which labor and money were incommensurable (because wage labor was thought shameful) and where certain products like millet and millet beer were *not* exchanged for money but produced to be exchanged for communal labor, as in help building a house. A monetary exchange sphere did exist where food and other useful items were exchanged for cash. Arab merchants came on the scene and, being outsiders not subject to local normative understandings, hired local workers to grow tomatoes, paying for the labor with beer. Since neither beer nor labor was exchanged for cash among the Fur, the workers were unaware that the cash value of the tomatoes in the commercial sphere far exceeded the value of the beer that compensated their labor, and the merchants reaped a large profit from sale of tomatoes.

For both Kirzner and Barth, the entrepreneur profits from arbitraging across a social structural gap and in the limited conception of power that informs exchange theory can be said to be more powerful than others since he gets better terms of trade. But might such entrepreneurs become powerful in more expansive ways? The answer to this question most likely lies in whether he can continue to benefit from the social structural gap exploited or whether it will close up, thus ending the source of profit. Both writers expected the latter outcome, which would dissipate the broker's power. Kirzner imagined the entrepreneur as a figure whose activity led to equilibrium by ending the inefficiencies caused by different prices in separated markets. His objection to standard neoclassical economic theory was not that it expected markets to equilibrate but rather that it imagined them to do so automatically, without a clear mechanism, relying instead on the fictional Walrasian auctioneer. In his account, equilibrium still occurs but through a dynamic process resulting from the agency of alert actors. Barth similarly argued that entrepreneurs, in the sense he defined them, were essential for the economic development of a country, since separated spheres of exchange represented a form of economic backwardness, which imposed drags on the best use of productive factors on account of information and mobility barriers. I think it fair to say that both writers, coming from quite different intellectual traditions, nevertheless represented variations on optimistic mid-twentieth-century modernization theory.

The problem with both accounts is that the entrepreneur who profits from bridging and brokering separated chunks of social structure or exchange has a strong incentive to keep those chunks separate, thus preserving advantage. There are two tasks that one must achieve in order to do so. One is to keep up ties into both chunks, and as Burt (2002) has noted, this is nontrivial, especially insofar as a tie is to an actor very different from oneself. Thus, he finds that ties that bridge structural holes have a much higher rate of early decay than other ties supported by mutual friends and colleagues, which are much easier to maintain. The other task is to keep the structural hole open by preventing other transactions from taking place across disconnected sectors. In Kirzner's view, this is unlikely because the trades performed by the arbitrageur are visible to other market participants, and they will quickly apprehend the information that led to profit and the possibility of advantage will disappear as the two separated markets are joined by enough trades to restore the single price that theory stipulates. In Barth's case, the Arab traders' activity and profits might have been sufficiently visible to generate resentment, and though his study breaks off without following the consequences, he does note that resistance to their activity was beginning to emerge (1967: 172). It may not be a coincidence that late twentieth- and early twenty-first-century turmoil in the Sudan has centered in part on the role of Arabs among the more historically rooted tribal groups.

Note the strong contrast between Kirzner's or Barth's image of the entrepreneur as an alert agent of economic progress, uncovering opportunities to profit by remedying inefficiencies, and the more swashbuckling image of entrepreneurs suggested by Schumpeter (1911) who characterizes them as engaging in "creative destruction." The larger-than-life figures like Rockefeller and Carnegie who fit the Schumpeterian mold were acutely aware of the need to sustain their advantages by restraining trades among others that would reduce their monopoly power, and anti-trust legislation of this period focuses on the inefficiencies and profits that result from what became illegal restraint of trade. The monopoly power that they reaped was not "natural" but resulted from their active manipulation of markets to preserve the disconnections that yielded their profits. Though such figures are far from the "sphinxlike" inscrutability of figures like Cosimo de Medici[9] and thus eventually provoked resistance in the form of legal constraints, they did nevertheless strive to cloak their activities as normal market action and would have been more successful had not a series of early twentieth-century "muckrakers" exposed what they did behind the scenes, as Ida Tarbell (1904) famously did for Rockefeller's Standard Oil, which was broken up by a landmark Supreme Court decision in 1911. I note also that Roger Gould's emphasis on the need for brokers to appear not to be feathering their own nests in order to be legitimate suggests one reason why those who do so generate the kinds of resistance faced by profiteering brokers from Arab traders to John D. Rockefeller.

To develop this argument further, we should note that although Kirzner and Barth share a conception of entrepreneurs as those who gain profit from bridging previously separated spheres of exchange, Kirzner imagines a figure who connects two markets that are similar to one another in every way but that are disconnected. Barth's protagonist, on the other hand, does something more complex, linking spheres that have completely disjoint sets of exchanges, different circuits of goods and services. In Kirzner's case, one imagines that there are no people in common between the two markets across which the entrepreneur arbitrages; in Barth's case, the people in the two spheres might be exactly the same or at least overlap, but the exchanges are different because of some preconception about what can be imagined to be commensurable with what. Thus, while Kirzner's figure engages in a transaction that is completely familiar to all concerned, Barth's is more creative, originating an entirely new kind of transaction, exchanging items previously imagined not to be commensurable or exchangeable. This creativity, however, is built on the transgression of previous moral prohibitions, suggesting still another source of resistance.

4.3.3 Brokerage, Power, Elites, and "Small Worlds"

Shifting our focus to larger settings, I note that questions of brokerage and entrepreneurship are related to the rapidly growing literature and discussion on complex networks and "small worlds." Stanley Milgram's clever 1960s experiments used a modified chain-letter technique that investigated the length of a chain of acquaintances connecting any two randomly chosen individuals in the United States. Milgram named this the "small world problem" after the obligatory cocktail party response of strangers who unexpectedly discover a shared acquaintance. His results suggested that average chain lengths connecting random individuals were surprisingly small, on the order of six, as confirmed by later research (see, e.g., Dodds, Muhamad, and Watts 2003 and my comment thereon, Granovetter 2003). Complex network studies took off in the 1990s, in part because of the exponential increase in computing power that arrived on most researchers' desktops. Watts and Strogatz (1998), in particular, breathed new life into the small-world problem by introducing more precise formulations and allowing new insight into the circumstances under which we might see results like those Milgram found.

The paradox of Milgram's research is that most people are more or less embedded in cliques, so it is surprising that path distances among randomly chosen people are so low. Watts and Strogatz (1998) pointed out that in a random graph—a network in which people chose their friends at random—there would be very few cliques, as these result from choosing or associating with others whom your friends already know, hardly random. Because it is cliquedness, or "clustering" (as it is called in this literature), that makes it harder to reach random others in the network, path lengths—the minimum number of links from one person to any other ("geodesics" in the language of graph theory)—should be low in a random network and conversely high in a very clustered one. Watts and Strogatz (1998) simulated highly clustered networks, and as predicted, path lengths to random others were high. But when they "rewired" ties in the clusters to random other network points in the overall network, they were surprised to find that after a *very* small amount of rewiring, just a few percent of ties, the average path length decreased so dramatically that it wasn't that different from a random graph, and yet the overall network remained highly cliqued; this was what they called a "small world." What had happened was that enough of the rewired ties created "shortcuts" between cliques that overall connectivity dramatically increased so that contrary to theoretical expectations, high clustering was accompanied by low path lengths, just as Milgram found for the actual empirical world.

While complex network researchers have stressed connectivity, the small worlds of Watts and Strogatz also look like the structures we have been discussing in relation to power, where individuals at either end of "shortcut" ties sit astride structural holes and therefore have the potential to become powerful, influential, and/or successful. This is just the flip side of the dramatically reduced path length: that reduction can be due to the ties of a small number of people, who are therefore in strategic network locations. So small-world networks present an opportunity to those in such locations to gain economic and/or political power. Research has begun in recent years on how and whether this may take place in the economy.

One reason this is interesting is because it links two research traditions on power that have proceeded rather separately and with very different emphases and levels of analysis. One is the work I have been discussing that analyzes the positional sources of power in social networks of exchange and economic/political action; the other is an older tradition of power studies that focuses on elites who dominate the political and economic institutions of societies and whose unity and cohesion are a longstanding subject of analysis and contention. This work is identified with such names as Vilfredo Pareto, Gaetano Mosca, and C. Wright Mills, whose 1956 book *The Power Elite* became a manifesto for many, especially on the left, who saw elites as maintaining an undemocratic domination of the many by the few. Much of this tradition suggested the importance of social networks but in an era without the tools of modern complex network theory. On the cusp between these traditions are works by Useem (1984) and Mintz and Schwartz (1985) that explicitly conceptualize elite dominance as a network phenomenon and begin to apply modern analytic tools to the problem.

The work of Mills has illuminating similarities and differences from explicit social network analysis. The studies of brokerage that I have described diverge from those of small-group exchange in introducing identity and institutional context as important and as a reason why brokerage matters. The work of Mills and other macro-level analysts of power leans heavily on the importance of institutional context. Mills stresses that to have power "requires access to major institutions" ([1956] 2000: 11) and that if you looked at "the one hundred most powerful men in America . . . away from the institutional positions that they now occupy . . . then they would be powerless and poor and uncelebrated" (10). Mills had especially in mind the power resulting from high corporate positions, and by the "power elite" he meant the "political, economic and military circles which as an intricate set of overlapping cliques shape decisions having at least national consequences" (18).

His interest in "overlapping cliques" is the link to our discussion. He stresses the importance of those who move easily between institutional contexts and by so doing occupy critical boundary positions, such as retiring generals who join boards of directors (214); the "admiral who is also a banker and a lawyer and who heads up an important federal commission; the corporate executive whose company was one of the two or three leading war materiel producers who is now the Secretary of Defense; the wartime general who dons civilian clothes to sit on the political directorate and then becomes a member of the board of directors of a leading economic corporation" (288). Because of their multiple roles, simultaneous or sequential, they "readily transcend the particularity of interest in any one of these institutional milieux . . . they lace the three types of milieux together" (289). He adds that in each of the elite circles there is a "concern to recruit and to train successors as 'broad-gauge' men, that is, as men capable of making decisions that involve institutional areas other than their own" (294–295). This overlap and interchange not only create a powerful central group but also unify that group in outlook, composition, and action. Here we should recognize brokers of the *tertius iungens* type discussed above and also the resemblance to Barth's brokers who gain by linking milieux and transactions of very different types previously thought unrelated or incommensurable. Their breadth of outlook also makes them more likely to be thought evenhanded rather than provincial or self-seeking.

Mills and his intellectual descendant G. William Domhoff (2013) are unusual in the literature on economic elites in stressing the overlap of elites between economic and other contexts, such as political and military. Most of the literature is far more focused on the question of whether there are centrally placed elites *within* the world of large corporations who are cohesive and influential. Much of this work derives from one particular research tradition on elites and their networks, on "interlocking directorates," the overlap in board of director memberships between firms, which since the early twentieth century was a lightning rod for suspicion of illegal coordination.[10] Because two firms with one or more directors in common can be considered "linked," the network of such firms and their linkages, usually just called the "interlock network," has been a frequent object of analysis.

Useem (1984) used such analysis as a platform to argue that in the United States and the United Kingdom, there is a corporate "inner circle" that dominates the political activity of large corporations and is thereby highly influential. Like other recent analysts, Useem rejects the idea that when one corporation places an officer on the board of another, it is to facilitate control or even sales or strategy. Instead, he argues they do so in order to achieve "business scan"—information that large corporations need about what is going on in government policy, labor relations, markets, technology, and business practices (41–48). So individual corporations allow their high officials to use valuable time on other boards for reasons that have to do only with their own goals. They have no larger purpose, but the result is a group that "can rise above the competitive atomization of the many corporations that constitute its base and concern itself with the broader issues affecting the entire large-firm community" (57), so that what Useem calls "classwide" interests rather than those narrower ones of individual corporations prevail when corporate leaders enter politics. He notes also that identifying individuals who hold multiple directorships is also a proxy for a "far broader and more intricate set of informal social relationships" such as club memberships (66–68). This is one reason why the "inner circle" has coherence as a group.

His research showed that directors who serve on multiple boards were twice as likely as others to serve in high government posts (1984: 78) and were generally more influential. For example, universities with more of these "inner circle" members as trustees got much more in contributions (85). This "inner circle" has a family resemblance to Mill's "power elite," as Useem stresses the broad outlook of such individuals, whose variety of experience and information makes them less parochial and, indeed, when in government positions, were subject to informal mores within their group that discouraged special pleading for their own sector or firm (95). On the one hand, the "classwide" interests of the inner circle, in Useem's account, resulted in more moderate political positions and some emphasis on overall social responsibility, and he argues that this group acted as the enforcer of overall social norms against firms that strayed too far from what was currently seen as socially acceptable (141–143). "Officers and directors who travel in the inner circle will be more open to arguments that their policies may be damaging for business as a whole," whereas those firms in peripheral positions are harder to bring into line (145). On the other hand, he argues that in part because the rise of the inner circle was in response to a decline in profitability and increase in regulation, this group helped channel business money increasingly into political campaigns and played a role in the United States and the United Kingdom in the 1980s in the conservative political transformation ushered in by Reagan and Thatcher, where both government spending for human services and social programs and regulation of business were throttled back.

Useem believed that the increased cohesion of the brokers of the inner circle, which he chronicles for the 1970s and the 1980s, "seems certain to continue. The inexorable movement of recent years has been toward more cohesion, less fragmentation" (172). And Useem related this trend not only to environmental challenges but also to the movement away from control of firms by families and later by managers to a situation where large institutions such as mutual and pension funds hold most stock in large corporations, so that the individual corporation becomes less important as a unit, a situation he calls "institutional capitalism."

But in recent years, students of elites and power have suggested that the trend that Useem observed was waning as he wrote. Mizruchi (2013), for example, argues that the corporate elite of the post–World War II period was declining in the 1970s. By the early 1980s, the "moderate, pragmatic and well-organized elite that had been present at the top of the corporate world since at least the 1940s [Useem's 'inner circle'] began to disappear" (221). And by the 1990s, the corporate elite had moved from being this inner circle to being a "collection of firms, powerful in their ability to gain specific benefits for themselves, but no longer able or willing to address issues of concern to the larger business community or the larger society" (269).

Writing at the same time as Useem, Mintz and Schwartz (1985) proposed that the inner circle of the economy was especially occupied by commercial banks and other financial firms, which were central in interlock networks in part because of controlling the vital resource of capital that so many industrial firms required. But Mizruchi and Davis (2009a, 2009b) show that during the late twentieth century, commercial banks became less central in interlock networks and less influential in the economy because firms in need of capital increasingly relied on commercial paper, which was intermediated by investment banks and bought up by money market and pension funds.

As regulation waned in the 1980s, finance became the major source of corporate profits, and investment banks facilitated a huge takeover wave, which saw one-third of the Fortune 500 disappear. In this new environment, CEOs became less secure, which gave them less leeway to consider the interests of the business community, let alone society, as a whole (Mizruchi 2013: Ch. 7). Both Mizruchi and Davis (2009a; 2009b) note the continuing decline of manufacturing in the United States, which means that "large corporations have lost their place as the central pillars of American social structure" (2009a: 27). Corporations are now increasingly owned by institutional investors. While these are "remarkably passive in corporate governance" (2009a: 32), as is argued also by Roe (1994), their wide holdings do mean that share price becomes the overwhelming measure of corporate performance—which is what is meant by the rise of "shareholder value" (Davis 2009a: 32–33; Davis 2009b: 77–88).

Mizruchi suggests that since institutional shareholders were concerned only with investment returns, as befitted their role as fiduciaries for investors, CEOs had to focus on stock price to avoid takeovers. This led to a vacuum of corporate leadership. In this context, the "inner circle" became rich but not cosmopolitan and business became "increasingly ineffectual" as a collective actor. He compares the 2008 crisis to that of 1907, in which J. P. Morgan rallied other elite actors' support for the financial system and worked to enact regulation that would stabilize the system. Had there been in 2008, he argues, a well-organized corporate elite able to work with the state to ensure that the system operated in an orderly and predictable manner, there would not have been a crisis (Mizruchi 2010). Instead, those in charge of the investment and commercial banks, who reaped enormous profits from what turned out to be dangerous and "toxic" investments and strategies, were not imbued with any sense of responsibility for the overall health of the system but focused instead on short-term profit, which they accumulated at dizzying rates until the structure finally collapsed as the "bubble" they had created burst. A similar argument is made by Johnson and Kwak (2010), who refer to six large banks as a new corporate "oligarchy"; this is, in their account, an elite that focuses only on its own advantages rather than those of the overall economy, so this is consistent with Mizruchi's account of the corporate elite's evolution.

Can research on "small worlds" offer a way to study such propositions quantitatively? I suggested above that the actors whose ties linked otherwise separated network clusters had the potential to accumulate power. But there is no assurance that they always activate this potential, so the question is whether and under what circumstances they do. Useem wrote before the 1990s' revival of interest in small worlds, but his argument about the "inner circle" as a core of individuals who tied together otherwise-disparate segments of the economy suggests that a necessary condition for such a circle to be influential is precisely the small-world property—a highly clustered network with a surprisingly low path distance among clusters because of a set of nodes that provides shortcuts between them. Later research on small worlds by Davis, Yoo, and Baker (2003) asked whether the loss of centrality by banks and the reduction in aggregate concentration of economic activity in the 1980s and 1990s would change the level of connectivity within the network of board interlocks. They found that small-world measures were virtually identical in 1982, 1990, and 1999.

This suggests the question of whether this finding could be consistent with Mizruchi's image of a structure with no coherent elite at the center. One critical clue is the observation that since a very small number of ties across clusters is sufficient to yield the small-world property (see Watts and Strogatz 1998), that property may be consistent with a variety of situations. Davis, Yoo, and Baker (2003: 322) suggested that it will occur simply when boards prefer to bring on directors who are well connected to other boards, no matter for what reason. So there is a disconnect between network measures and power outcomes; network position and structure alone, stripped of social and institutional context, will not tell us what we need to know about power. Useem, like Mills before him, posited not only that there existed a core of individuals who connected diverse clusters but also that this core engaged in social, economic, and political activities that brought them together, broadened their outlook, and created a cohesive and cosmopolitan leadership. Once the central core of commercial banks, large manufacturers, and military contractors fell from their dominant position, it may be that the set of potential brokers who were responsible for high small-world parameters no longer had enough in common to be cohesive or to evolve a broad outlook. If so, then the mere existence of a small world tells us only that it is possible for a central elite to form but is not a sufficient condition for such formation. Neither Useem, in his more qualitative account, nor Davis, Yoo, and Baker, in their more quantitative account, clearly identify and analyze the set of people responsible for creating small-worldness in the way that would be required to understand whether and how they wield power in the economy.

And, in fact, subsequent research on twenty-first-century network structures show that several forces have combined to reduce the significance and then the presence of small-world structures in the corporate economy. Some of these are noted by Chu and Davis in their paper seeking to answer the question: "Who killed the inner circle?" (2015). In order to understand whether those who create a "small world" through their links into otherwise-separated networks are a cohesive and powerful group, a necessary first step is to examine who they are and how they came to their position. Chu and Davis make clear that in the late twentieth and early twenty-first centuries, the way in which directors who created interlocks were chosen changed in two important ways: what kind of people they were and the importance of their preexisting ties.

Through most of the twentieth century, directors of large corporations were mostly white males, and those who created interlocks by virtue of serving on multiple boards were almost entirely so. This changed in the last quarter of the century, when women and minorities increasingly took their place on corporate boards of directors. Indeed, by 2002, four of the five best-connected directors in the 1,500 largest corporations as identified by Standard and Poor's were black (Chu and Davis 2015: 10). But as directors became increasingly females and minorities, the cohesive structures formed by an elite of white men who sat atop the corporate world gave way to a more representative collection of individuals, also of considerable achievement but who were not powerful individually, were not a cohesive group, did not con-nect different institutional sectors in the way that Mills and Useem identified, and increasingly were not even chosen for their multiple connections.

By the end of the twentieth century, banks had lost their position as the most central kind of firm in the network of corporate interlocks. But despite this, the corporate network still remained highly connected (short path lengths) because there was still a "highly connected core of directors" (7). But with the democratization of director choice and the selection of directors who were not powerful individuals in and of themselves, the incentive to choose as directors those who served on many boards declined. (This recalls C. Wright Mills's comment, cited above, that powerful individuals, without their institutional affiliations, would not be powerful at all.) Moreover, once corporate scandals became commonplace, director inattention to what cor-porations did became an issue; for institutional shareholder organizations interested in corporate governance reform, serving on too many boards was a red flag (Chu and Davis 2015: 10), and companies began to limit the number of boards their employees could serve on. Chu and Davis found that while in 2000, 62 corporations had more than 20 director interlocks to others, by 2010 only one did. In 2000 (15), 17 directors sat on six or more boards, 44 on five; by 2010, none sat on six and only 11 on five (16). With the decline of "prefer-ential attachment"—a preference to appoint to your board individuals already on many other boards—the overall network lost the "scale-free" property that made a cohesive elite a possibility (see Barabasi 2002). Scholars such as Useem and Mills had emphasized how interlocks and the presence of individ-uals linking or brokering among different institutional sectors created and socialized a leadership elite that fostered political unity and a relatively broad outlook; the new structure cannot do any of these things, and this is consistent with Mizruchi's portrait of an elite fragmented into segments, each of which pursues only its own interests. Chu and Davis conclude that the "interlock network no longer tells us much about who holds power in U.S. society" (2015: 38).

Another reason for caution about the link of "small worlds" to power in the economy is that corporations may seek to create small-world networks for a number of reasons that do not create power for those whose links knit these together. Thus, Baum, Shipilov, and Rowley (2003) find that Canadian investment banks that are peripheral may throw out ties to more mainstream cliques in investment syndicates in order to improve their overall position, whereas core firms may reach out to other core cliques in order to sustain their advantage. Any such cross-clique ties increase small-world measures but without creating powerful individuals. Gulati et al. (2012), in their study of collaborations among firms in the computer industry, suggest that understanding how small-world networks come about leads us to expect cycles of increasing and declining small-worldness. Unlike interlocking corporate boards, the collaborations they study involve a broad range of activities. Small worlds involve bridging ties between clusters of firms. The clusters here arise because organizations select as collaborative partners those with whom they are familiar either through prior collaboration or indirectly through prior partners (2012: 451). In the search for novel and nonredundant information, some firms then create ties that bridge between clusters. These ties cut average path length and create the small-world property. But eventually, the bridging ties increase in number sufficiently to "saturate the space between clusters" (452), which creates a single larger cluster and reduces the intellectual and technological diversity that separate clusters reinforced. This is then a small world in decline. In all of these partnerships, the individuals creating connections work on behalf of their firms and are not themselves powerful by virtue of creating a small world, and the collection of such individuals has no basis for cohesion.

So the bottom line here is that those individuals whose ties create a small world may indeed form a powerful cohesive elite, but whether they do so depends on historical and institutional circumstances and on the ways in which their linking ties have been created. In a more macro-social and macroeconomic framework, we will see that network structure still matters a lot for power, but the small-world property is important only under special circumstances, some of which I have suggested here. Future research on the links between small-world properties and the exercise of economic power will need to attend carefully to this larger framework.

4.4 Macro-Level Perspectives on Economic Power

Now to say a little more about this larger framework: individuals who wield power based on dependence (control of resources others deem critical), legitimate authority, or control of the agenda often appear to those in their thrall to be uniquely skilled and effective, as indeed they may be. But if we step back from the immediate situation, we may find that historical, political, and economic circumstance have played an outsized role in putting these individuals, however skilled, in a position to deploy their power.

So, for example, Padgett and Ansell, in their account of the enormous power wielded in medieval Florence by Cosimo de Medici, emphasized that a central source of his ability to do so was his strategic position at the intersection of separate political, economic, and kinship networks that he could deploy without the risk of their merging with one another. But it was a series of historical circumstances, which from the Medicis' point of view might be thought of as "accidents" in the sense that they represented a conjuncture of trends stemming from unrelated causes, over which the Medicis themselves had little power, that created this network situation. Padgett and Ansell comment that Cosimo had no plan to take over the Florentine city-state but that the social basis of what would be his political party "emerged around him," and then only during the early fifteenth-century war against Milan did he "suddenly apprehend the political capacity of the social network machine that lay at his fingertips" (1993: 1264).

And when we speak of controlling the agenda, we should ask how and when people with particular viewpoints on what the agenda should be are in a position to impose those views. In some cases, macroeconomic trends and legislative changes may create the circumstances that privilege one group's view over another's without any massive exercise of agency by the actors. Fligstein offers the case of what he calls the "transformation of corporate control" (1990). By tracing from what specialties CEOs and other top executives were recruited, he traces how control of corporations in the twentieth-century United States passed first from entrepreneurs to specialists in manufacturing, then to those in sales and marketing, and subsequently to those in finance. He argues that such individuals brought with them distinct "conceptions of control," ideas about how the market for their product could best be dominated and ruinous competition avoided. But whatever the personal skills of these sometimes-impressive individuals might have been—e.g., the redoubtable Alfred P. Sloan of General Motors—Fligstein argues that these transformations occurred because of macroeconomic or political upheavals that reshaped product and consumer markets. So the Great Depression changed the environment of corporations from one where what mattered was manufacturing efficiency to one where you had to persuade deeply apprehensive consumers that they wanted your product and only yours—which paved the way for the "sales and marketing conception of control" and for diversification reflected in the "multidivisional form" (1990: Ch. 4). And when the economy recovered and the post–World War II boom was in progress but new antitrust legislation (the Celler-Kefauver Act of 1950) discouraged horizontal or vertical mergers, mergers into unrelated industries remained permissible, and those who could assess the financial aspects of such unions and conceive of corporations as bundles of financial assets—viz. those with training in finance—came to the fore because it was their skills that were vital in the new environment (see Fligstein 1990: Chs. 5–8).

So these individuals' conceptions of the appropriate agenda mattered, but their particular conception dominated because of events beyond their control and at a larger scale than that of individuals or particular firms.

Fligstein's examples suggest that we should think of what I have called control of the "agenda" in broader terms than the 1950s political science debate about what people thought major issues were in large American cities. Beyond this lie more general conceptions of what is the best way to approach economic problems. Such conceptions are held not only by business executives but also by intellectuals who make it their business to think about the economy in general and abstract terms. And so it matters a great deal for public policy whether Keynesian or classical/neoclassical economists' conceptions dominate. An especially interesting case is developed by Christensen (2013 and see for more detail 2017). He notes the surprising fact that if one

considers four small countries—Denmark, Norway, Ireland, and New Zealand—the two of these that adopted highly neoliberal tax reform were Norway
and New Zealand, and the two where such reforms were determined by political rather than economic goals were Denmark and Ireland. So the apparently
similar Scandinavian countries adopted nearly opposite policies, and the
reason appears to be that in Norway and New Zealand, professional economists dominated the policy apparatus in a way they decidedly did not in Denmark or Ireland. And ironically, when this dominance took hold, before the
Second World War, the consensus among economists was Keynesian. But
once this consensus changed, by the 1980s, professional economists continued to dominate policy, even though by that time their preferred market-
oriented ("neoliberal") solutions were quite different from those of the
earlier period.

In a similar vein, Avent-Holt (2012) recounts the history of regulation
and subsequent deregulation of airlines in the United States from the 1930s to
the present. Professional economists became increasingly neoclassical from
the 1950s on, but this alone was not enough to turn around the conception
that had taken hold as early as the 1930s that regulated airline fares and traffic
would guarantee the best service to the public. An economic exogenous
shock, the deep recession and "stagflation" of the 1970s, when the Phillips
curve predicting an inverse relation between inflation and unemployment
was overturned by their unexpected positive correlation, wreaked havoc on
the economy. Because a spike in oil prices was a major cause of the crisis,
airlines were among the first and hardest-hit industries. This alone would not
have led to deregulation because before this crisis, challenger airlines framed
their mobilization within the "dominant cultural understanding that unregulated competition was destructive in the industry" (Avent-Holt 2012: 296).
But by the 1970s, neoclassical advocacy of free markets had challenged and
begun to displace the interventionist Keynesian framework. This made available an alternative understanding of solutions to the problems of airlines in a
cultural frame that came to seem more coherent than traditional industrial-
policy/state-centered action. This is thus a case where "culture interacts with
material interest in the policymaking process," so that even when actors have
clearly defined material interests, "what policies they pursue in those interests
is mediated by cultural factors" (298).

It is unlikely that we can effectively theorize or predict the arrival of exogenous economic shocks. But we can do more to understand their impact in conferring power on particular actors under different circumstances. When we ask how much power actors wield in *political* systems, the question posed at a national level is how to explain whether a political system is democratic, authoritarian, or totalitarian. We may ask similar questions for the economic arena. All formal business organizations have a hierarchy, as denoted in organization charts and as noted and perhaps reified by transaction cost economics, in contrast to something called a "market" where no unit exerts authority over any other. In practice, there is a question of over how wide an extent economic authority can be effectively wielded, as Barnard (1938) noted, drawing on his experience as president of New Jersey Bell Telephone and influencing organization theory for decades after.

Economists long avoided the general question of why firms become larger or smaller and what explains their size until Penrose ([1959] 1995) finally focused on this as a central issue. But even Penrose's pathbreaking work focused mainly on market conditions and resource constraints in explaining firm size rather than analyzing whether a firm's hierarchy could be stretched far enough to enable coordination of much larger numbers of people. The general problem in the exercise of either political or economic power is that no single individual can command many others simply by sheer force of his or her own physical resources. Some bureaucratic authority structure is needed in order to create the leverage that allows a single person to command dozens, hundreds, or, at the national scale, millions of others, and this leads us to analyze how actual hierarchies work to transmit authoritative orders through multiple layers or levels in such a way as to engender compliance.

This is a huge subject, and in some sense the focus of all political analysis, but its structural aspects have rarely been explicitly analyzed. In the classic studies of organization theory, such as Simon (1997) and March and Simon (1993), there is certainly discussion of hierarchies in organizations, and since the early part of the twentieth century there has been discussion of what the optimal hierarchy would look like and what was the ideal number of subordinates for any supervisor to have (the so-called "span of control" problem) and, beginning in the 1960s with the advent of "contingency theory—e.g.,

Woodward 1965—discussion of under what market circumstances steeper or flatter hierarchies would be superior for coordinating economic activity. But these discussions are confined to the question of how orders are best structured within a single organizational hierarchy and therefore do not address the larger question of how power is created, exercised, and sustained within a larger multi-firm economic framework.

Yet this is a critical question, and part of what makes it interesting and important is its purely structural aspects, though those aspects are incomprehensible outside a historical and institutional framework. My discussion that follows here is isomorphic with that in Chapter 3 on the way strategically placed ties of trust can allow trust relationships to extend far beyond primary groups and thus continue to be a force in large and complex modern structures, contrary to arguments that make trust relevant only in small, cohesive settings where interpersonal knowledge and affect loom large. In fact, that discussion, in Section 3.4, should be read as preface to what I am about to say, since most of the ties I mention there entail power as well as trust relations.

It has been well understood by social critics since the early twentieth century that one way to leverage economic power—to exercise power far beyond what might otherwise be expected from the resources under one's control—is to construct pyramids of ownership, in which an ownership interest (such as a family) controls one firm that has a controlling interest in a second firm, which controls a third firm, and so on. Note that for a block of stock to control does not require that it be a majority, but in many cases only that it be the largest block, which in some cases is less than 10 percent. The first of these firms may be an operating firm or may be organized purely for the purpose of holding stock in other firms, hence the name "holding companies," the successors of "trusts." Those controlling companies not only exercise much more power than would seem to flow from their resources but do so in a way that is quite difficult for outsiders to see if the pyramid has more than a few levels.

Critics from the left have often argued that such arrangements mask the power of a cohesive ruling class, as Zeitlin and Ratcliff (1988) propose for pre-Pinochet Chile. But even mainstream financial economists take note of the importance of chains of holdings—e.g., LaPorta et al. 1999: esp. 476–491—and offer definitions of pyramids and extensive examples and charts showing how very difficult it is to understand who are the actual owners of important large firms in numerous countries. It is very clear from their examples, discussion, and analysis that chains of ownership extend over large numbers of companies and may not uncommonly cross national lines. It is also clear though implicit here that corporate law and custom regarding stock ownership and control rights determine how such chains may be organized, so that only some imaginable structures can exist in fact.

Particularly illuminating here is Dukjin Chang's discussion of ownership patterns in Korea's business groups *(chaebol)*. Chang (1999) uses modern methods of social network analysis to illuminate strategies of control and emphasizes that these particular strategies are chosen from among all possible ones because of institutional and cultural constraints. The *chaebol* (e.g., Hyundai, LG, Samsung), like other business groups (see Granovetter 2005), consist of collections of firms that are legally independent but highly coordinated with one another. Unlike the (post–World War II) Japanese *keiretsu* (e.g., Mitsubishi, Mitsui, Sumitomo), whose component firms are only loosely coordinated and show no clear hierarchy, the Korean groups are typically dominated by single families, almost invariably that of the founder, and by a single dominant figure within the family. This authority is supported by complex network strategies in which the dominant family owns shares in group firms that own shares in other group firms, and so on. This "gives the owning family tremendous control because, sitting stop the multi-layered hierarchies, they can amplify their control often, say, one hundred times the original value of their owner's equity by means of crossholdings" (Chang 1999: 12).

Going beyond the illustrative examples of other analysts, Chang used data from the top 49 *chaebol* in 1989 and used blockmodeling techniques to find typical patterns of holdings. He found that firms play one of three possible roles in these ownership networks: "controllers," which send ownership ties but do not receive any back, and "intermediaries," which receive equity ties from the controllers and transmit them to those in the third role, "receivers." Those *chaebol* with intermediary roles have a much greater ability to amplify the family's control (1999: 117). Furthermore, he finds not just a hierarchy but a nested hierarchy in which hierarchical ownership relations within the intermediary set of firms are themselves nested in a larger hierarchy relative to controller firms. Such nesting is efficient because it means that, as in Hyundai, the controllers can "send strong ties [i.e., substantial stockholding] to a few firms located toward the top of the [intermediary] hierarchy instead of sending mediocre ties to every firm in the intermediary role-set," which is an extremely economical use of capital, and the family makes "use of minimum resources to achieve maximum control through the use of relations between actors" (139).

But to reiterate a theme that I argue is critical, this particular pattern is chosen and works so well not *only* for reasons of structural efficiency but also because it is so well matched to the cultural, historical, and institutional patterns of its setting. In particular, Chang mentions several factors. One is that the Korean state in the 1960s and 1970s encouraged the *chaebol* to expand with easy, state-sponsored credit, which led to very high debt-to-equity ratios. But 1986 antitrust legislation forbade a firm to hold more than 40 percent of its assets in the equity of another *chaebol* firm, and no pair of such firms could hold shares in one another (1999: 9). Finally, there is a very strong cultural emphasis in Korea on family control in economic enterprises, especially that exercised by the male family head. This long-institutionalized set of norms made the power of such heads seem legitimate and compelling to participants in these firms. This combination of elements led to efforts to put family control ahead of the profitability of any component firms in the groups, and the nested hierarchy was the most efficient structure to keep equity control within the family boundary while complying with all relevant legislation and taking advantage of the easy availability of capital at low and subsidized interest rates (142). Chang notes in subsequent work that although reforms promoted by international actors such as the World Bank, following the 1997 currency crisis in Asia, intended to weaken the hold of leading families over the *chaebol* and the overall economy, what happened instead is that although some already-marginal *chaebol* failed, other *chaebol* families became stronger, in part because they were able to refine the described networks of ownership in ways that made ownership leverage even more efficient (2000).

So a series of cultural and institutional influences created circumstances under which social units such as families—and in the Korean case the families are hardly internal democracies but are instead dominated by a single person—can exercise leverage in financial networks in such a way as to dominate a substantial chunk of the economy. These vertical ties are different from the horizontal ties of cohesion that Useem and others stress as creating a "power elite" in an entire economic system, and it is harder to see whether such horizontal ties exist in Korea. There is a widespread perception that the separate industrial empires of the *chaebol* are knitted together and to the political elite through ties of marriage, and this is a common theme in the popular press and could form the "small world" structure of elite cohesion. But there is little systematic investigation of this, and Han's exploratory study of marriage ties suggests that some power elite arguments are overblown, even though there is clearly more cohesion between *chaebol* in Korea than would be expected at random (2008).

An even more difficult question is what are the general initial structural, institutional, and cultural influences that make it likely that powerful individuals *will* emerge to dominate parts of an economic structure and that such individuals will cooperate to form a cohesive elite. In a 2002 paper, I suggested that structures of ties that are either extremely fragmented or extremely densely knit would both make it less likely that individuals could exert much economic power: in the first case because there is no way to pull together fragments that are wholly disconnected to one another so as to make them act in concert and in the second because no actors can attain power through brokerage in a situation where everyone is in contact already with everyone else, a point corresponding to the Gulati et al. (2012) discussion of the collapse of "small worlds" within an industry. So the potential for powerful actors depends on structures that have some degree of clustering with small numbers of connections between clusters, a description similar to that of "small worlds." In political sociology and history this is comparable to the argument of Marc Bloch and others that the emergence of national states in medieval Western Europe was more rather than less likely in spaces dominated by cohesive feudal manors than in places with less local structure because authoritative relations within clusters already existed and needed only to be pulled together by the right set of connections brokering between such clusters (Bloch [1939] 1961).

Finally, I note that some factors that impact which individuals wield power and how cohesively they do so reside at a macro level, well beyond the purview or control of individuals. It is not practical to treat all major macro-level sources of individual power here without a serious loss of focus. For example, macro-level geopolitical phenomena play an important role in determining the initial resource allocations that lead to economic power. One interesting case is when a comparatively small number of actors gain control of some resource that is by chance inhomogeneously distributed and highly valued, which is one way that comprehensive and long-term dependencies may arise. Some minerals fit into this category. Salt, for example, has been a longstanding source of economic and political power in numerous periods and countries including imperial China (see, e.g., Hucker 1975) and France from before the Bourbon period to modern times (see Kurlansky 2002: Ch. 14 on the infamous salt tax, the *gabelle*, a Revolutionary *cause célèbre*). The obvious current case is oil in the Middle East. Where movement of goods matters a lot, control of transport bottlenecks such as strategic waterways, critical points on caravan routes, or mountain passes can create substantial leverage and result from initial locations and endowments that confer economic power that is hard to dislodge. Military conquest can lead to the subjugation of entire populations that become unwilling economic agents of principals whose political power leads to enslavement or near equivalents such as the many varieties of serfdom and peonage.[11]

But it is clear that in a treatment such as the present book, factors of this kind can only be briefly noted in the background and left for others to investigate more fully. Thus, in my subsequent Chapters 5 and 6, I turn to general arguments about institutions and how they shape and are in turn shaped by the economy. These chapters link most directly to my discussion in Chapter 2 on the role of ideas, norms, frames, and culture in structuring the economy, and I will note how closely such "mental constructs" are linked to the occurrence of trust and the exercise of economic power and authority.

5

The Economy and Social Institutions

This chapter and the next follow those on norms, trust, and power—fundamental concepts but each offering only a partial account of what creates economic organization. Each of these separate discussions ended with consideration of how the subject manifested itself beyond the level of individuals, small groups, or self-contained communities. Such meso- and macro-level considerations inevitably led to some discussion of social institutions, but these accounts were truncated, and here I offer a more systematic argument.

I begin by observing that sociology as a discipline is distinctive in a number of ways, but I believe the most significant is its emphasis on *all* the major aspects of social life, economic, political, social, religious/ideological, and others, and in its assumption that no one such aspect has causal priority. I suggest that any such claim of priority—and such claims are common in the social sciences—foregoes the intellectual and analytical flexibility needed to explain social life. Institutions that impinge on the economy are invariably more than purely economic. As I argue in many particular cases, social, political, intellectual, legal, and family influences, among others, play key roles in shaping how the economy runs. This interpenetration of institutional sectors creates the unique texture of social life as we experience it, and this is what we need to keep in mind as we try to broaden our understanding of how people create, get, and use those objects and services that we define as meeting our needs. And we need always keep in mind, as I emphasized in the preceding three chapters, that important as what happens to individuals and small groups is, as important as single norms and cultural elements may be, neither individuals nor norms can exist or be understood without discussion of their larger social context and the structures that emerge from the interaction and aggregation of these elements. This leads us to the consideration of social institutions.

5.1 Institutions and "Logics"

We must begin by saying what we mean by "social institutions." The most typical definition is that they are sets of persistent patterns defining how some specified collection of social actions are and should be carried out. Mahoney and Thelen, in *Explaining Institutional Change,* describe institutions as "*relatively enduring* features of political and social life (rules, norms, procedures) that structure behavior and that cannot be changed easily or instantaneously" (2009: 4). This leaves open how large and what kind of boundary is drawn around what we call a single "institution," and here there is no standard practice, as analysts typically define as "institutional" that set of patterns they particularly want to understand. Thus the set of rules that govern a particular legislature, such as the U.S. Congress, may be the object of what comes to be called "institutional" analysis (cf. Sheingate 2010), but in some broader discussion this would be seen as a relatively small subset of the subject "political institutions." The "institutional theory of organizations" (cf. the seminal papers by Meyer and Rowan 1977 and DiMaggio and Powell 1983) has produced an offshoot that refers to "institutional logics," typically focused on single industries, which I discuss in more detail in the following section.

At the more macro level of entire societies, a typical twentieth-century way of identifying institutions was to list collections of social activities that carry out distinct social "functions," such as the economy, the polity, the family, religion, science, and the legal system. All of these can be transformed into adjectives modifying the term "institutions": "economic institutions," "legal institutions," and the like. But this leads to the question of exactly what set of institutions belongs on such a list and how to know whether it is complete. There was a time when this did not worry social scientists because they imagined they could discuss exhaustively what "functions" needed to be fulfilled for a society to "thrive" and "persist," terms whose meaning they once thought neutral and unproblematic. An early stab at such a list was Aberle et al. (1950), and this evolved into the eminent mid-twentieth-century sociologist Talcott Parsons's fourfold A-G-I-L scheme, where each letter stood for one of the four "functional prerequisites" he considered essential for a society: A (for adapting resources from the environment), G (for the execution of a society's agreed-upon goals), I (for integrating the various and possibly discordant elements of a society), and L (for "latent" pattern maintenance and tension management). Actual institutions that performed these functions were at a more concrete level of analysis, and generally Parsons argued that the economy was the main institutional source of adaptation, government the main source of goal attainment, the legal system the main source of integration, and family and religion the main motors of pattern maintenance. (See Parsons 1961 for one of his more compact expositions and Parsons and Smelser 1956 for an exhaustive account of how the economy fits into this scheme.) Left unspoken but critical to the argument was the assumption that societies were coherent social systems whose various parts fit together smoothly and where participants were in general agreement about the goals to be sought. One legacy of the political and cultural turmoil of the 1960s was an awareness that such assumptions, typical of midcentury "structural-functional" social science, left precious little scope for conflict and change, and the intellectual cross-currents that originated in such realization made such static arguments seem decidedly out of date and unsophisticated not just politically but also intellectually.

Thus, in the twenty-first century, few social analysts would still subscribe to some well-defined list of necessary social functions or think it makes sense to attempt compiling one. Moreover, though many would agree that all the institutions identified by lists like these are important, there are complexes of activities, such as science, that fit the general conception of having a coherent meaning and broadly understood sets of rules and rewards but would not be generated by a list of functional prerequisites, since many societies have functioned without scientific institutions. So it seems clear that we need to detach the idea of institutions from that of social functionality.

In the absence of functional moorings, ideas about institutions have moved away from definite constellations of activity oriented to a particular kind of outcome in a well-defined sphere such as the economy or the polity.

Consistent with increasing interest in cognition in the human sciences, analysts have focused on the idea that institutions not only are normative guides to behavior in defined spheres but also shape individuals' cognition about the choices and frameworks they operate in. For this reason, arguments about what are the main institutional spheres have come to draw on ideas from cognitive psychology about "schemas" (sometimes rendered as the Greek "schemata") that provide a framework within which one can make sense of events experienced (see esp. DiMaggio 1997 for elaboration of these connections). Very similar concepts about how individuals mentally structure their worlds are the ideas of "scripts" in social and cognitive psychology (see, e.g., Sternberg and Sternberg 2017: Ch. 8) and "frames," an idea developed by sociologists (Goffman 1974; Snow et al. 1986) and featured prominently in behavioral economics (e.g., Tversky and Kahneman 1981). These arguments do not abandon connections to defined sets of social activities but stress ways of thinking that may or may not fit easily into the boundaries of such traditional spheres.

Friedland and Alford (1991), for example, argue, in an influential paper, that the main social institutions are capitalist market, bureaucratic state, democracy, nuclear family, religion, and science (232, 248). Each of these "institutional orders" has a "central logic," a "set of material practices and symbolic constructions" that constitute its "organizing principles." The "institutional logic" of capitalism, for example, is

> accumulation and the commodification of human activity. That of the state is rationalization and regulation of human activity by legal and bureaucratic hierarchies. That of democracy is participation and the extension of popular control over human activity. That of the family is community and the motivation of human activity by unconditional loyalty to its members and their reproductive needs. That of religion, or science for that matter, is truth . . . and the symbolic construction of reality within which all human activity takes place. (248)

Note that the use here of "institutional logic" has a much broader scope than the typical industry-by-industry usage of that term as developed in the "new institutional theory of organizations" that I discuss in the following section. The absence of fixed and agreed-upon terminology for talking about institutions creates serious confusion in the form of scholars talking past one another with the illusory sense that they refer to the same subject. I do not attempt to standardize terminology but hope at least to make clear how I am using the relevant terms.

Boltanski and Thevenot (1999, 2006) discuss similar subject matter without reference to social "functions" or even "institutions." Instead, they talk about principles of "justification," assuming that all social actors need to *justify* their action to others and operate within a certain frame of reference that provides distinctive principles for doing so. They distinguish six such frames, or "orders of worth," or "worlds," each of which has its own principle of justification: the world of "inspiration," governed by aesthetic criteria such as those used by artists; the domestic world; the world of renown or honor; the civic world; the market world; and the industrial world (where worth is based on efficiency) (1999: 369–370).

All such proposals stipulate that the social world can be divided into realms, within which some set of implicit or explicit rules or criteria are generally agreed to apply in judging the value or appropriateness of behavior or social arrangements. Despite the appeal of such proposals, however, once the goal of matching institutions to social functions or even to well-defined sets of activities is abandoned, we have the problem that any such list appears arbitrary in the sense that it is not derived from any clear set of first principles, so we have no simple way to determine whether the boundaries drawn around sets of activities to identify them as institutions are correctly placed or whether there may be clusters of activity or logics or schemas that matter socially but do not appear on the list. For my purposes, I do not want or need to solve this problem and simply stipulate that in given contexts we can see empirically what sets of activities cluster together and can take that as a starting point for analysis. This is not merely an *ad hoc* criterion but corresponds to my preference for a pragmatist view of human action that sees people as problem solvers who are not as wedded to a particular set of institutional logics as we might imagine if we conceived institutions as defining reified and settled domains. This does not mean at any given time that existing institutions and logics do not matter. They are important reference points for action. And though it is difficult and challenging to talk about institutional change, it is also impossible to understand the dynamics of social organization without doing so (cf. Mahoney and Thelen 2009).

5.2 Institutions of the Middle Range: Institutional Logics in Industry

Among the earliest theorists to consider how clusters of norms regulated economic activity were sociological organization theorists who postulated normative models or "institutional logics" that apply to particular "organizational fields," a concept that loosely means a collection of organizations that interact with one another and in practice typically refers to a particular industry and those consumers, financiers, lawyers, legislators, regulators, and assorted other actors with whom it interacts.[1] The seminal article in this "new institutional" theory of organizations (as this term is used in sociology and management but quite far from the usage of the "new institutional" economics) is DiMaggio and Powell's 1983 paper that considers why organizations within a "field" imitate one another in so many ways, even when imitated practices do not seem particularly helpful or efficient. Scholars in this tradition argue that early adopters of innovations such as centralized human resources departments are sensitive to how this enhances efficiency but that once this becomes a model for how a modern organization should operate, adoption becomes detached from economic consequences and oriented instead to a general sense that it is more legitimate and modern to organize in this way (see, e.g., Tolbert and Zucker 1983; Baron, Dobbin, and Jennings 1986; for a general discussion of the history and progress of the "institutional" theory of organizations in the social sciences, see Scott 2014).

Far from arising from a "market for norms" or from some efficient selection process (cf. Ch. 2 in this book), such models are spread by consultants and professionals, whose training leads to their being taken very seriously, such as the increasingly professionalized human resources (early on dubbed "HR") specialists. These actors exert considerable power by their control over the agenda that organizations orient themselves to. The centralization of HR was also subject to pressures based on dependence on other organizations with which a firm interacted and from the requirements of the federal government, especially under the duress of materiel and personnel shortages during the Second World War (see Baron et al. 1986). Many subsequent studies in this tradition note organizational innovations that seem linked more to legitimacy than to efficient outcomes (though organizations considered more modern and legitimate may achieve better financial outcomes from the reputational effects that this produces). Note here the subtle shift away from a set of norms that tells economic actors what they are supposed to do to a more general conception of what a modern, cutting-edge organization looks like, which sets up a model whose pursuit creates rewards based on organizational status. So this becomes more of a cognitive schema than a set of detailed behavioral prescriptions, and this brings it into the orbit of the social psychology and behavioral economics of framing effects (see DiMaggio 1997 on culture and cognition) and even further away from the impact of separate, individual norms.

Thus the exercise of governmental power, the influence of society-wide increases in bureaucratization (Bendix 1956), and the interaction of firms with large industrial labor unions all impacted the organization of employment relations. There is considerable debate in the literature about the relative impact of these different forces. But they all have in common that they are not about the influence of a single, discrete operational norm but instead involve long-term historical trends, power relationships among actors, and the introduction of constellations of norms that, while they may all point in the same direction in some sense, are still not *definitionally* connected, such as the empirical correlation of time-and-motion studies in the manner of Frederick Winslow Taylor's "scientific management" with the adoption of centralized HR functions (cf. Baron et al. 1986).

Most of the "institutional logic" arguments that emerged from the new institutional tradition in sociological organization theory applied to particular industries in one country and, rather than making a blanket argument for the imperial sway of norms, often made arguments about how there were *alternate conceptions* of what was the most appropriate way for an industry to be organized that either were in competition with one another so that one gave way to the other over time or split the industry into sectors, each following a different normative/cognitive model. (For a general treatment of institutional logics, see Thornton et al. 2012.)

The more typical argument traces an evolution of logics over different time periods. So, for example, Thornton and Ocasio (1999) chronicle how higher education publishing moved from an "editorial logic" in the 1960s and 1970s, in which small publishing houses were privately owned and editors "engaged in publishing as a lifestyle and a profession" (808), to a "market logic" in which the goal was to build the competitive position and margins of the firm.

Like many authors in this "institutional logic" school they do not see the change they describe as isolated but rather link it to wider societal trends, in this case, a widespread societal shift away from professional conceptions of industries to a market logic in part encouraged by rapid expansion of demand and consequent expansion of the scale of production and markets (Thornton and Ocasio 1999: 816). Similar is the account of Haveman and Rao (1997) of changes in the American thrift industry in the late nineteenth and early twentieth centuries. Earlier California thrift associations were based on the "terminating plan," which emphasized mutuality and enforced saving for common goals (1997: 1613–1616) in a local community where people knew and trusted one another. (I note the similarity of such schemes to those embodied around the world in "rotating credit associations"—cf. Ardener 1964: 201–229, and for ethnic groups in the United States, see Light 1972.) These were supplanted by the 1930s by a different logic and "theory of moral sentiments" based on impersonality, bureaucracy, and voluntary saving (Haveman and Rao 1997: 1624). Here, the authors attribute the change to a general tendency in the United States linked to Progressivism and spelled out in Wiebe's classic *The Search for Order* (1967), which argued that the Progressive movement "imparted moral and theoretical cogency to a practical solution of bureaucratizing cooperation and allowing rational decision makers the freedom to save as they wished" (Haveman and Rao 1997: 1644)

In a rather different case, Rao et al. (2003) trace how the *nouvelle cuisine* movement in France contested with and eventually largely, but not entirely, displaced the classical gastronomy of Escoffier and the culinary schools such as Le Cordon Bleu from the late nineteenth to the mid-twentieth centuries—a social movement that emphasized freshness, inventiveness of the chef, simplicity, new techniques and ingredients, and a short menu changing with seasons and markets. They emphasize that the shift in institutional logics was in part the result of a social movement led by professional chefs whose names became synonymous with the new trends (e.g., Paul Bocuse), and much of the general literature on social movements then becomes relevant. So there is certainly a strong normative element here, but it is sustained in a larger frame of reference that defines an entire "school of thought."[2] Rao et al. go further, however, and propose that this change was not isolated to the economic sphere of cooking and restaurateurs but also was related to wider societal changes in France that moved it into a new cultural direction, an anti-authoritarian current that found its voice in the "new wave" in literature, film, and theatre and was exemplified in politics by the upheavals of 1968 in the streets of Paris (2003: 802–805).

It is easy to see why proponents of arguments about changes in "institutional logics" would not want to depict them as arbitrary or random but rather as emblematic of more general shifts in normative frameworks. But we may ask whether the shifts in question were so all-encompassing that they swept through every pattern in their path or whether it may be that the cases chosen for analysis suffer from a selection bias favoring logics that changed in a direction made familiar by well-known patterns or arguments but that might be counterbalanced by cases that changed little or in different ways despite iconic movements such as Progressivism.

Certainly arguments like Wiebe's 1967 contrast between isolated and decoupled small American towns in the nineteenth century and the post-Progressive bureaucratized and homogeneous America would draw more qualified response in the light of twenty-first century historiography and skepticism about the value of taxonomic dichotomies such as the distinction between liberal and coordinated economies—as in Hall and Soskice 2001 (cf. Herrigel 2005 on the application of this dichotomy to Japan and Germany), a concern prefigured in Kennedy's 1975 historiographic essay on Progressivism in which he notes Wiebe's failure to examine cases where the Progressive impulse also protected and promoted non or pre-bureaucratic patterns (Kennedy 1975: 463).

The larger point here, emphasized by Herrigel 2005, is that individuals creating new patterns are not necessarily concerned with being faithful to one particular side of a dichotomy or to a known social movement but are more likely to draw on a variety of sources to solve the problems they are addressing without much focus on ideological or theoretical consistency. So here again, I lean toward the pragmatist epistemology that I have mentioned before, closely related to depiction of actors as being syncretic, or engaging in what the French call *bricolage*.[3]

This concern is related to studies showing that rather than one prevalent logic giving way to another in a progression related to larger trends, a challenged logic may split the field with its challenger, each finding a niche. So Lounsbury (2007) gives the example of mutual funds, first organized in 1925 and routinized in the United States by the Investment Company Act of 1940. He notes that in the early twentieth century, money management was about wealth preservation and focused on conservative, long-term investing at low cost. This "trustee" logic led to very stable and somewhat mundane products, often based in Boston and steeped in the "financial culture of Boston and its Brahmin elites" (291). A competing logic emerged in 1950s New York, based on "performance" and involving more aggressive investing for higher short term returns—what became the "growth fund" movement. The appearance of "rock-star" investors occurred within the performance movement, but the rise of index funds in the early 1970s reflected a renewal of the trustee logic, and money management firms came increasingly to specialize in one or the other logic (293). So when logics compete, this competition may become an "enduring fixture of the industry" (302) in which the original geographic difference ends up imprinting and influencing the social organization of industry and market.

In all these arguments, and I have barely scratched the surface of the number of industries studied by the "new institutionalists," we should ask where new competing organizational or institutional logics came from and to what extent they were specific to the industry in question or were rather reflections of larger forces in the history and culture of the society. This in turn raises the question of whether the changes in practice induced by changing logics were inevitable consequences of normal economic, political, or social events or were variable depending on who acted as the entrepreneurs of new logics and with what techniques. This is a subject favored by scholars of social movements who remind us that while successful movements are typically piloted by skilled movement entrepreneurs, who operate in a social context that makes success possible, outcomes are still not inevitable but are contingent on leadership, external shocks, and other historical happenstance. This leads us to discuss institutions at a larger scale than an industry.

5.3 Institutions, Logics, and Regional and National Culture

In the literature on the "institutional logics" of organizations and industries, geographic space occasionally appears as the locus of one or another logic, as in Lounsbury's account of Boston's "trustee logic" for mutual funds versus the "growth logic" centered in New York. But many scholars go further and focus on geographic units as the main *carriers* of cultural, normative, and institutional differences that shape economic action, including any industries within that space. The complexes of norms that are said to govern different aspects of the economy go by names that correspond to the range of situations to which authors assume they apply. When the range is some economic sector, an industry or an "organizational field", then the complexes are called "logics." When that range is the nation, the typical rubric is that of national "cultures," but similar arguments are made for subnational regions, so we hear of regional cultures and at times of the clash or the contrast of cultures within a nation, affecting the economic performance of different regions (see, e.g., Locke 1995; Saxenian 1994). Although the national and the regional units of analysis are different, the arguments are similar. What is missing is a coherent argument about what geographic boundaries matter under what circumstances.

Although one might think that arguments about *regional* economic cultures are most likely to be applied to culturally heterogeneous nations like the United States and Italy, there is no generally accepted metric along which to measure such heterogeneity (as suggested by Lie's intentionally oxymoronic title for his book *Multiethnic Japan* [2001]), and though I chose Italy and the United States as examples of culturally heterogeneous nations, there is no shortage of claims about American or Italian "exceptionalism"—which implies a highly distinctive (rather than heterogeneous) national culture.

In line with the claims of heterogeneity are two well-known cases where arguments about distinctive subnational or regional industrial cultures have been made: for apparel in Italy and for high-tech (information technology) in the United States. For Italy, the stress has been on the distinct cultural and organizational capabilities of the "Third Italy" (neither north nor south—e.g., Piore and Sabel 1984), and in the United States, Silicon Valley versus the Route 128 (Massachusetts) high-tech complex (Saxenian 1994). The cultural story of the two more successful regions is that networks of interdependent small firms provide greater flexibility for innovation and less need for large sunk costs for in-house R&D: extensive subcontracting allows externalization of costs to state-of-the-art designers and producers, and local networks of loyalty and trust neutralize the risk that trade secrets will be betrayed.

But such accounts do not explain how and why regional cultures might vary from one another and how persistent such variations are. Regional cultural analysis is often less assertive than national about such persistence.[4] Although the initial work on the "Third Italy" suggested that the new patterns were the product of a powerful long-term pattern resulting from the end of mass production (the "second industrial divide"), empirical evidence that accumulated subsequent to Piore and Sabel's 1984 treatise on this subject suggested that towns and regions pursuing such strategies successfully for a time often failed to sustain them. Locke (1995) offers historical analyses to sort out which regions persisted in these patterns and details historical and political contingencies of a kind not easily encapsulated by simple cultural stories. Similarly, although Saxenian, whose influential discussion has strongly shaped discourse on the U.S. high-tech industry, at times suggests distinctive Californian cultural traits as a cause of Silicon Valley outcomes and practices, she also notes that in a 1980s crisis, local firms, more or less unaware of what was distinctive about the small-firm, high-trust, flexible networks model, nearly lost this cultural edge by reverting to a large-firm, mass production model. So it appears that Silicon Valley industrial leaders had little understanding of the cultural models she discusses and, absent the crisis spurred by Japanese mass production of semiconductors, might have lost the Valley's supposedly distinctive culture and industrial advantage by keying decisions and structures to a very different yet available cognitive model of production, the vertically integrated, autarkic model of Massachusetts. If this is right, then we should stress the fragility and contingency of cultural models for regions and the availability of quite different alternative models, or frames, rather than the inevitability of outcomes.

I also note that despite the continuing clear importance of flexible small-firm networks in Silicon Valley, large firms (e.g., Hewlett-Packard, Intel, Apple, Google, Facebook) have always played an indispensable role that is theoretically under-analyzed because this fits uncomfortably with the usual idea of a single, coherent model of organization. These firms' relatively "autarkic" qualities—especially prominent and indeed almost emblematic at the hugely successful Apple—more closely resemble the style that Saxenian associated with the less successful Route 128 (Massachusetts) region, and this suggests greater complexity of actual regions than simple cultural models can capture. (For a similar argument about the important but under-appreciated interplay of small and large firms in the Italian textile industry, see the provocative article by Lazerson and Lorenzoni 1999.) We can appreciate such apparently unlikely combinations of organizational forms more readily if we see cultural, structural, and normative patterns as assembled by actors from a variety of existing materials. This is far from saying that such assembly is random or that these patterns do not matter; rather, I argue that they are absolutely critical, but not unalterable, and subject to change over time as actors try to define and achieve their goals. Such an argument fits well with pragmatist or syncretist models of human problem solving.

I also note the selection bias in how regional-difference cases are chosen for analysis, typically contrasting a highly successful and a less successful region. Such dramatic contrasts may shape our understanding but not be the ideal way to assess the importance of national or regional models of innovation. I looked at a longer historical time span on the study of innovation in the United States and Europe to assess whether any distinctive patterns stood out (Granovetter 2009), following the argument of Mokyr (2005) that investment in human capital over long periods has high returns only in "settings where there existed connections among scientists, inventors, artisans, technicians and mechanics" (Granovetter 2009: 3). Economic historian Gavin Wright suggests that American technological dominance in some twentieth-century industries derived from the nineteenth-century emergence of an "indigenous American technical community" in which individual mechanics moved "repeatedly from one industry to another during their careers, applying a common set of skills and principles to a diverse set of challenges" and that this high mobility was a "powerful mechanism for diffusing new paradigms throughout the economy" (1999: 299–300). This high level of inter-firm mobility began with American industrialization and continues to exceed that in most of the world. Already in the nineteenth century, individuals with technical skills came to associate with other like-minded individuals, showing off their achievements in what we would now call a "nerdy" way, and where a high density of such individuals congregates in one industry and region, as in the "Homebrew Computer Club" that played such a central role in the development of the personal computer in Silicon Valley, this can make a huge difference in innovation (Granovetter 2009: 4).

Another essential ingredient in the success of Silicon Valley was the intense interaction of industry with Stanford University researchers. The university was founded in 1891 with a specific mission to educate in a practical way, and one can imagine that this was idiosyncratic to the great merchant/industrialist/Senator Leland Stanford and to the wide-open spaces of California. But a longer perspective suggests that this was hardly anomalous in the United States. From the nineteenth century on, American industrial firms, quite unlike European ones, interacted closely with educational institutions offering theoretical training in their industry, so that academic training was closely linked to practical problems (see Wright 1999 and Rosenberg 2000).

These two patterns, the intersecting networks of technical experts and the penchant for universities and industry to cooperate, epitomize what is supposed to be the unique culture of Silicon Valley as opposed to the more vertically integrated organization of knowledge in Massachusetts. Yet my survey suggests that in longer historical perspective, it may well be that the California pattern was more typically American and the Massachusetts one historically anomalous. If so, this sheds quite a different light on how one identifies what is actually a cultural pattern and what its significance is.

Many scholars argue that entire nations have distinct cultures that strongly shape economic actions and institutions. If "cultural" differences have this effect, then we have moved our discussion of norms and other mental constructs to a higher level of social organization, where we would again have to focus on the impact not of particular individual norms but of complex constellations of such conceptions that somehow cohere into collections of ideas that we denote as national "cultures." Economic theory does not explicitly make room for cultural differences and predicts the same outcomes under given economic conditions in any society where markets are allowed to function without impediments. One sees this view, for example, in the study of such economic practices as corporate governance. While some analysts expect empirically observed variations to persist because of "path dependence," part of which is culturally determined (e.g., Bebchuk and Roe 2004), others take the more orthodox economic view that such differences will disappear as market discipline enforces convergence to an optimal form that cultural differences cannot change (e.g., Hansmann and Kraakman 2004).

Interestingly, the hostility of convergence theorists to the idea of distinct, coherent, and powerful cultures that determine outcomes is shared by recent sociological analysts of culture, though for rather different reasons. Swidler, for example, in a well-known contribution, argues that the "reigning model used to understand culture's effects on action is fundamentally misleading. It assumes that culture shapes action by supplying ultimate ends or values toward which action is directed, thus making values the central causal element of culture" (1986: 273). Instead, she considers culture to be "symbolic vehicles of meaning, including beliefs, ritual practices, art forms and ceremonies, as well as informal cultural practices such as language, gossip, stories and rituals of daily life" (273) but notes that all real cultures contain diverse and conflicting symbols, rituals, stories, and guides to action. So it is less a "unified system that pushes action in a consistent direction" and "more like a 'tool kit' or repertoire . . . from which actors select differing pieces for constructing lines of action" (277). Rather than "cultural dopes," we should expect the "active, sometimes skilled users of culture whom we actually observe" (277).

So whereas rational-choice, market-based arguments dismiss the idea of powerful cohesive cultures as a way of downplaying their significance altogether, cultural theorists intend instead to understand culture as a powerful but complex and contextually determined influence on the behavior of actors who have particular problems they want to solve. This entails a view of human action consistent with pragmatist philosophy and epistemology, which is skeptical of simple means-ends frameworks of the kind that rational choice and game theory favor and which suggests that there are in any time and place usually numerous, but hardly unlimited, cultural models available to draw upon as ways of thinking about how to solve problems.

Such a view is broadly inconsistent with simple assertions that "the culture" of each nation is distinctive. One take on this is to characterize a nation's culture as measured by a series of discrete value-oriented questions such as those asked on the World Values Survey, so that typical responses to questions about trust, individualism versus collectivism, religious belief, and so on, become a proxy for the overall cultural framework. Among other issues, this hardly seems consistent with the idea that particular norms do not exist by themselves. Scholars take any observed correlations between such responses and actual economic practices and generate elaborate stories built so as to link culture causally to practices but without serious attempts to flesh out and specify empirically the mechanisms behind such a link, which remain as unsubstantiated and hypothetical speculation, as in the "adaptive stories" critiqued by Gould and Lewontin (1979). This was an important element of my critique of theories of trust in Chapter 3.

Precisely because these posited national cultures are so abstractly posed, the mechanisms linking them to actual economic practices are not immediately obvious. One take on this is to depict entire nations as having a distinct "institutional logic," which (unlike the usage by organizational institutionalists studying particular industries) refers to tendencies more abstract than any particular economic practice but that are more obviously and simply linked to such practices than are the abstract national cultures of surveys. So, for example, Biggart and Guillen (1999) argue that countries have distinct "organizing logics" that offer guidance as to how economic organizations are to be constructed. In some countries, they note, it is normal to raise business capital through family ties, while in others this is generally considered an inappropriate imposition. Such "logics" are the "product of historical development, are deeply rooted in collective understandings and cultural practices, and are resilient in the face of changing circumstances" (725). They assert that trying to organize an industry in ways that contravene a nation's prevailing logic will not make sense to actors, and economic and managerial practices not consistent with the prevailing institutional logic will not be readily recognized and incorporated (726). They emphasize that such logics are not merely constraints but also "repositories of distinctive capabilities that allow firms and other economic actors to pursue some activities in the global economy more successfully than others" (726). They take such capabilities to be a form of comparative advantage for nations and argue that this framework can explain why countries are more or less successful in particular industrial endeavors.

In particular, they argue that in the auto industry, assembly and export are most compatible with a logic that "favors large firms and vertical relationships, organized either by the state or by powerful private interests" given the large-scale capital investments and economies of scale and scope required, whereas the auto parts industry is more compatible with small-firm economies with horizontal networks that can develop responsive, "buyer-driven" links to the global economy—as when one must respond to the demand of large firms in a quick and nimble way (728). They analyze Korea, Taiwan, Spain, and Argentina, all of which have substantial auto industries, and argue that the distinct institutional logics of these nations explain why Korea and Spain are strong on the assembly side, Taiwan and Spain on the components side, and Argentina on neither (as of the 1999 writing). Institutional logics are here conceived as highly consequential, with the assertion that government policies that ignore them are bound to fail (740).

This argument about national "logics" is about how private enterprise actors are likely to think in some particular nation about how to organize their firms and industry, and it also suggests how public policymakers would approach their interactions with and support of major industries, suggesting that not following the prevalent national "logic" quite likely leads to economic failure. In his *Forging Industrial Policy* (1994), Dobbin suggests why states are quite likely to follow their own national logic because that logic shapes how policymakers think. He analyzes state policy toward the railway industry in its formative years from 1825 to 1900, in France, Britain, and the United States, suggesting that this is, in effect, a controlled experiment since railway technology is the same across countries, yet each approached the industry quite differently. In France, political actors assumed that only the national state could efficiently pull together a new industry such as railways; in the United States, the national government deferred to local authorities, and Washington was the "referee of the free market"; and in Britain, sovereignty was assumed to belong to elite individuals, and industrial policy thus first protected individual firms through laissez faire and later more actively against market and political forces (Dobbin 1994: Ch. 1). Dobbin argues that each country's political history and traditions were the source of its view of industrial policy. These traditions, what we might call the nations' "political culture," or, in other accounts, their "institutional logic," could in turn be traced to historical circumstances. In France, as Tocqueville ([1856] 1955) pointed out, the French Revolution, far from marking a dramatic turning point in France's political history, can be seen as continuing the relentless centralization of French polity and economy introduced by the Bourbon monarchs. Enlightened central planning could be seen to follow from Enlightenment philosophy and from the centralization of French higher education into the elite "grandes écoles," which have long dominated political and economic life. In Britain, political history was made by notables who clung to their power through historical thick and thin; and in the United States, the troubled knitting together of thirteen independent colonies, each jealous of its prerogatives, created a federal structure that centralized with great difficulty and against opposition that continued long after the Civil War (1861–1865) ended.

This argument that administration and politics drive the economy, rather than the opposite Marxist view, is broadly consistent with Max Weber's synthesis, except for the intervening variable of a political culture resulting from political history. Another variant is suggested by Mark Roe in his 1994 book whose title, *Strong Managers: Weak Owners,* signals skepticism that American corporations have converted their energies to the service of "shareholder value" because of the increasing ownership interest of large institutions such as banks, insurance companies, and pension and mutual funds. He argues that despite anecdotal evidence, this is in fact rarely the case, and the Berle-Means (1932) image of American corporations with fragmented shareholders who have little voice in governance compared to that of hired managers continues to be largely accurate. And he argues that this is by no means an outcome driven by economic efficiency, as often proposed by law and economics scholars, but rather that American political culture ultimately derived from "American discomfort with concentrations of private economic power" (Roe 1994: xiv), which made itself evident in the economic institutions created by the political process. At the core of the Progressive movement, for example, was the "sense that individuals must be protected against the large institutions then forming in business and government" (30), and so, American politics "deliberately fragmented financial institutions so that few institutions could focus their investments into powerful inside blocks of stock" (22).[5] And one could note that the surprising popularity of Bernard Sanders and Donald Trump in the 2016 presidential primary campaigns, and Trump's subsequent nomination as the Republican candidate, again illustrate resentment and suspicion of large concentrations of economic power.

Institutional logics and cultural understandings can be even more abstract and removed from consciousness than in these cases. For example, Biernacki surveyed the textile industry in several European countries from the seventeenth to the nineteenth centuries and concluded that Britain and Germany had quite different ways of conceiving exactly what kind of commodity labor was. For the British, it was measured by the appropriation of workers' materialized labor via products sold in the market, whereas for the Germans, it was the actual amount of labor as measured by the timed appropriation of actual labor power on the shop floor (see Biernacki 1997: Ch 1). He argues that this apparently subtle difference, articulated clearly though implicitly in many of the written accounts of both economists and industry participants in the two countries, had wide-ranging effects on how practices such as supervision and remuneration were organized on the shop floor and in the larger factory environment in the two countries.

Biernacki's case study is the textile/weaving industry, but he argues that the differences in how labor was conceived ran through these entire economies. I note that insofar as this is correct, the two different schemas for thinking about labor are more conceptual and cognitive than prescriptive and normative. They are not mental constructs that shape the perception of how things should be done but rather operate indirectly, quite unlike the norms as injunctions that typify most literature on "norms." They have their impact because if you conceive of labor in a certain way, it is more natural to organize compensation and supervision in ways that correspond to that conception. So the impetus is not a sense of what is morally appropriate but rather of what is cognitively consistent, and this is a very important distinction because it requires quite a different set of arguments to understand outcomes.

And though Biernacki's argument is exemplified by the practices of a single industry, it also moves away from that industry as a unit of analysis to the culture of entire societies, insofar as this impinges on economic activity.

This being the case, other critical issues are how much such cultural models change over time, where they originate, and whether the distinctive cognitive and cultural history of a society changes the processes through which they appear, persist, or disappear. Biernacki proposes that the distinctive conceptions of labor in particular European nations were, in effect, an accidental byproduct of the exact sequence in which certain political and economic events occurred in the transition to modern capitalism (see 1997: Chs. 5–7).

By moving away from discrete norms that simply tell people what they should or should not do to more complex cultural constructs that shape how we perceive our options and code the data of everyday experience, we loosen the causal reins in such a way as to make it more problematic whether there is a simple and direct relationship between the relevant mental constructs and behavior and open the way to consideration of human agency. Any argument about how cultural patterns or schemas impact action will need to include a more elaborated discussion of how and with what certainty such causation operates. This leads to quite different arguments than those elicited from the "moral dilemmas" that psychologists impose on individuals who undergo an fMRI scan. Such dilemmas are clear-cut and well defined between two possible alternatives, and the moral issues are front and center, as in the famous "trolley problems" that moral philosophers and psychologists focus on—see Cushman et al. 2010. While individuals may well encounter some such simple situations in their everyday economic life, most actual decisions entail far more complexity and contextual subtlety, with consequent uncertainty as to what set of rules is appropriate. This brings us again to the landscape of action that pragmatist psychologists and philosophers propose, where individuals are trying to figure out what problems to solve and with what available tools and the process of decision-making is ongoing and co-evolving with the situation at hand.

Despite the value of arguments about the institutional logics or economic cultures of regions or nations, our enthusiasm should be tempered by how deterministic they are and how little attention they afford to the role of active agents who may be able to create policies and structures that do not look plausible in the context of what informed actors think they know about logics or cultures. Thus in the literature on national development, there is a tendency to suppose that the institutions and cultures of some nations predispose them to "modernization" while those of others do not. This idea was a staple of mid-twentieth-century modernization theory, which suggested that there was only one road to economic development (namely that followed by the West) and that newly developing economies should be measured by how far they had traveled along that road (see esp. the enormously influential Rostow 1960). But later and more nuanced work suggests that active and savvy national policy, in a favorable structural situation (cf. Evans 1995) may achieve results that appeared unlikely to observers before the fact, given what they knew about a particular country. Such surprises are not uncommon: for example, the efforts of General Park Chung Hee in South Korea from 1961 on to make his country a world power in heavy industry were thought by economists and other experts on Korea in this period to be wholly inconsistent with Korean traditions and institutions and therefore little more than a fool's errand. But as subsequent events showed, carefully planned uses of power, including heavy doses of coercion, along with a big push toward institutional development, especially in the form of technical education and huge government-supported loans to favored capital intensive industries, can achieve results that appeared impossible before the fact. On a smaller scale, Sabel (1993), Locke (2001), and Whitford (2005: esp. Ch 6) offer examples of regions where well-conceived efforts by government to bring counterparties together who normally would never have interacted well (if at all) created relations of trust in areas and industries notorious for chronic mistrust and resulting economic incapacity or adversarial relations suboptimal for efficiency and innovation, and Whitford (2012: 267) notes that government is only one of an array of third parties that plays this role.

In the twenty-first century (and arguably in earlier periods as well), another relevant question is whether national economic policies or cultures are the main determinant of outcomes in industries where supply chains are increasingly globalized. In this regard, the auto industry is an interesting case study, and the following section on how the craze for "modular" production affected that industry tells us a lot about the rise and fall of institutions and logics and about the increasingly global rather than national reach of new industrial developments and influences.

5.4 A Case Study in the Rise and Fall of Institutions:
"Modular" Production and the Automobile Industry

The automobile industry is particularly interesting because it has been refer-
enced in discussions of national cultures or logics but also because in recent
years its supply chains have become increasingly globalized. This being the
case, production may be scattered among a number of countries, and if
national cultures matter, then one may ask whether it is only the national
culture of the final assembler ("OEM") country that matters or whether the
OEM has to figure out how to integrate activities carried out under diverse
national cultures. As it happens in the case I describe here, that is typically
not a big issue, though it can be in industries such as apparel where the lead
firm (e.g., Nike) brings together components sourced from multiple countries in its supply chain where practices vary in ways that provide severe challenges to "corporate social responsibility" and difficulties in ensuring that
labor is utilized in ways that satisfy emerging global standards. (See, for
example, the excellent account in Locke 2013.) In this case we also see a conflict between national practices (some of which may be "cultural," and others
the outcome of local systems of inequality and political institutions) and
those that would follow from internationally accepted standards that shape
and reshape those of nation states (see, e.g., Meyer et al. 1997). The auto
industry is also of interest because its leading firms can be found in a variety
of countries whose "cultures" are usually thought quite different from one
another: the United States, Japan, Germany, South Korea, France, and Italy.
The case of "modular" production shows how a set of practices can sweep
through an industry with little impact from particular national cultures, with
some exceptions as noted below.

I present the story of modularity and its impact on the auto industry as
one about *institutions* because a set of ideas about how production *should* be
managed came to be widely accepted in an industry that had previously
arranged production rather differently. It is an interesting story in that it show-
cases the importance of the power of experts and consultants to create a normative framework that influences those within an industry who, in turn, have
the power to insist that production be rearranged around it. Without that
organizational power, auto production might have continued to be vertically

integrated, the classic pattern, in which large assemblers either owned the companies that provided parts or dominated them through market power. The story is also of interest as a case where less-than-optimal outcomes, helped along by the latent but not forgotten resistance to modularity on the part of some affected parties, eventually resulted in what we might call a process of deinstitutionalization, where auto firms returned not to a vertically integrated arrangement but to one in which ideas of modularity had been largely set aside. So this reminds us that institutions are made by humans and are not cast in stone. Actors impacted by institutions use them to solve problems, and if they are not successful in this, they then cast about for workarounds that do provide solutions, and these may eventually undo the institutional aura of the practices they move away from. In saying this, I echo the arguments of "constructivists" like Herrigel (2010) who emphasize the "creativity of action" of those trying to solve problems in industrial settings and argue against what they see as the exaggerated determinism of institutions as conceived by some scholars. But contrary to some constructivist arguments, I also suggest that even if institutions are fragile and subject to change, they still have a considerable impact on behavior and a certain reality of their own that makes them critical to consider in studying how economic frameworks evolve.

The case of modularity in autos is also interesting in showing how humans create institutions by transposing models that seem to work in one setting to others where they think they will work just as well, if suitable modifications are made. Some such analogies are highly successful, as mass production in a few industries was then adapted to many, though not all, and the vertically integrated and subsequently multidivisional firm spread as an organization form to a large part of the industrial economy through the mid-twentieth century, as chronicled by Chandler (1962, 1977) and theorized in the "new institutional economics" (Williamson 1975). Yet some analogies turn out to be troublesome in their application, for reasons that are hard to see until they are put into practice.

Modularity is a strategy of production based on the example of the computer industry. As Baldwin and Clark (1997) explain, computers are extremely complex, and by breaking up the product into subsystems or "modules," different companies "can take responsibility for separate modules and be confident that a reliable product will arise from their collective efforts" (85). The first modular computer was the mainframe IBM System/360, which IBM announced in 1964 and which came to dominate the industry. The Baldwin and Clark paper, in the *Harvard Business Review,* an outlet whose purpose is to influence practicing managers, has a clear exhortatory tone. Its title is "Managing in an Age of Modularity," and it contains in large print the statement that "Many executives will have to learn what computer executives have long known" (84). And the authors specifically state that automakers would benefit greatly from a modular design, especially when firms separate from the OEMs make modules for which they take on most of the design responsibility (87); then (by a typical free-market argument) competition among module suppliers will intensify and lead to better performance and innovation. They also note that financial services have benefited from modularization since financial services are intangible, without physical complexities, and thus easier to modularize. They say, for example, that designers can "split up securities into smaller units that can then be reconfigured into derivative financial products. Such innovations have made global financial markets more fluid" (88). (As we now know, later events severely jolted the confidence of observers in the success of this particular modularization.)

Sturgeon's 2002 article refers to modular production networks as a "new American model of industrial organization" and refers to modular production as a "paradigm" in the sense of Thomas Kuhn, who famously applied the term in his discussion of "scientific revolutions" (1962). The term "paradigm" as applied to industrial production is closely related to my usage of "institution," as it is a framework that provides cognitive guidance as to how production would best be managed. Sturgeon suggests that through the mid-1980s, the dominant economic paradigm was the "modern corporation" as defined by Chandler, and it was "assumed that successful firms would tend to come closer to its image over time" (2002: 452), but in the 1970s and 1980s, Asian competition created a new paradigm based on the economies created by ongoing interaction between firms—the "production network paradigm" (452). And from the 1990s, a new American model arose based on modular production, electronics being the first example. In the "modular production network," linkages between firms are achieved by the transfer of codified information about how the separate modules made by separate firms have to be made in order to fit together in the overall architecture. Sturgeon suggests that modularity is increasing in apparel, toys, home furnishings, food processing, and auto parts. In the auto industry, he says that U.S. automakers have spun off their in-house parts subsidiaries and "outsourced the design and manufacture of entire automotive subsystems to first-tier suppliers" (454), and these become "turn-key suppliers" that provide the full range of services without much assistance from or dependence on lead firms, so "turn-key suppliers and lead firms co-evolve in a recursive cycle of outsourcing and increasing supply-base capability and scale" (455).

Early articles on modularity saw as one of its advantages that it simplified and made less intense the relationships of trust and the dense ongoing communication between lead firms and suppliers of the sort that were known to be characteristic of the Japanese auto industry and often thought a big part of their success (see, e.g., Nishiguchi and Beaudet 1998). In the ideal type of modular production, the codification of rules as to how modules must be made in order to fit together eliminates the need for intense communication between firms. Sturgeon notes that turn-key contracting allows for looser and thinner interactions because the supplier decides how to make its module, and so there is less need for interaction or for social or spatial closeness and trust. Where trust is needed, he suggests, it is a barrier to progress because the "trust required to enter the system takes a long time to build up" (486), and this need is greatly reduced by modular production that relies on "widely accepted standards that enable the codifiable transfer of specification across the inter-firm link" (486). These highly codified links allow the system to "attenuate the build-up of thick tacit linkages between stages in the value chain" (486–487). This reduced mutual dependence "lowers barriers to network entry and exit" (488), and this is more flexible than captive or localized industrial networks.

These accounts assume that technical properties of the products drive what is the most efficient way to produce. For example, the computer is a product that can easily be assembled from separate modules that don't have to be made by the same company. As long as the makers of modules obey the "architectural" rules specified by the lead firm, which are then codified in the entire industry, then the module can be a black box. Moreover, this modular "architecture" naturally leads to a certain way of organizing the firms in a production network. The "mirroring hypothesis" emerged as a statement that the organization of firm networks would come to mirror the productive technology, as Sturgeon spells out.

Subsequently, more sobering appraisals of this technologically determinist expectation about the organization of production networks mirroring the technical properties of the production process were offered by, e.g., Frigant and Talbot (2005) and Colfer and Baldwin (2016), and we will see more in my account below of events in the auto industry. But a careful look at the original sources reveals what should perhaps have been cautions about the inevitable evolution of modularity, even in computers, the original source. So, Baldwin and Clark note that IBM developers had no idea initially how difficult it would be to actually ensure the integration of modules with one another, and had they realized this, especially given that they underestimated the likely market value of the System/360, they might never have pursued this approach at all (1997: 86). At a later stage in the evolution of computers, another thing IBM did not realize, which would have likely stopped in its tracks the pursuit of modularity in making PCs, was what its impact would be on its own position in the computer market. Delegating the operating system to Microsoft and the design and creation of chips to Intel left IBM in a much-weakened market position relative to these module suppliers. Indeed, Jacobides and Macduffie refer to IBM's decision to embrace the modular production model for the PC as the "outsourcing blunder of the century" (2013: 97) and note that Microsoft and Intel "quickly amassed market capitalizations that eclipsed those of IBM and the other OEMs that had dominated the market" (93).

Another idea influencing the pursuit of modularity, which was featured in the management literature in the 1990s, was that firms should pursue their "core competencies" rather than fritter away resources on activities better pursued by others. The highly influential article on this subject, Prahalad and Hamel (1990), appeared in the *Harvard Business Review,* as did important articles on modularity. While not every *HBR* article has an outsized influence on business practice, there is nevertheless an aura of legitimate authority from this outlet, which makes a given article much more likely to set an agenda for firms and influence practice than if it had appeared elsewhere. Even though the "core competencies" argument does not give precise instructions for determining just which of a firm's competencies are "core," it is still consistent with modular product design, which in almost any specification will relieve a lead firm of some functions. Still another influence was Christensen's idea of "disruptive innovation," first developed in his 1997 book *The Innovator's Dilemma,* whose subtitle made clear its mission: *The Revolutionary Book Which Will Change the Way You Do Business,* published by the Harvard Business School press. Modularity looked to some observers like an excellent example of a "disruptive" technology or innovation.[6]

And so, we find that by the late 1990s, major auto assembly firms, including Ford, Chrysler, General Motors, Hyundai, and Fiat, had embraced modular production as the wave of the future. And we do not have to speculate as to whether these firms were influenced by the new management ideas because we have evidence for this. The International Motor Vehicle Program, a cooperative research project between industry and academia run out of MIT, had a project between 1998 and 2003 called "Modularity and Outsourcing," which "attracted many sponsors, allowing researchers to conduct fieldwork at OEMs and Tier 1s worldwide" (Jacobides et al. 2016: 1952). IMVP researcher Daniel Whitney "observed the ubiquity" of the Christensen book and another by Baldwin and Clark (2000) (in effect an expanded version of their HBR article on modularity) "on the shelves of product engineers during a 2000 visit at one of the Big Three OEMs," and he noted that certain words "were obligatory, and one of these was modularity. . . . I was told that the Christensen and Baldwin & Clark books had been declared required reading" but also noted that his contact at this OEM "felt that it oversimplified a complex situation and forced people to agree with top management's decisions instead of working through the problem themselves" (quoted in Jacobides et al. 2016: 1953). One of the central academic figures in the modularity movement is quoted as saying that in the late 1990s, Kim Clark and Clay Christensen "were in evangelizing mode and the [modularity] frameworks were just out. Kim in particular had a longstanding relationship with the Ford CEO, and I know they discussed our work" (quoted in Jacobides et al. 2016: 1953).

I note here the similarity of these events to what DiMaggio and Powell (1983), in their seminal article on the "new institutional theory of organizations," indicate is a major source of "mimetic isomorphism," by which they mean the tendency of organizations to imitate innovations they see in other organizations because they come to be seen as the most "modern" way to organize in an uncertain environment. They note that "models may be diffused unintentionally, indirectly through employee transfer or turnover, or explicitly by organizations such as consulting firms or industry trade associations" (151) and that large organizations "choose from a relatively small set of major consulting firms, which, like Johnny Appleseeds, spread a few organizational models throughout the land" (152). But despite some similarity, our case here is different in that rather than some firms imitating others, it appears that all were following the lead of the same set of experts and consultants who originally stated the case for modularity in a way that inspired top executives (but less so product engineers) of large OEMs to reorganize according to this new model, and the site of adoption was not a single firm but much of an industry across multiple countries.

Top executives pushed the frame of modularity even though product engineers had serious misgivings. Consistent with this point, the management literature has begun to discuss "framing contests" that occur within organizations (the first systematic statement is that of Kaplan [2008], and see Whitford and Zirpoli 2016 for an account of framing contests within Fiat relating to modular production). What is new in my account here, compared to existing "framing contests" literature, is emphasis on the idea that proponents and opponents of modularity were engaged in a framing contest that went well beyond the boundaries of individual firms and impacted an entire and very major industry.

Compared to the examples popular in the new institutional theory of organizations, such as the adoption of centralized HR functions in large organizations, the manufacture of physical products is different in that there are relatively simple ways to measure whether products made in one way work better or worse than those made in another. In the case of HR, so many factors enter into the success and failure of organizations that it is very hard to measure whether an organization that has revamped its human resources is better or worse off for having done so. But a manufactured product like an automobile is rated constantly by experts, by regulators, by final consumers, and even before these by production engineers as to how well it works, so that if a particular mode of production results in vehicles that work less well than others, this will become clear relatively soon. And this is critical to remember as I convey some detail as to why modular production in autos encountered organizational and quality difficulties that became clear to all concerned, including initial proponents of the modular model. Our understanding of the auto industry also benefits from it being the focus of attention of numerous management scholars who have specialized in it and provided trenchant and detailed accounts that I draw on here.

Before I offer details on the rise and fall of modularity in large auto OEMs, I suggest some of the reasons why the modular strategy was not a good fit for the auto industry—though in fairness, few saw these issues clearly before the experiments in modular production. The opposite of modularity is integrality, a system of production in which each part depends on and must be designed along with each other major part. Macduffie and Helper observe that auto product architecture has proved resistant to moving away from integrality because a car "is vastly more complex than a PC, it must use space much more tightly, and it is highly dependent for marketing on a distinctive visual identity" (2006: 425–426). And in autos, a "module" is quite different than in a computer. In fact, the sections of autos that came to be treated as modules were originally specified *before* ideas of modularity came on the scene, as for Fiat in the 1980s (Jacobides et al. 2016: 1950). These were basically chunks of "physically proximate components that could be subassembled independent from the rest of the vehicle, tested for functionality after subassembly and then installed on the final assembly line in a single step" (MacDuffie and Helper 2006: 426). This violates the formal definition of modularity in several ways. One is that more than one function is performed by these chunks, there is no standard definition of the functions they perform, and thus no standardized interface can be specified that allows the modules to be connected to one another. And this means that in violation of the strict definition of modularity, where a module should have interdependence within each module but only standardized connection rules between modules, there was instead functional interdependence *between* modules because most functions of, for example, the instrument panel, required components elsewhere in the vehicle in order to be operable (MacDuffie 2013: 19). And across companies, "differences in design philosophy meant widely different numbers of defined modules and no agreement on modular boundaries" (MacDuffie and Helper 2006: 426). MacDuffie also notes that the definition of modules was "idiosyncratic from the start"—e.g., the instrument panel, the front end, seats and the rolling chassis" (2013: 15). Modules were defined not by their simple functions, as in a computer's CPU or memory, but "following the logic of combining bulky or heavy parts" like the front end (15). Still another reason that it was difficult to assign design and production of major modules to first-tier suppliers is that the OEM firms ultimately had regulatory responsibility and legal liability for all parts of the auto as well as "ownership of the customer experience and/or distribution" (Jacobides et al. 2016: 1962), factors that hardly arose in the computer industry, where user safety was a nonissue.

Despite these problems that became more clear after years of experimenting with modularity, OEMs were initially enthusiastic as were suppliers, especially in the first tier, since the modular process would give them major new functions and expand their business substantially. Jacobides et al. suggest that OEMs at the outset were "quite oblivious to the strategic risk" that suppliers might, as had happened in the computer industry, capture the lion's share of industry value (2016: 1953). MacDuffie discusses the case of Ford, whose CEO and top managers were enthusiastic about the prospects of saving, as in the computer industry, by outsourcing design to suppliers, whereas many Ford engineers saw this as a risk to product performance and brand identity (2013: 25). MacDuffie chronicles how Ford redefined its entire vehicle in terms of nineteen modules rather than the thousands of parts or "components" that suppliers previously had produced.

An interesting case is the design of the instrument panel, which was outsourced around 1999–2000 to first-tier supplier Visteon (previously spun off from Ford). Visteon redesigned the panel to greatly reduce the number of parts and thus the weight and size, consolidating many electrical functions onto a small number of integrated circuit boards. A hinge on the back edge allowed the top half of the panel to open up so as to replace boards or software. So in principle, this was a great design improvement of the kind that you would expect from modular production. But because it had been designed in isolation from the rest of the vehicle, unforeseen problems emerged, such as major vibration problems with the installed prototype module, poor performance under extreme conditions of temperature, and difficulty in installing new boards because the windshield blocked the opening. A senior manufacturing executive noted that neither Ford nor the suppliers "really understand how the electronics in an instrument panel module need to interact with the electrical system in the rest of the vehicle. Plus the suppliers need to understand a whole lot more about the customer, the warranty system, our dealers, etc." (MacDuffie 2013: 26). Similar issues arose with other modules or were foreseen even before they were contracted out (22–23, 25). A chief engineer, referring to the newly defined modules, explained that the original goal "was to use all 19 . . . But in the end, after many false starts, we didn't use a single module" (23). And in 2001, Ford's modularity task force was disbanded. Though some modules continued to be produced at supplier plants, the more ambitious goal to make the entire vehicle modular was abandoned.

Whitford and Zirpoli (2014) report a case where a module that seemed to have been successfully produced for Fiat by a first-tier supplier surprisingly led to the return of design responsibility for this system to Fiat itself. This story is more complex and nuanced than those for Ford but in its way even more compelling as an account of fundamental problems in the concept of modular production for autos. One of the modularization projects undertaken by Fiat was to delegate to a large supplier firm, here denoted as TIER1, all the responsibility for developing the occupant safety system—air bags, seat belts, sensors, etc. TIER1 was happy to have this opportunity and undertook, as was consistent with the modularization paradigm, to supply Fiat with a 'black box"—a system that Fiat did not need to understand, just know how to integrate with the rest of the vehicle. Moreover, standard Euro NCAP crash tests would measure how successfully the module had been designed (1826–1827).[7] In reality, however, development of this module was more complicated. It became clear, for example, that if the system did not get the top score of five stars, it would not be obvious whether the fault was with the module or with other parts of the car that interacted with it in practice and were not working properly or interacting with it in a way that made occupants safe. Among the components that might affect crash test performance were the seats, door coverings, the dashboard, brakes—all could affect whether airbags deployed successfully, and all were made by suppliers other than TIER1 (1827). This required informal communications with other suppliers.

In 2005, the occupant safety system that TIER1 had designed was highly rated in the Euro NCAP crash tests, which one might have thought would be taken as validation of the modular paradigm. Yet this is not how TIER1 engineers responded. Instead, they were concerned that they did not actually understand *why* the test was so successful because they did not control the design of all the subsystems that affected safety and were not "responsible or even competent for the design of the chassis, the engine layout and packaging of components and systems that affect the performance of the occupant safety system." (1829). So they discussed the problem with Fiat engineers, who concluded that it would be a mistake to leave the fate of the next occupant safety system to "serendipity." Subsequent to these discussions, the overall responsibility for the safety system was returned to Fiat, while "TIER1 engineers stepped back into their previous role and were therefore again responsible for the performance of parts and components, rather than for the system as a whole" (1829).

This turnaround in the face of successful performance is puzzling because one might imagine that TIER1 engineers would be loathe to admit ignorance of why their product worked so well, as this might lead to the "implication that they were simply not as competent as they maintained" (1829). Whitford and Zirpoli suggest that to understand why they acted as they did, we need to know that much of the work had been done by TIER1 personnel located in Italy, who had "long-standing relationships with Fiat engineers at multiple levels," and moreover, they knew that many of those engineers had "grown unhappy with the broad strategic shift from component to system supply" (i.e., with modularization), "which had also generated problems for Fiat elsewhere in the network" and were "little enamored of their own plight in a company they believed had committed too much to the pursuit of a modular product architecture." Thus one Fiat engineer, referring to the idea that the lead company's role should be to create "architectural" rules for how to integrate modules, told the authors that the experience with modularity had taught him that you "cannot integrate component performances you know very little about . . . if you have never designed a component or a system it will be very difficult to understand the subtle interactions with the rest of the vehicle" (1830). Structured relationships among firms during the modularity experiment had not

> obviated the need for situational recourse to informal 'embedded' ties and a reliance on goodwill trust in the pursuit of workarounds.

> And that proved fortunate because the existence of that goodwill trust meant that TIER1 engineers could . . . reveal that they did not quite know why the crash test had worked, confident that they were in the presence of parties with whom they had long-standing working relationships and who would therefore believe their revealed ignorance to reflect systemic rather than individual deficits. (1830)

So we have the irony that while one virtue ascribed to the modularity paradigm was relieving firms of the need to establish close, trusting relations with suppliers, in fact, it was precisely the existence of that trust, based on historical patterns of relationships, that led to the virtual undoing of modularity based on the fear that continuing with modular production of safety systems would sooner or later lead to a major failure based on lack of understanding as to how they worked in conjunction with other modules.

Whitford and Zirpoli (2016) also note that the transition away from modularity was not determined only by technology but also by coalitions within and across auto firms that were organized around competing cognitive frames. When Fiat first embraced modularity in the late 1990s, the modularity frame was contested by a group consisting mostly of engineers who were skeptical of the idea (as product engineers had been at Ford) and who joined with supplier engineers at strategic moments. This group was largely submerged during the ill-fated alliance of Fiat with General Motors from 2000 to 2005 but could resume its "counter-mobilization" once that alliance was unwound. They note that even while formally disbanded, this group still pursued its strategy, which "was greatly aided by thick social relations between project teams and key suppliers maintained only as an accidental byproduct of the company's balkanization between 2000 and 2002" (17). The existence of this group and its known attitude toward modularity, together with its ties to TIER1 engineers, made possible the reversal of strategy.

A case where the modular strategy worked much better is revealing because it belies the argument that a virtue of modularization is that it facilitates the efficient, arm's-length interaction between lead firms and suppliers. Quite to the contrary, this case shows that modularity can work *only* in the context of close and trusting ties between suppliers and the lead firm. South

Korean auto assembler firm Hyundai Motor is "arguably the automaker most heavily engaged in using modules to manage complexity, improve quality and reduce costs" (MacDuffie 2013: 26). The most interesting bit of background information here is that Hyundai has a unique and close relationship with its sole-source module supplier, the "mega-supplier" Mobis, which was once a division within Hyundai. After the spinoff, it turned out that Mobis was the official holding company for Hyundai Motor as well as its largest shareholder, and in fact, the CEO and other senior executives at Hyundai Motor worked previously at Mobis. Mobis is located close to Hyundai and Kia (a Hyundai subsidiary) assembly plants and makes chassis, cockpit, and front-end modules. It is the tenth-largest global auto supplier and more profitable than Hyundai Motor itself (27). From the outset, the "relationships between Hyundai and Mobis have stayed closely integrated" (29) involving frequent contact as well as equity cross-holdings and overlapping governance structure. So we see a "quasi-vertically integrated relationships market by tight interpersonal and interorganizational ties across firm boundaries," and this collaboration has intensified over time (29).

This constant collaboration, facilitated by personnel overlap and mobility between the two firms (one Mobis manager explained to MacDuffie that 30 to 40 percent of its engineers came from Hyundai—2013: 28), is needed because, as with other auto assemblers, modules continue to be interdependent *across* module boundaries—especially when considering problems of "NVH"— noise, vibration, and harshness—as those issues cannot be resolved without collaboration with the assembler, which has the best sense of how different modules affect one another. As one Mobis manager indicated, "We can't address NVH issues within chassis alone: it is tied to many other aspects of product design. When we have NVH issues, Hyundai and Mobis engineers meet frequently to resolve them" (28). MacDuffie notes that contrary to the ideal type of modularity in which there is high interdependence within modules and little or none between, the performance of modules "increases as they become more internally integral in terms of product architecture and as increased learning about cross-module inter-dependencies leads to an ever-more-integrated organizational architecture" (28).

So the irony here is that modularity does not work according to the ideal type set out by engineers and business professors in the 1990s, in which separate companies make modules that are independent of one another and later connected by "architectural" rules that are standardized in an industry. Instead, in the case of autos, and perhaps many other products such as financial instruments, interactions *across* modules are significant, complicated, and idiosyncratic, requiring close cooperation between the lead firm and its suppliers, facilitated by network ties between the firms' personnel and the trust that results from longstanding relationships. So modularity works best exactly in the situation that it was supposed to make unnecessary.

Note also that the closeness between Hyundai and Mobis that makes this possible results from the overall structure of Korean *chaebol*—the groups of firms such as LG, Samsung, and Hyundai that cooperate closely within a group. The characteristics of a *chaebol* make the evolution of Hyundai and Mobis easier to understand. Each *chaebol* (often misleadingly referred to as a "conglomerate") is a collection of firms that are legally independent of one another but typically highly interlocked in ownership and governance, with a single group such as a family providing overall leadership across firms despite their legal independence from one another. (For an overview of business groups around the world, see Granovetter 2005, and for more on the power structure within the *chaebol,* see Ch. 4 in this book). Thus, the "spinoff" of Mobis from Hyundai, while technically the creation of a separate firm, leaves it squarely within the Hyundai sphere of influence, much like all the other legally separate firms in the group, as is made clear by the interlock of ownership and control between it and its former parent, Hyundai Motor. This is hardly unique within the *chaebol* structure, as firms are spun off or brought back in, listed or unlisted, for reasons related to strategic aims of the central controlling group (see the excellent account of these activities in Sea-jin Chang 2003). Yet the legal separation of the firms offers certain advantages, as the distinct identities confer the ability to develop separate policies toward employees, such as paying nonunion rather than union wages (MacDuffie 2013: 27). So it may be that such an arrangement is optimal for modularity to actually work. But insofar as it works, it looks quite different from the ideal type of modularity originally proposed. This deviation from ideal type is not of much concern to personnel who are trying to solve problems set out for them and are not particularly concerned about fulfilling an idealized description of a productive "paradigm." So the institutional structure of modularity ends up looking quite different from its origins in the computer industry because pragmatic actors in the process of solving problems create structures that work, and in the end, the revised modularity paradigm might spread, insofar as firms can meet the requirements of the new model. So the bottom line is that models, paradigms, or institutions really do matter and shape behavior, but the agency of those who follow those models reshapes the institutions in critical ways, and this is something very important to understand about institutions at every level.

Finally, I note that the paradigm of modularity had less influence on Japanese automakers than elsewhere, and I suggest this is because the close interaction that already existed between assemblers and suppliers within Japanese vertical business groups such as Toyota (cf., e.g., Nishiguchi and Beaudet 1998) was productive in a number of useful ways, including that of design innovations, so that a model that promised to end the need for such interaction would likely meet more skepticism. The closeness of relations between such firms was consistent with themes typical of Japanese culture, but as Nishiguchi and Beaudet emphasize, inter-firm cooperation is hardly automatic but requires many years of trial and error to get the patterns to work (consistent with Swidler's idea that while a given culture may provide tools for its members to use, it is not a set of simple prescriptions that are automatically followed). Jacobides et al. note that in 1999, in a "rare moment of candor, one Toyota executive . . . [stated that] 'Our competitors will pursue modules and they will have quality problems as a result and our advantage over them will only grow.' Our fieldwork suggests that Toyota was not ignoring modularity, but viewed it as something to explore first internally, particularly with respect to design. Toyota was more cautious, experimented within its own boundaries, and didn't subscribe to the new vision—rightly so, as it turned out" (2016: 1952n).

6

The Interplay between Individual
Action and Social Institutions

The previous chapter offered general arguments and characterization of institutions as patterns of ideas or norms that influence but only incompletely determine how actors approach the problems they mean to solve. I did not there try to deal with the fact that in any social setting, more than one institutional pattern may appear relevant to the same set of social activities, and actors implicitly or explicitly need to sort out what is the appropriate pattern they should call on for guidance. This multiplicity of institutional guidance is quite common and presents another reason why it is so important to consider the thought processes and active consideration that actors give to problems they face. In this final chapter, I offer some ideas to cope with this pivotal but difficult issue and end with discussion of how in any particular setting, the menu of institutions that actors see as relevant in their situation came to be as it is. That discussion is necessarily comparative, historical, and conducted at a macro level.

Actors who cast about for ways to deal with some problem, economic or otherwise, become aware of various approaches, where I use "approaches" as a way of talking about institutions as they appear to individuals. Roughly speaking, there are three alternative ways that they can settle on a particular institutional approach to help solve a problem: (1) they can think about alternative approaches from different institutional arenas and decide that one is the most appropriate way to frame their situation; (2) they can take a solution that is usually applied in an institutional realm different from the one relevant to their problem and transpose it, repurposing it for the occasion; and they can transfer not only institutional patterns but also resources from another realm for their purpose; or (3) they can mix and match bits and pieces of various institutional approaches, which is what one might expect from a pragmatist epistemology. I consider these in order in the next three sections, followed by a section treating the emergence of institutional alternatives that follow from political turmoil, war, and revolution. Although I pose these three ways that actors use institutions as conscious decisions for the sake of exposition, it seems likely that in many if not most cases, much of this framing is below the level of conscious thought. Like most normative patterns, institutions are more influential the less they are brought to conscious awareness.

6.1 Institutional Intersections and Alternative Schemas

In some situations, actors choose one institutional approach from among those available to solve some problem they want to deal with. One way that multiple approaches become relevant is when an activity intersects multiple institutional spheres. I begin with the homely, almost trite, example of a Wall Street financial analyst whose hundred-hour weeks analyzing mergers and acquisitions establish her reputation as brilliant and hardworking. But were she to allocate her activities and commitments by the standards of obligation to her suburban spouse and children, she would likely re-deploy some of her strenuous efforts in lower Manhattan to the family sphere.

This is the classic elementary textbook stuff of "role conflict," but for our purpose, it is more interesting that our analyst lies at the intersection of two institutional domains, that of business and the economy on one side and that of family and marriage on the other. If we treat these domains as circles in Venn diagrams, then the intersection is the place where the norms and standards of evaluation of either institution *might* govern, and the individual has to figure out which ones to apply. Many issues lie outside the intersection: how to balance the interests of client against employer lies entirely within the economic domain, and how to divide labor in your household is a family matter. But how to allocate your time *between* family and career lies squarely in the intersection. This case entails a quantitative decision, but sometimes a more qualitative choice is required, as when a government official is in a position to favor his relative for a permit to engage in some economic activity and must consider whether the guideline of bureaucratic efficiency or that of family loyalty should govern action. Here, the standards of "justification" proposed by Boltanski and Thevenot loom large. And such decisions are central to imputations of "corruption," as I discuss in more detail in the sequel volume. This case may also, to the extent that the multiple frames of judgment become clear but are held by different and possibly competing groups, result in a "framing contest" of the kind referred to in the previous chapter, and this has quite commonly come about when contesting groups disagree as to what behavior is "corrupt," as I argue in more detail in my sequel volume and in Granovetter 2007.

So where individuals act in situations which they could code as being guided by the norms and standards of institution A or alternatively by those of institution B, then which code, frame, schema, or script they deem relevant will determine what action seems appropriate and proper. A typical such choice is that between career and family, as for our Wall Street analyst. The inverse of this choice occurs when a "wife views her household labor through a marketplace logic of explicit exchange, whereas her husband imposes a family logic of selfless service upon the situation" (DiMaggio 1997: 277), and in this formulation we see also a *clash* of institutional logics embedded in and providing scripts for a family power struggle, a very special kind of framing contest, and indeed the uncompensated market value of household labor is a recurrent theme in feminist politics and theory.

The situation here is that both spouses appeal to well-known and accepted norms, but these derive from different institutional frames or schemata, and the spouses disagree about which frame is appropriate to their situation. Because this disagreement reflects a conflict of interest as well as an intellectual divergence, this might also be thought a case of people using culture strategically, as is emphasized by such theorists of culture as Swidler 1986. But this does not mean that the disagreement is not "really" about norms or that the norms are mere fig leaves concealing the underlying struggle of interests, as rational-choice reductionists or Marxists might argue. Instead, the conflict of interests is conducted around normative arguments precisely because these *do* matter and carry enough emotional freight to be persuasive if one side can successfully frame the situation in a certain way. Which side is successful in making its frame prevail depends in part on its ability to set the agenda, a critical aspect of power as emphasized in Chapter 4 and related to the ability of those with this agenda to achieve actual political power positions of the sort that resulted in 1960s and subsequent legislation on gender discrimination in the United States.

A similar conflict of institutional logics is suggested by Boltanski and Thevenot (1999: 374) in their example of disputes on workers' rights, where one side draws on the logic of the "civic world," a frame that stresses the rights of citizens, and the other on the logic of the "industrial world," based on economic efficiency. The existence of conflicts suggests that when individuals have to choose which institutional frame should govern their action, they typically do not make such choices in isolation, and others connected to them may make different choices that are inconsistent and conflicting, as with husbands and wives or workers and employers.

This raises the issue of how people facing conflicting institutional logics or principles make their choices. The examples above are easily categorized as driven by rational interests, but we should be wary of pushing this too far, as interests, even if the proximate cause of outcomes, are not always self-evident and given. The "interests" of housewives, which figure in the above examples, came to be dramatically redefined in the course of the twentieth century by macro-social trends and widely visible social movements. Nor is it always obvious *which* of an individual's interests a given situation engages. Peter Hall offers the example of a voter considering a party's proposal to change environmental rules. Such a voter "has a multivariate preference function," i.e., has different interests as a consumer, a worker, a parent, and a citizen and must decide "which of the corresponding concerns to weigh more heavily when taking a position on the issue," and this will depend in part on "which of his identities are engaged most intensely in debates about the issue" (2010: 211–212).

The focus here on individual identities is forced by the focus on voting, something *individuals* do, but also points up the parallelism between institutions and role identities, as the most important norms of an institutional sector are typically those that specify proper behavior and responsibilities for its various role incumbents, consumers and workers in the economy, parents, children and spouses in the family, citizens in the polity. Moreover, Hall points out, even when outcomes do turn largely on material interest, as they might in this case, issues of identity can still be "important determinants of the result. The presumption that identity politics has little to do with the politics of material interest is generally false, and normative beliefs figure prominently in identity politics" in determining which interest identity is triggered (2010: 212).

DiMaggio offers a more abstract account, suggesting that faced with the need to "invoke one among the many schemata available to them in a given situation," people are "guided by cultural cues available in the environment" and that a schema is "primed or activated by an external stimulus" such as conversation, media use, or the physical environment (DiMaggio 1997: 274). He refers to framing effects in social surveys, where questions are answered differently depending on what precedes them—e.g., "whites are more likely to accept negative stereotypes of African-Americans if the question is preceded by a neutral reference to affirmative action" (274).

6.2 Transposition of Logics and Resources across Institutional Boundaries

In some situations, actors with an economic problem to solve may not see any obvious institutional pattern that offers guidance and instead analogize their problem to one of a different institutional kind that does have culturally understood patterns of action and transpose these for an economic purpose. In other words, the pragmatic actor with problems to solve does not have a limitless number of templates to draw on, and one way to approach a new problem is to transfer a template from another institutional setting, which is to say, a different aspect of their own lives. In discussing business groups, I have referred to this as "cross-institutional isomorphism" (Granovetter 2005: 437).

For example, in my discussion of East Asian economic organization (437), I follow the argument of Dukjin Chang (1999) that family and kinship institutions differed significantly among Korea, China, and Japan and that these differences spilled over into the way businesses and business groups were organized in these countries. In particular, he notes strong differences among the three in inheritance patterns and the flexibility of a family in adopting heirs.[1] Of the three countries, Korea was the only one where the eldest son received essentially the entire inheritance ("primogeniture"). In China, equipartition among sons was the rule; and in Japan, one son, not necessarily the eldest, inherited the entire estate, but there was great flexibility in who might be considered a son, including adopted children, often chosen for inheritance if they appeared more able than natural ones (Chang 1999: 26). Chang shows that the way Korean business groups *(chaebol)* are organized, including patterns of succession in management, the unquestioned authority of the patriarch in these family-led conglomerates, and the complex ways in which equity crossholding ties among member firms are arranged, closely follows the patterns of norms previously well established in family relations and inheritance (1999: Ch. 2). He suggests that family dynamics come to shape the world of business because the normative patterns of kinship "create lenses through which actors view the world, and categories of structure, action and thought that enhance the legitimacy of their behavior, that are taken for granted prescriptions and that do not even need monitoring by a third party" (47).

While the way the *chaebol* were organized had a clear resemblance to well-known patterns from the domain of family and kinship, the immediate catalyst for this to occur was a political upheaval in which General Park Chung-Hee seized power in 1961 from the last of a series of ineffective and corrupt post Korean War governments and embarked on a policy of dramatic industrial development in which he dragooned the *chaebol* to overhaul their operations and gear up for a big push into heavy industry and exports (see, e.g., Kim 1997). Although a few of the *chaebol* that became prominent in the ensuing period were already in operation (e.g., Samsung was founded in 1938), most did not exist in the 1950s (Kim 1997: 97). The organizational patterns modeled on kinship were readily understandable to *chaebol* family leaders, which made them easier to adopt, but were also useful in establishing centralized and unified *chaebol* leadership, particularly helpful in dealing with a powerful and determined political leadership that was itself quite centralized. So the political upheaval was the immediate and critical stimulus for relations from the kinship domain to be transposed to that of business in a way that transformed the Korean economy.

This theme of upheaval leading to transposition is developed systematically in the work of John Padgett and his collaborators on economic innovation and invention in medieval Florence. In particular, Padgett and MacLean (2006) analyze the invention of the partnership system in late fourteenth- and early fifteenth-century Florence, which was important in vaulting it to a position of world economic leadership. An analysis of this invention that did not see its relation to politics might stay entirely within the economic realm by adopting the common view that new inventions are simply economic reactions to the need to solve economic problems and that actors do find economic solutions in such situations, since those who do not are competed out of the market. Such an argument has several liabilities. One is that it is Panglossian (cf. Gould and Lewontin 1979), assuming that all problems are solved and indeed solved efficiently, which is belied by the frequent market and institutional failures that we observe. It is also problematic in its assumption that the economy is an insulated sector, operating in a competitive market not highly impacted by politics or social organization. Only in such situations can we imagine that competition will stimulate best outcomes, and even under such assumptions it is unclear how actors are supposed to figure out what these are.

More typically, institutional realms are intertwined, and actors are not infinitely clever in imagining abstract solutions but gravitate instead to patterns familiar from other arenas of their lives. So innovation and invention rarely arise *de novo* but are built instead with materials that already exist, just as biological evolution does not create forms that use entirely new building blocks; variation, selection, and retention, the mantra of biological evolution, imply selection from *existing* variations, which provide a substantial but hardly an unlimited resource base for new forms.

Correspondingly, Padgett and MacLean (2006) show that the invention of the Florentine partnership system was the outcome of a series of political upheavals that led pragmatic actors to import existing patterns from outside the economy to solve new economic problems. The partnership system resembled the modern business group (Granovetter 2005) being a "set of legally autonomous companies linked through one person or through a small set of controlling partners" (Padgett and MacLean 2006: 1465), and it was highly consequential for the Florentine economy because it facilitated diversification into multiple markets by a single set of companies. By contrast, the earlier unitary companies of the fourteenth century, based on patrilineages, had been generalists that carried out whatever activity seemed needed, whereas within the partnership, each separate company specialized in a single market, improving the efficiency and market power of the group and laying the foundation for subsequent Florentine economic dominance.

To sum up Padgett and MacLean's argument, they attribute this development to strategies adopted as the result of political upheavals in the late fourteenth century. After the working-class Ciompi revolt of 1378 was quashed, elites returned to power and mobilized domestic ("cambio") bankers into the state apparatus to shore up their own position. These bankers' new role in politics exposed them to an internationalist perspective previously unfamiliar to them, and they set about rebuilding the export trade damaged by the civil war. Earlier, they had built their firms according to a "master-apprentice" logic, itself borrowed from guilds, in which they had short (e.g., three-year) renewable partnerships with ex-apprentices who were expected eventually to split off and form their own firms. In the new international setting, these bankers transposed this logic to set up partnership systems in the form of formal contracts between themselves and branch managers who might be in different industries (2006: 1508). Instead of a sequence of contracts as before, there evolved a series of simultaneous contracts in different places and industries, which displaced previous forms of international merchant banking. This transposition and "refunctionality," as Padgett and MacLean refer to these developments, became truly transformative when partnership came to be embedded with intermarriage. Displacing an earlier logic based on patrilineage—direct descent in the male line—what now became important was who your in-laws were, with the result that *cambio* bankers became integrated into the elite. They refer to this as "network catalysis," where "social incorporation brought the logic of marriage, and hence dowry, out of the world of popolani [Florentine elite] banking, reinforcing and rewiring the social embedding of banking partnerships into the elite" (1520), and dowries then came to be used as start-up capital. Before the Ciompi revolt, marriages were just about kinship, not so much about politics and economics, and at the center of the constitutional stage of the state were guilds and patrilineages. But post-Ciompi, the guilds were "defanged" because of their suspect role in the revolt, and marriage became an important tool for previously elusive elite cohesion.

The ensuing partnerships were hugely successful, and lead partners shifted from entrepreneurial to financial activities, since the branch partners were chosen for their expertise in specific domains. In this respect, they looked like modern venture capitalists, and the wide range of interests that they had to pursue encouraged them to become what came to be known as "Renaissance men." Padgett and MacLean conclude that significant organizational inventions, like the partnership system, may result from political upheavals that create difficult problems for actors with economic, political, and kinship interests. They deal with these by transposing relational logics from one domain to another "which attain new purposes in the new domain, whose reproduction is positively reinforced to the point that it alters interactions among others in the new domain. Florentine inventions were more than good ideas. They were discontinuous system tippings, rooted in reproductive feedbacks among dynamic multiple social networks" (1544; for other cases of "transposition," see Padgett and Powell 2012).

Another important aspect of intersecting social institutions is that actors may transfer resources originating in one so as to gain advantage in another. A familiar example is when employers recruit through the social networks of existing employees. They gain from doing so because friends and relatives feel an obligation to help one another find the most suitable employment, and new workers, once hired, feel bound by their social ties to perform in a way that will not embarrass their informant/sponsor. The key point is that employers do not, and indeed as a matter of principle *cannot,* pay to create the trust and obligations that benefit their recruitment strategy, as these originate in the institutional domains of kinship and friendship, and any economic efficiency gains that result are a byproduct of the way that economic activity happens to intersect that of family and friendship obligations.

A common situation where intersections matter is when social occasions develop economic import because participants, not making any particular effort to segregate institutional sectors, exchange economic information in settings where their main goal is social. Adam Smith famously complained that people of the same trade "seldom meet together, even for merriment and diversion, but the conversation ends in a conspiracy against the public, or in some contrivance to raise prices" (1776: Book 1, Ch. 10, par. 82). In our own period, people typically attend parties with nothing more in mind than a good time. It would be implausible to imagine their partying as instrumental economic behavior; the expected economic gain from loud and intense socializing is unlikely to be anyone's main reason for attending. Yet information about jobs can and does pass among partygoers (Granovetter 1995). Labor markets and expressive socialization routines are separate institutions whose intersection depends on structural elements of social organization whose explanation lies well beyond that of individual incentives.

So whether or not participants are aware of the transfer of resources between institutional sectors, such transfer may still dramatically alter the cost of economic activity. When the activity is coded as corruption or rent-seeking, that cost may be increased, as noneconomic activity is subsidized by economic. But it is less frequently remarked on that the reverse often occurs as when employers, in effect, free-ride on noneconomic resources put to economic use or better job placements result from party attendance.

The transfer of resources between sectors is a general case of a more specific phenomenon that I discussed in Chapter 4 on power, namely the gaining of advantage from securing a resource from one social setting relatively cheaply and using it to gain more than it cost in another. The classic case is arbitrage between unconnected markets, which Austrian economists have taken as the type case of "entrepreneurship."

In this context, I mentioned Barth's conception of entrepreneurs as arbitraging across "spheres" or "circuits" of exchange. In the simplest case, in principle, the unconnected spheres, across which trade is inconceivable, might not look at all like what we have referred to here as "institutions"; they might simply be sets of goods that a group considers to be exchangeable only against one another and not against those in another sphere, as Firth describes Tikopians' likely incomprehension at the notion of exchanging bonito-hooks for food (see Ch. 4 in this book). But in practice, institutional considerations go into the very definition of spheres—differences between them typically involve ceremonial considerations or moral judgments—in which the monetary or barter sphere is typically ranked as inferior to others having more to do with intimate relations or ceremonies—as when modern individuals find it hard to understand the question of for what sum of money they might sell their children[2] or to condone the setting of a price for the sale of a political favor, even though these cash values could be calculated in fairly straightforward ways. Resistance to such calculations signals that different sets of norms attach to different kinds of activities, which shades over into the institutional choices and frames I discuss in this chapter.[3]

This is clear in Barth's case of Arab traders who bridged separate economic spheres to exploit differences in the cost and market value of tomatoes grown by Fur tribesmen whom they compensated with beer, as was traditional in an economy where wage labor was shameful. The outside traders' power derived from the institutional separation between communal practices, such as mutual housebuilding help, to be compensated ceremonially with beer, and market trade, where food was sold for cash in a more purely economic transaction. The advantage for those who could see these institutional barriers not as moral guides to action but as possible sources of profit depends first on there being clear institutional definitions and boundaries in place, second on their devising transactions that arbitrage across these boundaries, and finally on the presence of those who for whatever reason did not consider themselves bound by the normative structure that defined these institutional rules, as "outsiders" typically do not.

It may be helpful to think about the activity of securing resources cheaply in one institutional setting and using them to profit in another as generalized arbitrage. Classic arbitrage across separated markets makes public the opportunity available from market separation, and this draws in more traders so that the market gap and resulting opportunity vanish. In Chapter 4, I noted that contrary to this standard expectation, the entrepreneur/arbitrageur may become powerful from his activity and leverage that power to prevent others from taking advantage of this opportunity. In effect, they use their power to maintain the separation of spheres.

When the spheres are clearly identified with significant social institutions, there is still another reason why the use of extra-economic resources to gain profits need not close the gap between economic and other social activity. This is because, as I have argued,

> separate institutional sectors draw their energy from different sources and consist of distinctly different activities. Many authors have argued that economic activity penetrates and transforms other parts of social life. Thus, Karl Marx asserted (for example, in chapter

1 of *The Communist Manifesto*) that family and friendship ties would be fully subordinated under modern capitalism to the "cash nexus." But despite intimate connections between social networks and the modern economy, the two have not merged or become identical. Indeed, norms often develop that limit the merger of sectors. For example, when economic actors buy and sell political influence, threatening to merge political and economic institutions, this is condemned as "corruption." Such condemnation invokes the norm that political officials are responsible to their constituents rather than to the highest bidder and that the goals and procedures of the polity are and should be different and separate from those of the economy. (Granovetter 2005: 36)

When arbitrage is between institutional sectors, early or first movers, just as in classic arbitrage, may profit handsomely. Some dramatic successes in industrial organization can be seen as the result of such activity. Our study of the early American electricity industry suggests, for example, that Samuel Insull, the leading early twentieth-century entrepreneur (see Granovetter and McGuire 1998) stood out from others in having extensive social contacts into several separate and institutionally defined networks: tinkerers/inventors, financiers, and politicians. His career featured his deft movement of resources back and forth between these networks and the institutional sectors of which they partook. So he was the first to mobilize political resources successfully on behalf of his particular industrial model—large, integrated central station companies, transporting electricity over great distances. (It did not hurt that his base was Chicago, legendary still for its porous boundaries between politics and business.) His financial contacts in the United States and his native England enabled him not only to finance his schemes but also to transfer innovative financial instruments and accounting techniques, such as balloon depreciation, not previously used in this industry, in such a way as to support his favored technical path.[4]

Insull also wielded influence in the voluntary association sector, shaping the ostensibly nonpartisan National Civic Federation study of municipal and privately owned power companies in such a way as to advance utility regulation at the state level and disadvantage public power in relation to that provided by investor-owned utilities (Granovetter and McGuire 1998: 165–166 and, in more detail, McGuire and Granovetter 1998). Although Insull shared his innovations within a relatively closed circle, he actively combated the efforts of those outside that circle, such as sponsors of isolated generation, decentralized systems, and municipal ownership—i.e., he was the prototypical entrepreneur doing all he could to prevent others from following in his footsteps. And Insull was widely acknowledged to be one of the most powerful economic figures in his generation, so much so that he was denounced in a famous campaign speech by Franklin Roosevelt in 1932 to the Commonwealth Club of San Francisco (Roosevelt 1932).

Another interesting case is the rise of venture capital financing in Silicon Valley. In the older model of financing innovation, financiers were at arm's length from the industries they financed, knew little of the technical detail, and were not linked to its social and professional circles. Finance and industry were largely decoupled, except for specific loan transactions. This mattered little because due diligence required only an assessment of ability to repay a loan, which could be gleaned from analysis of balance sheets and an assumption of stable markets going forward. But these standard financial tools faltered in an industry undergoing rapid technical change, and beginning in the 1960s, a new model emerged. Engineers and marketing specialists from Silicon Valley firms who had made huge fortunes from their innovative products used these to become a new breed of financier—the "venture capitalist," whose extensive technical knowledge and personal networks allowed them to quickly assess new ideas. Given their skills, they were not averse to taking substantial equity positions, sitting on boards of directors, and taking active roles in management, all roles that traditional bankers typically avoided.

In effect, they moved their resources from the industrial and family spheres where they had been accumulated into a newly organized financial sector where they could deploy them in such a way as to multiply them manyfold. And their early success helped them attract huge new inflows from limited partners such as pension funds and wealthy individuals, who had no connection to technical circles (see Kaplan 1999: Chs. 6 and 7). This institutional development resembled the activity of early nineteenth-century business families who founded banks in New England to fund expansion of industries by drawing in funds from nonfamily sources (Lamoreaux 1994). In this special case of moving resources across institutional sectors, many new venture capital players continued to emerge, but traditional finance never was able to reassert its dominance because the venture capital sector developed a complex network of resources and information that could not be duplicated. Thus, although there are many new players compared to the early years, the sector remains more or less self-contained and dominant in these industries (see Ferrary and Granovetter 2009). And top figures in venture capital are well known and considered extremely powerful, at least in determining the fate of high-tech companies.

6.3 Multiple Institutional Frameworks as Resources for Pragmatic Actors

I want to repeat that though I may talk about how individuals choose one institutional frame to guide their action, "choose" implies more conscious thought than is likely. Which norms govern depends on what cognitive schema is triggered, and such schemas, if they are truly guides to action, are unlikely to be actively pondered, which would make them less potent in structuring perception. Awareness is more likely when frames collide as part of conflicting visions and interests. In some cases, individuals may benefit from ambivalence and ambiguity about what frame is relevant, and such ambiguity is typical because institutions interpenetrate each other in real life and rarely occur in pure and isolated form.

I return to the concept of "robust action," originated by Leifer in his study of chess players (1991) and developed by Padgett and Ansell (1993) to explain the extraordinary political achievements of Cosimo de Medici in coming to dominate politics in fifteenth-century Florence, as I discuss in Chapter 4. Recall that Cosimo had interests, and, as Peter Hall would say, identities, in several institutional contexts—financial, familial, and political. Padgett and Ansell argue that he was "sphinxlike" and "multivocal," and by making it obscure *which* of these interests he was pursuing in any given situation, he preserved flexibility for himself while reducing it for others. And his networks of supporters from each institutional realm could not coalesce with one another because their divergent origins made them socially incompatible and mutually contemptuous. So Cosimo straddled these varying frames without fully committing himself to one. He did so, it seems, instinctively rather than consciously, the ultimate pragmatic actor, assembling resources from wherever he could to solve his various problems but without clearly labeling his activity, which would have made it easier to attack.

David Stark elaborates this theme in the context of transition economies (1996, 2009). Drawing on fieldwork in post-transition Hungary and ideas from Boltanski and Thevenot's "modes of justification," he notes that actors in firms where the environment is uncertain may face a situation where it is unclear according to what principle or logic their result will be judged. Where your "success is judged, and the resources placed at your disposal determined, sometimes by your market share and sometimes by the number of workers you employ . . . you might be wise to diversify your portfolio, to be able to shift your accounts. . . . To gain room for maneuver, actors court and even create ambiguity. They measure in multiple units, they speak in many tongues" (Stark 1996: 1014–1015).

In emphasizing that actors may strategically maneuver among principles of justification or frames of evaluation, Stark does not mean to argue that these frames merely obfuscate. On the contrary, the only reason it makes sense to maneuver in this way is that people take the frames seriously, so that if you can persuade them that your preferred frame is appropriate, you will gain advantage. Moreover, this ability to redefine the agenda is a typical example of that aspect of power described in Chapter 4 and shows how power interacts with norms by creating frames in which the norms favored by those who persuade go on to guide others' behavior far more efficiently than would coercion. I return to this theme in my chapter on corruption in the sequel volume.

In later work, Stark generalizes this argument to propose that effective organizations often adopt a strategy of "heterarchy," by which he means artic-ulating and maintaining "alternative conceptions of what is valuable, what is worthy, what counts" (2009: 5). Having multiple performance criteria avail-able to invoke can produce a resourceful dissonance, and especially when the organizational environment is turbulent, what it means for an organization to be entrepreneurial is for it to "keep multiple principles of evaluation in play and to benefit from that productive friction" (6). He suggests that the rivalry among performance criteria makes it "possible to break out of the lock-in of habituated unreflective activity" (19). This results in a noisy clash as "proponents of different conceptions of value contend with each other. The latent consequence of this dissonance is that the diversity of value-frames generates new combinations of the firm's resources" (27).

Different institutional complexes and principles of justification may clash in consequential ways even if individuals are not aware of the conflict. So George Strauss (1955) studied a work group of women painting toys and paid by the piece, whose productivity (and thus pay) improved dramatically when a consultant gave them more freedom to arrange their work as they liked. But because the factory's other departments were staffed heavily by their husbands, male relatives, and friends, other groups quickly learned that the women's wages had skyrocketed and objected strenuously because this violated the existing status order of groups in this establishment. The information flow patterned by social relations and the conceptions of fairness in wage differentials rooted in underlying social distinctions made the new economic developments untenable, and the innovations were abandoned. Gartrell, in his discussion of how sanitation workers in Cambridge, Massachusetts, evaluated the fairness of their pay, noted the importance of discussions they had in social contexts with their friends and relatives in nearby cities and suggested the importance of such intersections of work and residential socializing for the evolution of inflationary pressures (1982: 134–136).

It seems unlikely that the workers in these two examples would easily articulate the way that institutional intersection of kinship/friendship/residence with economy and work affected their perceptions of wage fairness, and many such intersections operate far below the level of consciousness. For example, Burawoy, in his ethnographic study of a Chicago-area machine shop, argues that local conceptions of masculinity in working-class culture unwittingly added value for employers (1979). "Scientific management," pioneered in the early twentieth century by Frederick Winslow Taylor and others, used time-and-motion studies to determine how to speed up workers' production by raising quotas if it turned out that they were capable of faster work. Many of the famed industrial relations studies of the 1930s documented worker resistance to such strategies, in which workers informally set upper limits on how much should be produced and punished or ostracized "rate-busters" (cf. Homans 1950). But nothing of the kind occurred in Burawoy's machine shop, since the status currency of the male machinists was precisely skill, demonstrated by fast and effortless execution of the machinist's tasks. Burawoy, who worked in this shop in order to observe it closely, notes that until he "was able to strut around the floor like an experienced operator, as if I had all the time in the world and could still make out [produce the quota assigned by management] few but the greenest would condescend to engage me in conversation" (1979: 64).

Burawoy articulates the Marxist lament that this status system led workers to cooperate with management "in the production of greater surplus value" (64). This occurred because of the way that a particular male working-class status culture happens to intersect with the needs of the industrial system. Employers did not invest in creating these values, and it seems unlikely that either side is much aware of the way the culture supports profitability. But if employers did understand that the local culture supported their goals, they would have had still another reason to recruit through social networks since the culture would operate with more consensus and strength in cohesive work groups.

Finally, I should say that when actors draw on more than one set of institutional rules or patterns in their attempt to solve problems, some of which come to be defined as a result of that effort, there is a range of intentionality that we may see. It may be in some cases that, as Stark suggests for Hungarian factory managers, they more or less intentionally assemble a diverse "portfolio" of possible ways to justify their actions so as to have the best chance to get support based on those justifications. But it may also be that actors assemble bits and pieces from different institutional frameworks because, as pragmatist philosophers and social scientists maintain (Dewey 1939; Joas 1996; Whitford 2002), most actors have less concern for the purity of institutional design than they have for resolving the situation they are in, and this may result in solutions that would look Frankensteinian to the purist but that work in their context.

I can make this point more clearly in developing some historical and comparative arguments about "national cultures." Recall that the arguments of Biggart and Guillen, described in Chapter 5, suggest that the "logics" of certain countries more likely favor either assembly of autos as an OEM or the production of parts. But note that the logics in question did not mainly concern cars but rather the ease with which individuals in a country slotted themselves into large hierarchical operations such as assembly plants or were able to nimbly adjust to the demands of external actors in the supply chain whose requirements changed quickly, as in fashion or in auto parts. So they suggest, for example, that patrimonialism has deep roots in Korean society, and this creates an institutional logic that "legitimates centralized control by competing elites and . . . confers on the state the legitimate right to target industries for development" (1999: 733). In Taiwan, by contrast, they argue, firms did not grow by enlarging but by spinning off, resulting in a collection of densely networked family firms "ill suited to a capital-intensive enterprise such as auto assembly. It is ideal, however, for capital-light but knowledge-intensive products" (735).

One of the interesting points about such claims is that they do not rest on cultural exceptionalism for particular societies but rather imply that any society with similar institutions or logics would have a similar economic outcome, and there would then be then nothing distinctively Korean or Chinese that would explain such outcomes once the institutions in question were taken into account. So we here go beyond the idea that each country has a particular culture that determines outcomes, which would allow for few if any generalizations, to the position that we can identify certain kinds of institutional logics that might in principle appear in any country with similar effects. In fact, one might say the Biggart/Guillen argument allows cultural peculiarities of a country to matter only insofar as they lead to a particular institutional logic, but once in place, such a logic strongly determines outcomes. This general way of thinking is similar to that of more abstract theoretical arguments that there are a finite and identifiable number of "varieties of capitalism" (esp. Hall and Soskice 2001, and for an overall summary of such literature, see Streeck 2011 and the critical symposium on the "varieties of capitalism" literature in the *Business History Review* [2010]).

Hall and Soskice make a distinction common in this literature, under a variety of labels, arguing that there are, broadly speaking, two main "varieties" of capitalism, which they label "liberal market economies" (LMEs) and "coordinated market economies" (CMEs) (2001: 23). Coordinated market economies involve many forms of nonmarket coordination among firms, "patient capital" depending on close-knit corporate networks "capable of providing investors with inside information about the progress of companies that allows them to supply finance less dependent on quarterly balance sheets and publicly available information" (29), and considerable attention to non-market economic goals relating to social solidarities and traditional obligations. So access to "patient capital," for example, allows firms to retain workers in downturns and make long-term investments that will not pay off quickly. The usual type cases are Germany and Japan. In liberal market economies, market relations resolve coordination problems, corporate networks are far less close-knit, and "shareholder value" is a more critical consideration, with other stakeholders being only residual claimants.

I will talk in more detail about related issues in the sequel volume in a chapter on corporate governance. But for now, the more immediate point is that scholars with a pragmatist or "constructivist" perspective challenge such typologies, arguing that this way of thinking about economic institutions presents too simple a picture that does not do justice to the ability of most economic actors to navigate troubled economic waters without concern as to whether their behavior meets any particular institutional mandates. I would add that although it may seem plausible to suggest that state economic policy inconsistent with a society's institutional capacities or logics cannot succeed, we should consider whether the cases cited to support this argument suffer from the selection bias of known success and failure. Counterexamples might be cases where state policies flew in the face of apparent capacities but somehow succeeded. Thus, as I have mentioned above, Western economists found General Park Chung Hee's 1960s push to make Korea a major force in heavy industries such as steel and chemicals to be bizarrely misguided and incompatible with the society's known capacities; yet the subsequent success story is now well known, which should give us pause in supposing that societies have only one story to tell or pattern to fall into (see Amsden 1989; Kim 1997).

The claim for the potency of a few ideal types of capitalism assumes that national culture and the historical peculiarities of particular countries that may have produced a collection or, as I would like to say, a "menu" of institutions clearly different from that of others do not matter once we understand what "type" of capitalism we are observing. A debate on these issues emerged around two edited volumes on the economies of Japan and Germany: Streeck and Yamamura's 2001 volume *The Origins of Non-Liberal*

Capitalism: Germany and Japan in Comparison and Yamamura and Streeck's 2003 volume, *The End of Diversity?: Prospects for German and Japanese Capitalism*. In these volumes, a variety of essays, with framing commentaries from the editors, consider Japanese and German capitalism to be of the "non-liberal" or "solidaristic" variety, closely related to the distinction that Hall and Soskice make between "coordinated" and "liberal" market economies. In particular, Streeck and Yamamura note that "non-liberal" economies feature a higher level of "embeddedness" than liberal ones, which means that the "transactions by which it is made up either are also supposed to serve other than economic purposes (in other words are constrained by noneconomic objectives such as social cohesion or national defense) or are supported by noneconomic social ties" (Streeck and Yamamura 2001: 2). In the 2003 volume, the authors focus on the enormous pressures on Germany and Japan to conform to the liberal market model, with a consensus that this is unlikely to occur—that Germany and Japan "will continue to be able to defend the values that their institutions were designed to support. These include, in the German case, politically negotiated social cohesion and high social equality and, in the Japanese, the protection of internal solidarity and external independence through politically guided economic development assuring equal status with the West, while avoiding the social disruptions associated with rapid modernization" (39).

In a review symposium on Streeck and Yamamura's volumes, Gary Herrigel praises the authors for pointing to "dimensions of social action and transformation that many constructivists . . . have long emphasized: i.e., that actors confront considerable uncertainty, which in turn makes the meaning of rules ambiguous, thus making interpretation and creativity an inescapable dimension of social action and institutional change" (Herrigel 2005: 560). Rather than treat institutions as "static systems of constraining rules," Herrigel observes, real actors treat them more as "provisional solutions to commonly defined problems" (560). But Herrigel goes on to complain that the very distinction between "liberal" and "solidaristic" economies is problematic because it distracts from a "wide array of other kinds of struggles over institutional alternatives that are neither of a liberal nor of a segmentalist or solidaristic character" (562), such as those in Germany between small and medium-sized firm forms of industry, federal/regional struggles over centralization and sovereignty and regional heterogeneity, Catholic versus social democratic ideas of vocation and local community, and radically localist Syndicalist ideas in unions and the socialist party. These alternatives, he argues, and this is the crux of the matter, do not "fit neatly into either a solidaristic or segmentalist frame and they are plainly not liberal. The fact that they fall out of the portraits that the individual authors provide of the German system is a problem" (563). If one "only looks for the limitations on liberalism or for turning points for solidarism and segmentalism, one invariably overlooks alternative processes of borrowing, recomposition and hybridization that are going on" (564).

Herrigel worries that the authors have a strong tendency to "view the institutional systems in Japan and Germany as highly coherent, unitary systems of interconnected and complementary institutional realms of governance" (564). This creates the impression that "such institutional systems exist 'on the ground' as clear bright line rules that guide behavior" (565). But the actual systems are much more incoherent, non-unitary, and provisional. They are "composed of a patchwork of different institutional solutions to a wide array of political economic problems. The range of solutions work alongside one another not only (or not even) in complementary ways, but also in relations of non-paralyzing juxtaposition. Indeed, it is difficult, on the ground, to identify a coherent, stable system of constraining rules in Japan and Germany (or anywhere else for that matter)" (565). Societies, he concludes, are "rich assemblages of historically accumulated dispositions and rules, not coherent complexes of complementary (and constraining) institutions. Theory should point to possibilities that are emerging from actors' experiences, rather than systematically blend them out" (566).

Reviewing the same volumes, O'Sullivan points out that it is misleading to cite the United States and United Kingdom as type cases of "liberal" capitalism, reminding us of the important role of the U.S. government in the promotion of technology, the history of military support, and the importance of noneconomic objectives, and concludes that "some of the outcomes that these typologies of capitalism link to liberal institutions of capitalism, such as success in radical innovation, are in fact a product of distinctly non-liberal institutions" (554). Pempel similarly criticizes the volumes for their neglect of political explanations of institutional outcomes, mentioning as an example the far greater political power of labor unions in Germany than in Japan (2005).

In response to these critiques, Streeck agrees that institutional types must be conceptualized in a very loose way and that the distinction between "liberal" and "non-liberal" economies may indeed be highly misleading. But he does worry that in Herrigel's conception, institutions don't exist at all, and social action must be "conceptualized as completely voluntaristic." Institutionalized rules may not determine everything, but they are still "protected by social sanctions that may be effectively applied in their defense" (Streeck 2005: 584).

How then can we find a position that balances the need to accommodate problem-solving action (in the pragmatist tradition) and not overestimate the coherence of institutions yet meets the concern that Streeck articulates by making a systematic and coherent theoretical argument? I argue that the way to thread this needle is to analyze for a country or region what the likely alternative frames or "logics" are that actors are *likely* to choose among in organizing economic activity and that seem conceptually available, determine the extent to which they are separate and autonomous from one another or overlap, explain how this particular range or "menu" of options arose, and theorize the process by which actors assemble solutions for the economic problems they face from among these available materials—that is, to understand what in the social and economic environment keys actors into the frames or logics that they do use. The cultural peculiarities of regions or nations might become salient at any of these stages. This strategy is consistent with the theoretical argument that culture, including norms, is more of a "tool kit" than an inflexible recipe for action and also with a variety of empirical observations that nations not infrequently act in ways that seem surprising given typical stereotyped ideas about their possibilities.

Japan, for example, is often considered to have a strongly distinctive culture predisposing to harmony and hegemony of the group over the individual. Japanese institutions such as permanent employment and quality control circles were often imagined to be "natural" outgrowths of these immanent tendencies. But then observers are perplexed to see "permanent employment" evaporate quickly in deep recessions, while other elements, such as organization into the collaborative business group form of *keiretsus,* change in form but have staying power beyond that imagined in neoliberal ideology. (See Lincoln and Gerlach 2004 for details.) The picture is further confused by historical reflection that shows recent "characteristic" Japanese labor institutions to have originated only in the mid-twentieth century, whereas earlier periods, such as the 1920s, had high labor turnover and considerable labor-management conflict (see, e.g., Taira 1970).

6.4 Comparative Historical Case Studies of How Institutional Alternatives Emerge from Turmoil, War, and Revolution

I want to pursue these themes by examining cases in which national economic and political systems undergo dramatic reconstruction under traumatic historical conditions, as such cases reveal a lot about the interplay between broad historical forces, strategic action, and institutions, both those on the ground at any given moment and those in the historical record whose residues, carried through personal and institutional memory, make them available as plausible models for addressing problems at the present moment. I could conduct such a discussion through a broad, synthetic treatment drawing on all available sources, but the topic is so big that this alone would require a book-length treatment. Instead, I proceed through a dialogue with two books that cover these issues from somewhat different angles and offer many useful insights: Arndt Sorge's *The Global and the Local: Understanding the Dialectics of Business Systems* (2005) and Gary Herrigel's *Manufacturing Possibilities: Creative Action and Industrial Recomposition in the United States, Germany, and Japan* (2010).

Sorge's treatment focuses entirely on Germany and traces modern institutions far back into medieval times. But rather than asserting a simple, deterministic relationship between medieval institutions and modern patterns (as, e.g., in Putnam 1993), Sorge argues that economic and political history over long periods of time lead to a multiplicity of institutional patterns that individuals construct, in part in response to the exercise of political and military power of their own and foreign governments and armies, in order to solve ongoing problems. This multiplicity, though rich, confusing, and contradictory, is not random nor unlimited but takes certain discrete forms that may be mixed and matched over long historical periods, even when such mixtures fall well outside the ambit of typologies such as coordinated versus liberal market economies. Herrigel (2010) considers a much more compressed time period, from the end of the Second World War to the present time, in three countries deeply affected by the war—the United States, Germany, and Japan—and weighs the balance of impact on economic institutions of individual and group strategic action, technology and markets, and the backdrop of long institutional history.

Herrigel begins with a focus on the steel industry in the three countries and frames his discussion around the debate as to whether globalization pressures will cause convergence in "practices, rules and governance forms across advanced political economies" (2010: 1). He frames his own pragmatist or "constructivist" view as reflecting dissatisfaction with neoliberal emphasis on atomized individuals' rational calculations, on the one hand, and institutionalism's emphasis on "constraining rules and sanctions in shaping industrial change," on the other (2). He notes that the United States, Germany, and Japan, in the steel industry after World War II, all pursued, as neoliberals would predict, "remarkably similar strategies" but argues that they did so in different ways that "recast or re-create differences between the political economies" (28). He argues against versions of "institutionalism" that make institutions powerful and irresistible influences on behavior, noting that "creative agency leads to the circumvention of institutional constraints" (28). Here I note that my own version of how institutions work, as developed in this and the previous chapter, is softer than the versions that Herrigel critiques, such as the "varieties of capitalism" school, and I argue not that institutions create "bright line" guides to behavior but only that they shape how actors think about their situations and create normative pressures to act in certain ways that are part of the background that they take for granted as they figure out how to solve their problems. This softer version is still quite different from the idea that actors face economic problems in an institutional vacuum, that their own local social context has no impact on what they do, which is influenced only by the costs and benefits inherent in technical and economic parameters of their situation. I hope to make this clearer in the empirical cases that follow.

Critical to understanding how the Japanese and German economies evolved post-1945, including particular industries such as steel, is the simple fact of American occupation of these countries. This occupation meant to impose American conceptions of the limits of government domination of the economy, in line with the general goal of restoring or creating democratic institutions in societies where they had been lacking or had been destroyed. In response, Germany and Japan created the "mutual limitations between state and economy that the Allies desired, but in ways that were inescapably and insidiously informed by their own peculiar understandings of the categories and relations that Americans imposed" (Herrigel 2010: 32–33). In particular, the Americans stressed the importance of private property as part of market competition in liberal-democratic pluralism, but German industrialists, Herrigel observes, conceived private property to entail a certain status in society and a range of mutual obligations to other social groups, the nation, and the state and believed that ownership of property entailed authority (62). Moreover, they considered themselves a corporate group contributing to the greatness of the nation, not the state—thus the state's power should be limited with regard to property just as their own power over workers was limited by obligations. So these industrialists "highlighted elements of their traditional view that resonated with the American one" (63) such as the important role that private organizations play in limiting state power. But they kept the traditional German view of "society being composed of deeply entrenched functional groups" that involved "complex notions of status, entitlement and mutual obligations" (64). So the "Germans and Americans were nodding their heads in agreement when the content of what they agreed upon differed quite radically" (64)—for the Germans, private property in industry was "still understood to be crucial for the maintenance of social order and hence deserving of respect and recognition. The American view denied that distinctions of status and entitlement could be politically drawn among private actors, while the adapted German view assumed this to be a foundational dimension of what was meant by private control of industry. In both forms of understanding, however, private property constituted a countervailing power against the authority of the state—and this was crucial for Allied approval" (64).

Thus, in steel, as in other industries, through the 1950s, contrary to what Americans understood and wanted, both management and labor in Germany "understood themselves to be corporate groups with social and political status in the broader society and with an understanding of mutual obligation and responsibility" (69), and in fact this led to flexibility in steel in ways that American plants did not have, including the institutions of codetermination between labor and plant owners, which was a "tremendous advantage for the steel producers during the great postwar economic boom" and "gave steel producers remarkable flexibility in work and production" (66). So German producers "embraced the vocabulary and practices of Americanism and pluralism, but in doing so creatively recomposed them in ways that either were consistent with their own prior understandings and practices of Americanism and pluralism, or extended the received principles in ways that were not in evidence in the United States nor foreseen by the Allied reformers." (70). So although the industry "adopted or was forced to adopt American principles of market order and production and was profoundly changed by this encounter, this in no way resulted in an erasure of distinctively German features in the production of steel" (70).

I would translate these passages as showing that institutions—in this case traditional German understandings of the roles and responsibilities of such status groups as owners and workers—created the conceptual framework within which Germans adapted their practices to the demands of the American occupation forces, in the process transforming industrial institutions that nevertheless remained recognizably German. This is consistent with the way I would like to portray institutions, as having a serious influence on behavior and framing but without tightly or completely controlling the behavior of individuals who, within the framework of given institutions, can still create new solutions to their problems in a context where external power strongly shapes what is possible.

In the case of Japan, as in Germany, "defeat and reform created spaces in the debate for the rearticulation of abandoned, defeated, or unrealized conceptions of social and industrial order from the past that the wartime regime had suppressed" (70). And so the Japanese "reinterpreted and recomposed the American understanding of oligopolistic competition" by mixing cooperation with competition among steel industry actors. Rather than abandoning the cooperative exchanges among firms and between firms and government bureaucracy that had been typical in the prewar period, they "recast the method of cooperation . . . away from . . . cooperation between a state monopoly and broadly diversified holding companies to cooperation among relatively equal rival steel firms" (75). This return to prewar practices fit with the American ideas of democracy in the economy.

Herrigel's account takes for granted that there is a well-defined institutional framework at any given time. But we should ask where such frameworks come from, and this is typically a story of long-term historical development and is one that Sorge (2005) tries to tell for the case of Germany. Sorge's attitude toward institutions is to take them quite seriously but also to note, as does Herrigel, that they are "regularly decoupled and recombined into novel forms and constellations" (28) so that to

> stylize pervasive institutions as covering an entire society across multiple actors, situations and subsets has very limited value. Institutions differ greatly between domains and situations. [In fact there may be] very distinct and even opposing patterns existing in close proximity [Fundamental values are therefore] only an initial approximation used to provide meaning for the complete range of behavioral repertoires of different types of people in one society. (38)

In other words, people are "naturally born syncretists, meaning that they adapt new beliefs, ideas, practices, techniques etc. to those they already have. They have an amazing capacity to make things compatible that at one stage or at first sight appear radically different" (11). Sorge thus asks how it can that Germany, a country "known for idolizing authoritarian father figures and goose-stepping, exalting all things military, and meting out corporal punishment in the family . . . could subsequently develop a company and work organization featuring few superiors and a great deal of lateral coordination and co-determination?" (23). Suggesting strong limits on the idea of cross-institutional isomorphism or transposition across institutions, as I discussed above, he argues that in practice, societies "do not do things in a uniform way across many domains, institutions, settings and situations. Instead, they have an uncanny capacity to combine situationally differentiated opposites with one another" (25). Institutions are "regularly decoupled and recombined into novel forms and constellations" (28). To "stylize pervasive institutions as covering an entire society across multiple actors, situations and subsets has very limited value. Institutions differ greatly between domains and situations"

(38). In fact, there may be "very distinct and even opposing patterns existing in close proximity" (38). Fundamental values are therefore "only an initial approximation used to provide meaning for the complete range of behavioral repertoires of different types of people in one society" (38). Norms are "inherently ambiguous. As interactionists emphasize, action is always built on the selective interpretation and activation of norms and other knowledge" (53).

This leads me to characterize all the possible institutions that people can draw on at any given moment, some of which conflict with one another in their pure form, even if actors manage to combine them, as a "menu" of possible institutional forms that can be mixed and matched. But there is a danger in theorizing such menus, which is that of falling into historicism, where every case is unique and anything can happen. To avoid this requires us to explain where and by what mechanisms institutional menus originate. Here, Sorge points back to medieval historical patterns as the primordial soup from which emerged the modern collection of institutional solutions to problems that Germans would now recognize. Feudal Germany, for example, had its own classic pattern of rivalry between central rulers and their more or less independent vassals and other powers (84). Feudal rule included "older measures of social coordination, such as peer control through guilds" (88), and so the historical Germanic tendency was to "achieve coordination by lateral but constraining association between 'peers" rather than by *fiat* from above" (89), and rulers presided uneasily over such arrangements. So you had a blend of restricted autocracy and guild control and a distinctive trait of societal order in South Germany was that "hierarchical rule was never far away but it also intimately incorporated the countervailing and older principle of self-government through guilds" (92), which led to a "partitioning of institutional space" in which the sovereign focused on general politics and external relations while economic institutions featured self-government by guilds—a "distinctive fusion of . . . autocratic rule with peer control, of 'democratic' or republican legitimation with the 'divine right to rule'" (94). So this led to a South Germanic "metatradition" that "closely intertwined two opposing forms of control, namely autocratic rule and peer groups" (97). This means that from the beginning of modernity, German socioeconomic history has been marked by recombinations of liberal and corporatist economic institutions—of hierarchical subordination and lateral association, though, in some periods, one or the other has prevailed—liberalization in the first half and the end of the nineteenth century and after the Second World War and corporatism in various periods including the Third Reich.

Sorge argues also that a critical way that a society comes to have "distinct societal institutions and culture" is internationalization—the impact of other societies on some particular one. I note that to the extent this is correct, it cuts against versions of "exceptionalism" that mean to characterize a society's essence without reference to the outside. Certainly if one thinks about the United States, a nation often considered "exceptional," it is clear that its institutions were forged in part from its ultimately violent interaction with its erstwhile parent, Great Britain. And Herrigel notes the important ways in which Japanese and German economic and political institutions were reshaped by interaction with the occupying Allied forces, who brought their own institutional agenda. In the case of Germany, whose "national character" has long been a source of discussion, Sorge notes how easy it is to forget that it is a "nation of immigrants to the same extent that the U.S. or Australia are" (25). The impact of internationalization is especially clear after the Peace of Westphalia in 1648, ending the Thirty Years' War, with the most striking cases being responses to Napoleon's incursions a century and a half later.

In particular, the areas conquered by Napoleon's forces were subjected to the rigors of the Napoleonic Code, which imposed liberalization in the form of establishing legal equality of citizens and thereby undercutting the power of guilds and estates, i.e., of corporatism. Before Napoleon, Prussia was strictly divided by estates, where the Junkers (elsewhere known as "gentry") were the ruling class. Yet *within* corporatist groups, peer control was typical. Napoleon's representatives eliminated feudal privileges, introduced the concept of citizenship, and abolished serfdom. Sorge notes that in fighting against France, the military took on French characteristics, including the "importation of general civil rights and duties and commercial freedom" (113). Subsequently, swings between liberalization and the reassertion of the corporatist order were recurrent, a "seesawing." Economic liberalization in Prussia was radical because it came from above, initially the result of conflict with and the influence of Napoleonic France but in later periods as well, rather than emerging gradually as in English towns (115), and this is why it was not connected to political liberalization. All through the nineteenth century, Prussia seesawed between liberalism and corporatism, and Sorge suggests that such seesaws are typical because "human beings need trial and error" (120).

After the Franco-Prussian War of 1870–1871, Prussia entered a period of imposed liberalism, with corporatist eruptions from below especially from small artisans and firms adversely impacted by free trade, a "grassroots" drive back to corporatism (123). And cartelization, an iconic feature of late nineteenth-century German economy, was a case where businesses were able to take "important instruments from the toolbox of the old guilds, namely price-fixing and the stabilization of supply and profits, and to enact them by formal agreement or contract, rather than on the basis of statutory privileges" (124), and this was a reaction against pervasive liberalism. In the end, this led to a "new synthesis of capitalism, corporatism and mercantilism" (128), a collection of traditions that do not seem compatible with one another, with an ongoing theme of a "lateral peer control that is closely articulated with hierarchical control within a societal space" (140), all closely related to conflict, war, and its aftermath.

And some of these traditions survived the Nazi period, so Sorge notes that Harbison's early 1950s study of steel plants in Indiana and Germany showed that the "social coordination of work was clearly more lateral and rooted in professional autonomy and mutual adjustment between skilled workers" in Germany (154)—that such coordination, despite its suppression during the Third Reich, remained in the German repertoire or "metatradition."

Yet another striking case of dormant institutional elements reasserting themselves after a long hiatus can be found in the recent history of China. Capitalism went into hiding after the 1949 accession of the Communists to power and especially after savage attacks on any remaining signs of capitalism in the Cultural Revolution from 1966 to 1976 (see Esherick et al. 2006). Yet, after the famous opening to market processes implicit in the policies of Deng Xiaoping in the late 1970s, capitalist practices came roaring back and made China what is arguably the most thoroughly capitalist advanced industrial society in the world. Part of why this was possible is that important elements of market capitalism had a very long history in China, especially along the southeast coast, where Freedman's essay shows how the financial sophistication of market participants in this region gave them an enormous advantage both locally and overseas (Freedman 1959, and more generally on the Chinese in Southeast Asia, see Lim and Gosling 1983). And perhaps even more striking as a throwback to long-dormant traditions is the way that current Chinese entrepreneurs like to invoke Confucian principles in the course of doing business as alleged justifications of their practices. This is surprising not only because Confucian ideas were stigmatized under Communism but also because in the Confucian worldview, commerce and moneymaking are a distinctly second-best kind of activity, thought to be much below the realm of scholarship or even thoughtful administration that was in theory infused with Confucian principles. This then serves as another example of how actors, trying to solve the problems that their environment presents, will assemble principles and practices from a variety of sources without much regard for consistency or apparent conflict between those principles and their own place in society.

My argument, then, as partly exemplified by these cases, is that norms, culture, and institutions are important influences on economic action but far less coherent and more variable than often portrayed. Complex combinations of economic practices are assembled by actors in ways that may not be easily anticipated but that are by no means random. Like all structures, economic institutions have to be built out of existing materials and cannot simply be invented *de novo* out of our theorizing about the best possible solution to some stated objective. We need much more theoretical attention to the processes that create over long periods of time in a society the particular set or "menu" of perceived viable alternatives that actors call upon in solving economic problems, how they use their social networks to assemble solutions, and how these solutions themselves then circle back to impact norms, culture, and action in ways that shape future activity.

Finally, one might ask how it can be that despite my frequent warnings about the perils of selection bias in cases chosen to make a certain theoretical point, I rely here on the highly selected cases and accounts of Germany, Japan, and China. A parallel question would be how far my arguments, supported by such cases, go toward a fully satisfactory theory of how the menu of institutional elements that actors perceive to be relevant in their situation really determine institutional evolution. And the answer is clearly that this is only a beginning of such a theoretical argument, a useful beginning to be sure, but one that needs much more work supported by a much wider range of cases.

And to add a further cautionary note, one might conclude from these particular cases, and from the tone of much pragmatist or constructivist theory, that actors typically are so creative in assembling bits and pieces of institutional solutions from hither and yon that they always pretty much solve their problems in a creative and syncretic manner. But it is easy to falsify such a Panglossian assumption. Think, for example, about how African societies reacted to the incursions of colonial powers. It is hard to imagine an account in which those subjects of colonization could be seen as having creatively recombined existing institutional templates so as to construct new institutional solutions to their problems. And if this did not happen, it cannot be because the needed elements were not present in their history, since the continent had considerable political and economic development in the previous millennium and was the scene of numerous storied and powerful empires—see the brief account in https://en.wikipedia.org/wiki/African empires. Instead, the obvious answer to the question of why indigenous groups did not engage in creative institutional solutions to the problems posed by colonialists is that occupying nations quashed any such attempts with overwhelming military power.

And as to why they did so, consider the difference in the goals of Napoleon Bonaparte in his conquered territories from those of the colonial occupiers in Africa. Military conquest was, of course, always Napoleon's first goal. But in governing conquered territories he acted not merely as an occupier but also as a child of the Enlightenment, abolishing serfdom and liberalizing laws and practices, as embodied in the Napoleonic Code, that stressed the rights of citizens to pursue their enterprises and activities without interference from entrenched interests of the kind that corporatism protected, abolishing guilds and other powers intermediary between the citizen and the state. Colonial rulers had quite a different attitude toward their colonies, regarding them principally as a source of cheap labor and abundant raw materials while also viewing Africans as a benighted and inferior race, incapable of attaining European standards of development. This combination produced, with some variations, colonial rule that did not countenance autonomous development of economic or political institutions from below.

And with few exceptions, even though all the former African colonies are now independent states and thus out from under the grip of colonial rulers, these new states have rarely succeeded in putting together economic institutions that are productive internally or competitive in the modern industrialized world. One reason we might cite is that many such new nations are the result of rather arbitrary amalgamation of tribes that do not naturally have much to do with one another and, in addition, are riven by religious conflict among Christians, Muslims, and more locally native cosmologies. But this in itself does not seem compelling, if we note that the situation in what we now call Germany was not much different in 1648 after the Treaty of Westphalia. A historical atlas of this area at that moment shows dozens of tiny principalities and other kinds of political units, none of them especially prepossessing in its ability to assemble economic resources and riven among themselves by continuing religious conflict that the Thirty Years' War channeled but did not remove. Ironically, one of the main forces that pulled many of these units together was the Napoleonic Wars and the continuing rivalries with France and Great Britain, which eventually spilled over into two World Wars. For many reasons, it seems unlikely that similar developments will occur in Africa, though such a discussion is beyond both my space and my competence.

The example of Napoleon Bonaparte also suggests some limits to the pragmatist/constructivist image of many individuals creatively assembling bits and pieces of solutions to the problems they see from available menus of institutional elements. While it is clear that actors do so under many circumstances, it is also clear that at some critical times, to paraphrase Orwell (1945: Ch. 10), some actors are more equal than others, so that Napoleon and his goals had a lasting and complex impact on legal, political, and economic institutions in areas that his representatives governed. While their decrees and interventions blended with and made use of institutional elements already present, they did so in a way that the elements alone could not have fully predicted or determined. The case of General Park Chung Hee in South Korea, from 1961 to his 1979 assassination, shows clearly again that while the set of available institutional raw materials matters, it does not by itself predict or preclude particular outcomes, as General Park used traditional Korean patterns to achieve economic outcomes that experts had thought impossible.

6.5 The Dynamics of Trust, Norms, and Power in Economic Action, Networks, and Institutions

At this point in a book it is conventional to have a final chapter, a conclusion that summarizes all the main arguments and attempts to show how they all hang together in some coherent fashion. I resist doing so, in part because I do not want to pretend to coherence that does not exist and in part because I can make the excuse to the reader that I have promised a sequel volume of topics that will present applications of special cases, such as corruption, organizational forms, and corporate governance, where I will try to show how the framework developed here illuminates in ways that more standard theories do not. On the matter of coherence, I have argued that the themes of trust, power, norms, and institutions are implicated in virtually every economic activity and that few topics can be fully and satisfactorily analyzed in the absence of these considerations.

But as to exactly how these elements of economic and indeed all social life interact with one another in a given case, I have presented no completely general guidance to draw on. In the sequel volume, I hope in the context of particular topic chapters to explore what such larger generalizations would look like for the constellation of related topics. I am enough of a positivist to think that, ultimately, the goal of good theory is precisely to develop general guidance in the form of regularities in the way that the main influences on economic life interact with one another and lead to outcomes. So moving farther in that direction will be one goal of the sequel. But to do so in full generality is a very big goal that takes us well beyond where modern economic and sociological theory have traveled, despite frequent claims to the contrary. And so what I hope to have done here is to present informed researchers with an assemblage of crucial concepts that must be combined in ways that particular cases dictate with the larger goal of creating generalizations that will inform future theory. The detailed historical, cultural, and at times ethnographic work that this entails, in addition to the more typical statistical analysis of data, which remains critically important, is harder work than to spin abstract models from abstract principles and then assert that the relevant data from a case can be fitted to the model with suitable mathematical skill. I do not underestimate the value of imaginative and well-crafted models in helping to illuminate economic life, as this seems quite clear and amply demonstrated. But in the end, our understanding of the economy needs to combine both of these styles of research and learn how they can inform one another. If this book and its sequel encourage this kind of creative and synthetic activity, that is all I could hope for.

Notes

1 Introduction: Problems of Explanation in Economic Sociology

1. Historical accounts of how relationships between sociology and economics evolved over the nineteenth and twentieth centuries can be found in the introduction to Granovetter and Swedberg 2011 and also in Granovetter 1990.

2. Modern economics follows Robbins in abstracting away from this, frequently arguing that actors with economic motives act "as if" making a rational calculation, even when no such subjective state can be attributed to them, as when difficult calculations are obviously beyond their ability, or can be empirically shown to play no part in their conscious decision-making. I will have several occasions to address these issues and will be especially interested in what justifications may be given for this "as if" stance. For now, I simply treat "individual economic action" as action oriented to the provision of "needs" as defined by individual actors, in situations of scarcity, without taking any position on the actor's subjective understanding of the economic situation or his degree of calculation. This mixture of Weber's and Robbins's stances will serve for heuristic purposes. Below I say more on the important issue of whether one implication of this stance, that action should be studied in a means-end framework, may not have important limitations, as pragmatists such as Dewey (1939) and their modern followers would argue.

3. A brief account of such arguments and their tendency toward dualism or mysticism is offered in Kontopoulos 1993: 23–24.

4. The idea that economic life can be studied and explained entirely by attention to social networks should be clearly set aside, and in fact it is doubtful that anyone has ever argued for such an extreme position. But the frequent focus on social networks by proponents of the "new economic sociology" has sometimes led critics to this conclusion. See the exchange in Krippner et al. 2004.

5. The particular setting, the parochial interests that actually led to the practice of limited liability, and the situations in which it is counterproductive are detailed in Marchetti and Ventoruzzo 2001: 2804–2805.

6. This rhetoric morphs easily into the joke that an economist is someone who, upon seeing a twenty-dollar bill lying in the street, ignores it because if it were *really* a twenty-dollar bill, someone would already have picked it up. This is a special case of the definition of an economist as someone who knows that something is true in practice but remains skeptical because he cannot see how it could be true in theory.

7. It is interesting that the intellectual history of recent institutional economics replays of that in social anthropology from about 1890 to 1940. Structural functional anthropologists of the 1930s and 1940s attacked earlier anthropological accounts grounded in (sometimes rather speculative) history and defended static functional analysis on the grounds that one needed to explain any social pattern as part of the coherent social whole to develop a full and sophisticated understanding of how the social system fit together. Thus, Malinowski attacked the notion that some social patterns were vestigial "survivals" of earlier periods. "Take any example of 'survival,'" he challenged. "You will find first and foremost that the survival nature of the alleged cultural 'hangover' is due primarily to an incomplete analysis of the facts. . . . The real harm done by this concept was to retard effective fieldwork. Instead of searching for the present-day function of any cultural fact, the observer was merely satisfied in reaching a rigid, self-contained entity" (1944: 30–31).

8. The rather rigorous competitive conditions that make evolutionist arguments plausible are carefully presented in Nelson and Winter 1982. See also the cautionary tales of "permanently failing organizations" in Meyer and Zucker 1989.

9. Latin for "that which is to be explained"; a typical usage in the philosophy of science literature.

10. I treat the example of "trust" in detail in Chapter 3.

11. I speculate that since Parsons had been thoroughly trained as an economist and was thus conversant with the classical and neoclassical literature but was less well trained in the utilitarian tradition, he took the philosophical stance he found in economics to have necessarily resulted from its roots in the utilitarian tradition and thus projected that stance backward.

12. Thus, Ricardo's *Principles* is relentlessly stylized, like much twentieth-century neoclassical writing. The single place where he makes room for the influence of social relations is in his treatment of international trade. Faced with the necessity of explaining how countries might differ in efficiency of production of the same good—impossible if capital and labor were perfectly mobile, as he otherwise assumes—he comments: "Experience shews that the fancied or real insecurity of capital, when not under the immediate control of its owner, together with the natural disinclination which every man has to quit the country of his birth and connexions, and intrust himself with all his habits fixed, to a strange government and new laws, check the emigration of capital. These feelings, which I should be sorry to see weakened, induce most men of property to be satisfied with a low rate of profits in their own country, rather than seek a more advantageous employment for their

wealth in foreign nations" (1821: 143). It seems clear that Ricardo allowed this exception into his theoretical system because he approved of its consequences; a perfectly competitive market in international trade implies the absence of patriotism or attachments to home, family, and country, the desire for which falls well outside the orbit of classical liberalism.

13. This implies that the solution offered by Parsons (1937) to the failings he attributed to utilitarian thought is not nearly as radical a break from the position he attacked as he supposed it to be.

14. The standard reference, encyclopedic in detail, is Wasserman and Faust (1994). An excellent guide for the novice is Scott 2010 and, with more detail, Scott 2013. A useful online account of social network principles is Hanneman and Riddle 2005. The reader who wants general guidance on network ideas along with software that does network analysis and visualization should look at de Nooy, Mrvar, and Batagelj 2011. Those interested in economic models using social network analysis will find useful Jackson 2010 and Easley and Kleinberg 2010. A comprehensive handbook with articles on many social network subjects is Scott and Carrington 2011.

15. "Density" of a social network, the simplest and perhaps most important quantitative measure available, is the proportion of the possible $n(n-1)/2$ ties that link the n nodes in a network, where the nodes may be individuals or collective entities such as organizations and the ties may represent any relationship the analyst defines, such as friendship, antagonism, domination, or the sharing of corporate directors. For details on the technical aspects of social networks, see Wasserman and Faust 1994.

16. That economists came to see this separation was only part of a more general process by which intellectuals, government officials, and parts of the general public came to envision economic activity as involving only economic motivation. This is the process that Dumont (1977) calls the "triumph of economic ideology" and Reddy (1984) the "rise of market culture." Reddy's account of French textile markets in the eighteenth and nineteenth centuries is particularly illuminating in showing how public officials revised data collection procedures to conform to their assumption that the textile industry followed market principles, despite ample evidence that workers and owners were still strongly influenced by traditional noneconomic motives. These motives were greatly obscured by the new forms of economic data.

17. In personal correspondence with Richard Swedberg, Samuelson acknowledges that this comment reflected Pareto's influence.

2 The Impact of Mental Constructs on Economic Action:
Norms, Values, and Moral Economy

1. For consideration and rejection of the argument that the emotions are merely further costs to be calculated in deciding whether to conform to a norm and that, in general, norms are "really optimizing mechanisms in disguise," see Elster 1989a: 130ff.

2. This appearance is partially misleading since the definition of "incest" varies greatly across societies, but there does seem to be a universal basic core, which is the prohibition of sexual relations among siblings or between children and parents.

3. Results of these experiments are presented and analyzed in great detail in the somewhat grandiosely titled *Foundations of Human Sociality* (Henrich et al. 2004) and summarized more compactly in Henrich et al. 2005.

4. One especially interesting finding in the UG literature is that "about one-third of autistic children and adults offer nothing in the UG . . . ; presumably their inability to imagine the reactions of responders leads them to behave, ironically, in accordance with the canonical model" (Henrich et al. 2005: 799). The authors do not go on to conclude that only autistic individuals follow the rational actor model, but some critics of neoclassical economics hold this view, as one heterodox organization, the "post-autistic economics" network, published an online journal called the "Post-Autistic Economics Review"; see www.paecon.net. The journal was subsequently and less derisively titled "Real-World Economics Review," though the sponsoring organization retains it original name.

5. This definition obviously suffers from being vague, but more seriously, it is defined circularly in terms of the *consequences* of close-knittedness rather than in terms of what close-knittedness actually means in terms of network structure, as the concept requires. Moreover, the equality of power distribution is extraneous to structure and merely grafted onto it here.

6. But see the rebuttal in McAdams 1997: 357n85. We might also question the costless conferral of esteem by referring to the mid-twentieth-century sociological literature on the limits to the time and affect that one has available to confer on others—the so-called "lump" or "fund" of sociability. See, e.g., Nelson 1966.

3 Trust in the Economy

1. A "decision dilemma" is an interactive situation in which individuals, acting either simultaneously or sequentially, must choose among actions that are in varying degrees selfish or cooperative. The dilemmas are constructed in such a way that each individual deciding rationally (i.e., selfishly) would produce an outcome worse for all than if each had been less rational and instead chosen the cooperative action, which, however, would only pay off if one could "trust" that others would also cooperate.

2. A Pareto-optimal outcome is one in which no one can be made better off without someone else becoming worse off.

3. I would add that when trust concerns people who know one another, there is another aspect to it that is rarely noted explicitly but that I think is important: to trust another is to expect that she will not deceive or betray you. I suggest that deception and betrayal evoke emotional resentment of a kind that is of exceptional importance when it occurs and leads people to responses that may be hard to give

instrumental accounts of, as actions of revenge typically lack clear calculations of costs and benefits and result instead from emotions (cf. Elster 1999).

4. See http://en.wikipedia.org/wiki/You_Always_Hurt_the_One_You_Love

5. A literature in social psychology on "commitment" in exchange relations followed the lead of Lawler and Yoon (1996). Sahlins (1972: Ch. 5) discusses a range of commitment in "primitive" exchange, from "freely bestowed gift to chicanery" (196), typically based on kinship distance.

6. So the diamond trade has also been the scene of numerous well-publicized "insider" thefts and of the notorious 1982 "CBS murders" in New York In this case, the owner of a diamond company was defrauding a factoring concern by submitting invoices from fictitious sales. The scheme required cooperation from his accounting personnel, one of whom was approached by investigators and turned state's evidence. The owner then contracted for the murder of the disloyal employee and her assistant; three CBS technicians who came to their aid in the parking garage where the murders took place were also gunned down (Shenon 1984).

7. The importance of structural embeddedness for trust corresponds to what Hardin (2002: 14, 22) refers to as "thick" group or societal relations, but the mechanisms by which this "thickness" works need to be unpacked.

8. But controversy continues within economics as to the costs and benefits of family-run firms and often depends on what outcome measure is selected for analysis and what institutional constraints are considered. See, e.g., Bennedsen et al. 2007 and, for the special circumstance of China, Bennedsen et al, 2015.

9. A systematic attempt at bringing these concepts together is the work of Alejandro Portes and his collaborators on the concept of "enforceable trust" (e.g., Portes and Sensenbrenner 1993).

4 Power in the Economy

1. For an exhaustive discussion of the translation issues, see Roth's note 31 in Weber ([1921] 1968): 61–62.

2. In organization theory, a similar position is taken by Chester Barnard (1938), who argues that the authority of executives entirely depends on the cooperative attitude of those to whom orders are given. This argument is dismissed by Perrow, a theorist who stresses the importance of power in organizations and who observes that superior authority is "hardly a fiction if one can be fired for disobeying orders or shot for not moving ahead [on a battlefield] on orders" (1986: 71).

3. I suspect that one reason Weber found the subject of power based on a "constellation of interests" relatively uninteresting was that he imagined the need for resources that made such constellations important to be more or less objectively given.

4. To be more consistent, Weber ought probably in this discussion have talked about two diametrically contrasting types of power rather than of domination. His argument about the force of constellation of interests explicitly does not require that

anyone actually issue "commands," as in his definition of "domination" cited above, as a special case of power. In fact, during this discussion, Weber refers to the term "domination" as being used in the "quite general sense of power, i.e., of the possibility of imposing one's own will upon the behavior of other persons" (1968 [1921]: 942). I note that the later discussion was actually written first, and the definitional chapters, written later in order to collect and systematize the concepts, were put at the beginning of *Economy and Society* by the editors who assembled the bits and pieces after Weber died before being able to bring the manuscript to completion or sort out possible inconsistencies.

5. This is roughly comparable to Steven Lukes's third "face of power" (1974).

6. Bonacich (1987) summarizes and formalizes this argument by introducing a parameter β in the measure of power, for which a positive value indicates that being connected to powerful others makes you more powerful and a negative value means it makes you less powerful. The latter corresponds to "negatively-connected networks."

7. The importance of the distinction between negotiated and reciprocal exchange and its relation to early classic formulations of exchange theory was first clearly noted by Molm (see her summary in Molm 2003), whose research program emphasizes the distinction between the two kinds of exchange.

8. This German city, whose pseudonym was "Altneustadt," had factions defined by Christian Democratic (CDU) and Social Democratic (SPD) affiliations.

9. See, for example, Nevins's illuminating 1953 biography of John D. Rockefeller. It may be that the Medicis could be "sphinxlike" because the separated networks that they sat astride were naturally antagonistic to one another in the highly socially differentiated setting of medieval Florence, with its myriad ranked social distinctions. In the more homogeneous social setting of nineteenth-century America, sphinxlike behavior may have been a luxury that the "robber barons" could hardly afford if they were to keep others from ganging up on them.

10. This is why the 1914 Clayton Act forbade interlocks between firms in direct competition with one another.

11. For an ambitious attempt to chronicle the various sources of social power in long-term historical perspective, see Mann 1986, 1993. For the definitive treatment of slavery, see Patterson 1982.

5 The Economy and Social Institutions

1. My use of the term "middle range" in the heading title is a perhaps not-so-sly nod to the usage by Robert K. Merton (1957) of "theories of the middle range," which was his way of nudging sociology away from grand theory and minor close-range observation to a more fruitful and workable theoretical location.

2. The social movements literature also then appropriated the conception of organizational "fields," with special emphasis on "strategic action fields," as in Fligstein and McAdam 2012.

3. For *bricolage,* www.oed.com—the Oxford English Dictionary website—lists: "Construction or (esp. literary or artistic) creation from a diverse range of materials or sources. Hence: an object or concept so created; a miscellaneous collection."

4. But Herrigel 1996 is an exception.

5. But see Becht and deLong (2007) for a more complex argument about the absence of blockholding in the United States, which they believe began only in the twentieth century. Though they agree with Roe that American political culture mattered, they also introduce a series of other causal factors that cast doubt on the inevitability of this outcome.

6. But see Lepore's skeptical view of the concept of "disruptive" innovations (2014).

7. For details of these tests, see http://www.euroncap.com/en.

6 The Interplay between Individual Action and Social Institutions

1. I note that these differences were pointed out long ago in a landmark but now often neglected article on Japan and China by Marion Levy (1954).

2. But there have been many historical periods in which the poor sent their children to live as servants in the homes of the better off and were compensated for doing so in a transaction that has some resemblance to a sale. As Zelizer points out in great detail (2005), transactions in which intimacy is implicated often involve financial transfers as well, and the existence of these does not seem to make intimacy felt any the less strongly.

3. Cf., for example, the Trobriand Islanders studied by Malinowksi, who focused much of their energy on the ceremonial exchange of armshells and necklaces in the "kula" ring and whose withering disdain for someone who did not make these exchanges with the proper etiquette and ceremonial niceties was expressed by saying that they "do it as if it were *gimwali* [barter] ([1922] 2014: 103)."

4. Such transfers are not, however, without risk. Insull's use of balloon depreciation, for example, was used as part of the rationale for accusing him of massive fraud in a set of trials that ran through the 1930s. See the detailed (but hagiographic) account in McDonald's 1962 biography of Insull.

References

Abbott, Andrew. 1983. "Professional Ethics." *American Journal of Sociology* 88: 855–885.

Abend, Gabriel. 2014. *The Moral Background: An Inquiry into the History of Business Ethics*. Princeton: Princeton University Press.

Aberle, D. F., A. K. Cohen, A. K. Davis, M. J. Levy Jr., and F. X. Sutton. 1950. "The Functional Prerequisites of a Society." *Ethics* 60(2): 100–111.

Aghion Philippe, Yann Algan, Pierre Cahuc, and Andrei Shleifer. 2010. "Regulation and Distrust." *Quarterly Journal of Economics* 125: 1015–1049.

Amsden, Alice. 1989. *Asia's Next Giant: South Korea and Late Industrialization*. Oxford: Oxford University Press.

Anderson, Ronald C., and David M. Reeb. 2003. "Founding-Family Ownership and Firm Performance: Evidence from the S&P 500." *The Journal of Finance* 58: 1301–1328.

Ardener, Shirley. 1964. "The Comparative Study of Rotating Credit Associations." *Journal of the Royal Anthropological Institute* 94: 202–229.

Arrow, Kenneth. 1974. *The Limits of Organization*. New York: W.W. Norton.

Arthur, W. Brian. 1989. "Competing Technologies and Lock-In by Historical Events." *Economic Journal* 99: 116–131.

Atran, Scott, and Robert Axelrod. 2008. "Reframing Sacred Values." *Negotiation Journal* 24(3 July): 221–246.

Avent-Holt, Dustin. 2012. "The Political Dynamics of Market Organization: Cultural Framing, Neoliberalism, and the Case of Airline Deregulation." *Sociological Theory* 30: 283–302.

Bachrach, Peter, and Morton Baratz. 1962. "The Two Faces of Power." *American Political Science Review* 56: 947–952.

Baldwin, Carliss, and Kim Clark. 2000. *Design Rules, Volume 1, The Power of Modularity*. Cambridge, MA: MIT Press.

Banfield, Edward. 1958. *The Moral Basis of a Backward Society.* New York: The Free Press.

Barabasi, Albert-Laszlo. 2002. *Linked: How Everything Is Connected to Everything Else.* New York: Perseus.

Barnard, Chester. 1938. *The Functions of the Executive.* Cambridge, MA: Harvard University Press.

Baron, James, Frank Dobbin, and P. Deveraux Jennings. 1986. "War and Peace: The Evolution of Modern Personnel Administration in U.S. Industry." *American Journal of Sociology* 92: 350–383.

Barth, Fredrik. 1967. "Economic Spheres in Darfur." In *Themes in Economic Anthropology,* edited by Raymond Firth. London: Tavistock.

Baum, Joel, Andrew Shipilov, and Tim Rowley. 2003. "Where Do Small Worlds Come From?" *Industrial and Corporate Change* 12: 697–725.

Bebchuk, Lucian, and Mark Roe. 2004. "A Theory of Path Dependence in Corporate Ownership and Governance." pp. 69–113 in *Convergence and Persistence in Corporate Governance,* edited by Jeffrey Gordon and Mark Roe. New York: Cambridge University Press.

Becht, Marco, and J. Bradford deLong. 2007. "Why Has There Been So Little Block-holding in America?" pp. 613–666 in *A History of Corporate Governance around the World: Family Business Groups to Professional Managers,* edited by Randall Morck. Chicago: University of Chicago Press.

Becker, Gary. 1976. *The Economic Approach to Human Behavior.* Cambridge, MA: Harvard University Press.

Ben-Porath, Yoram. 1980. "The F-Connection: Families, Friends, and Firms in the Organization of Exchange." *Population and Development Review* 6: 1–30.

Bendix, Reinhard. 1956. *Work and Authority in Industry.* New York: Wiley.

Bendor, Jonathan, and Piotr Swistak. 2001. "The Evolution of Norms." *American Journal of Sociology* 106: 1493–1545.

Benedict, Ruth. 1946. *The Chrysanthemum and the Sword: Patterns of Japanese Culture.* Boston: Houghton-Mifflin.

Bennedsen, Morten, Casper Nielsen, Francisco Perez-Gonzalez, and Daniel Wolfenzon. 2007. "Inside the Family Firm: The Role of Families in Succession Decisions and Performance." *Quarterly Journal of Economics* 122: 647–691.

Bennedsen, Morten, Joseph P. H. Fan, Ming Jian, and Yin-Hua Yeh. 2015. "The Family Business Map: Framework, Selective Survey, and Evidence from Chinese Family Firm Succession." *Journal of Corporate Finance* 33: 212–226.

Berger, Peter and Thomas Luckmann. 1966. *The Social Construction of Reality: A Treatise in the Sociology of Knowledge.* Garden City, NY: Doubleday.

Berle, A. A., and G. Means. 1932. *The Modern Corporation and Private Property.* New York: Macmillan.

Bewley, Truman. 1999. *Why Wages Don't Fall during a Recession.* Cambridge, MA: Harvard University Press.

Biernacki, Richard. 1997. *The Fabrication of Labor: Germany and Britain 1640–1914.* Berkeley, CA: University of California Press.

Biggart, Nicole, and Mauro Guillen. 1999. "Developing Difference: Social Organization and the Rise of the Auto Industries of South Korea, Taiwan, Spain, and Argentina." *American Sociological Review* 64: 722–747.

Blau, Peter. 1964. *Exchange and Power in Social Life.* New York: Wiley.

Bloch, Marc. [1939] 1961. *Feudal Society.* Chicago: University of Chicago Press.

Blumer, Herbert. 1969. *Symbolic Interactionism: Perspective and Method.* Berkeley, CA: University of California Press.

Bohannan, Paul, and George Dalton, editors. 1962. *Markets in Africa.* Evanston, IL: Northwestern University Press.

Boltanski, Luc, and Laurent Thévenot. 1999. "The Sociology of Critical Capacity." *European Journal of Social Theory* 2: 359–377.

———. 2006. *On Justification: Economies of Worth,* translated by C. Porter. Princeton, NJ: Princeton University Press.

Bonacich, Philip. 1987. "Power and Centrality: A Family of Measures." *American Journal of Sociology* 92(5): 1170–1182.

Boorman, Scott A. 1975. "A Combinatorial Optimization Model for Transmission of Job Information through Social Networks." *Bell Journal of Economics* 6: 216–249.

Burawoy, Michael. 1979. *Manufacturing Consent: Changes in the Labor Process under Monopoly Capitalism.* Chicago: University of Chicago Press.

Burt, Ronald S. 1992. *Structural Holes: The Social Structure of Competition.* Cambridge, MA: Harvard University Press.

———. 2002. "Bridge Decay." *Social Networks* 24: 333–363.

———. 2005. *Brokerage and Closure: An Introduction to Social Capital.* New York: Oxford University Press.

Business History Review. 2010. "'Varieties of Capitalism' Roundtable." 84: 637–674.

Camic, Charles. 1979. "The Utilitarians Revisited." *American Journal of Sociology* 85: 515–550.

Carruthers, Bruce. 1996. *City of Capital: Politics and Markets in the English Financial Revolution.* Princeton, NJ: Princeton University Press.

———. 2013. "From Uncertainty Toward Risk: The Case of Credit Ratings." *Socio-Economic Review* 11(3): 525–551.

Castilla, Emilio, Hokyu Hwang, Mark Granovetter, and Ellen Granovetter. 2000. "Social Networks in Silicon Valley." pp. 218–247 in *The Silicon Valley Edge,* edited by C.-M. Lee, W. Miller, M. Hancock, and H. Rowen. Stanford, CA: Stanford University Press.

Chandler, Alfred. 1962. *Strategy and Structure.* Cambridge, MA: MIT Press.

———. 1977. *The Visible Hand: The Managerial Revolution in American Business.* Cambridge, MA: Harvard University Press.

Chang, Dukjin. 1999. "Privately Owned Social Structures: Institutionalization-Network Contingency in the Korean Chaebol." Ph.D. dissertation, Department of Sociology, University of Chicago.

———. 2000. "Financial Crisis and Network Response: Changes in the Ownership Structure of the Korean Chaebol since 1997." Working Paper: Ewha Women's University, Seoul, Korea.

Chang, Sea-jin. 2003. *Financial Crisis and Transformation of Korean Business Groups: The Rise and Fall of Chaebols.* New York: Cambridge University Press.

Chase, Ivan. 1974. "Models of Hierarchy Formation in Animal Societies." *Behavioral Science* 19(6): 374–382.

———. 1980. "Social Process and Hierarchy Formation in Small Groups: A Comparative Perspective." *American Sociological Review* 40(4: August): 905–924.

Christensen, Clayton. 1997. *The Innovator's Dilemma: The Revolutionary Book That Will Change the Way You Do Business.* Cambridge, MA: Harvard Business School Press.

Christensen, Johan. 2013. "Bureaucracies, Tax Reform, and Neoliberal Ideas in New Zealand and Ireland." *Governance* 26(4): 563–584.

———. 2017. *The Power of Economists within the State.* Stanford, CA: Stanford University Press.

Chu, Johan, and Gerald Davis. 2015. "Who Killed the Inner Circle: The Decline of the American Corporate Interlock Network." SSRN paper uploaded October 23, 2015: http://papers.ssrn.com/sol3/papers.cfm?abstract_id=2061113. Forthcoming, *American Journal of Sociology.*

Chung, Chi-Nien. 2000. "Markets, Culture and Institutions: The Formation and Transformation of Business Groups in Taiwan, 1960s–1990s." Doctoral dissertation, Department of Sociology, Stanford University, Stanford, CA.

Coase, Ronald. 1960. "The Problem of Social Cost." *Journal of Law and Economics* 3: 1–44.

Cole, Robert. 1979. *Work, Mobility and Participation: A Comparative Study of American and Japanese Industry.* Berkeley, CA: University of California Press.

Coleman, James. 1990. *The Foundations of Social Theory.* Cambridge, MA: Harvard University Press.

Colfer, Lyra, and Carliss Baldwin. 2016. "The Mirroring Hypothesis: Theory, Evidence, and Exceptions." Working paper 16-124, Harvard Business School.

Collins, Randall. 1980. *The Credential Society: A Historical Sociology of Education and Stratification.* New York: Academic Press.

Cook, Karen, and Richard Emerson. 1978. "Power, Equity, and Commitment in Exchange Networks." *American Sociological Review* 43: 721–739.

Cook, Karen, Richard Emerson, and Mary Gillmore. 1983. "The Distribution of Power in Exchange Networks: Theory and Experimental Results." *American Journal of Sociology* 89(2): 275–305.

Cook, Karen, and Russell Hardin. 2001. "Norms of Cooperativeness and Networks of Trust." pp. 327–347 in *Social Norms,* edited by M. Hechter and K.-D. Opp. New York: Russell Sage Foundation.

Cook, Karen, and Eric R. W. Rice. 2001. "Exchange and Power: Issues of Structure and Agency." pp. 699–719 in *Handbook of Sociological Theory*, edited by Jonathan Turner. New York: Kluwer Academic/Plenum Publishers.

———. 2003. "Social Exchange Theory." Chapter 3 in *Handbook of Social Psychology,* edited by J. Delamater. New York: Kluwer/Plenum.

Cook, Karen S., Russell Hardin, and Margaret Levi. 2005. New York: The Russell Sage Foundation.

Cook, Karen S., Margaret Levi, and Russell Hardin, editors. 2009. *Whom Can We Trust?: How Groups, Networks, and Institutions Make Trust Possible.* New York: The Russell Sage Foundation.

Cooter, Robert. 2000. "Economic Analysis of Internalized Norms." "Economic Analysis of Internalized Norms." *Virginia Law Review* 86: 1577–1601.

Crenson, Matthew. 1971. *The Un-Politics of Air Pollution: A Study of Non-Decision-making in the Cities.* Baltimore: The Johns Hopkins Press.

Cushman, Fiery, Liane Young, and Joshua Greene. 2010. "Multi-System Moral Psychology." pp. 47–71 in *The Moral Psychology Handbook,* edited by John Doris. Oxford: Oxford University Press.

David, Paul. 1986. "Understanding the Necessity of QWERTY: The Necessity of History." pp. 30–49 in *Economic History and the Modern Economist,* edited by W. N. Parker. London: Blackwell.

Davis, Gerald. 2009a. "The Rise and Fall of Finance and the End of the Society of Organizations." *Academy of Management Perspectives* August: 27–44.

———. 2009b. *Managed by the Markets: How Finance Re-shaped America.* New York: Oxford University Press.

Davis, Gerald, Mina Yoo, and Wayne Baker. 2003. "The Small World of the American Corporate Elite, 1982–2001." *Strategic Organization* 3: 301–326.

Deane, Phyllis. 1978. *The Evolution of Economic Ideas.* Cambridge, UK: Cambridge University Press.

de Nooy, Wouter, Andrej Mrvar, and Vladimir Batagelj. 2011. *Exploratory Social Network Analysis with Pajek.* 2nd ed. New York: Cambridge University Press.

Dewey, John. 1939. *Theory of Valuation.* Chicago: University of Chicago Press.

DiMaggio, Paul. 1997. "Culture and Cognition." *Annual Review of Sociology* 23: 263–287.

DiMaggio, Paul, and Walter Powell. 1983. "The Iron Cage Revisited: Institutional Isomorphism and Collective Rationality in Organizational Fields." *American Sociological Review* 48: 147–160.

Dobbin, Frank. 1994. *Forging Industrial Policy: The United States, Britain and France in the Railway Age.* New York: Cambridge University Press.

Dodds, Peter S., R. Muhamad, and D. S. Watts. 2003. "An Experimental Study of Search in Global Social Networks." *Science* 301(5634): 827–829.

Domhoff. G. William. 2013. *Who Rules America? The Triumph of the Corporate Rich.* 7th ed. New York: McGraw Hill.

Dumont, Louis. 1977. *From Mandeville to Marx: The Genesis and Triumph of Economic Ideology.* Chicago: University of Chicago Press.

Durkheim, Emile. [1893] 1984. *The Division of Labor in Society,* translated by W. D. Halls. New York: The Free Press.

Easley, David, and Jon Kleinberg. 2010. *Networks, Crowds, and Markets: Reasoning about a Highly Connected World.* New York: Cambridge University Press.

Eggertsson, Thrain. 2001. "Norms in Economics, with Special Reference to Economic Development." pp. 76–104 in *Norms*, edited by M. Hechter and K.-D. Opp. New York: Russell Sage Foundation.

Eisenstadt, Shmuel. 1963. *The Political Systems of Empires: The Rise and Fall of the Historical Bureaucratic Societies*. New York: The Free Press.

Eisenstadt, Shmuel N., and Luis Roniger. 1984. *Patrons, Clients, and Friends: Interpersonal Relations and the Structure of Trust in Society*. New York: Cambridge University Press.

Ellickson, Robert. 1991. *Order without Law: How Neighbors Settle Disputes*. Cambridge, MA: Harvard University Press.

———. 1998. "Law and Economics Discovers Social Norms." *Journal of Legal Studies* 27: 537–552.

———. 2001. "The Evolution of Social Norms: A Perspective from the Legal Academy." pp. 35–75 in *Social Norms*, edited by M. Hechter and K.-D. Opp. New York: Russell Sage Foundation.

Elster, Jon. 1983. *Explaining Technical Change*. New York: Cambridge University Press.

———. 1989a. *The Cement of Society: A Study of Social Order*. New York: Cambridge University Press.

———. 1989b. "Social Norms and Economic Theory." *Journal of Economic Perspectives* 3: 99–117.

———. 1990. "Norms of Revenge." *Ethics* 100: 862–885.

———. 1999. *Alchemies of the Mind: Rationality and the Emotions*. Cambridge, UK: Cambridge University Press.

———. 2000. "Rational Choice History: A Case of Excessive Ambition." *American Political Science Review* 94(3: September): 685–695.

Emerson, Richard. 1962. "Power-Dependence Relations." *American Sociological Review* 27: 31–41.

Esherick, Joseph, Paul Pickowicz, and Andrew Walder, editors. 2006. *The Chinese Cultural Revolution as History*. Stanford, CA: Stanford University Press.

Espeland, Wendy, and Mitchell Stevens. 1998. "Commensuration as a Social Process." *Annual Review of Sociology* 24: 313–343.

Evans, Peter. 1995. *Embedded Autonomy: States and Industrial Transformation*. Princeton, NJ: Princeton University Press.

Farrell, Henry. 2009. *The Political Economy of Trust: Institutions, Interests, and Inter-Firm Cooperation in Italy and Germany*. New York: Cambridge University Press.

Fehr, Ernst, and Simon Gaechter. 2000. "Fairness and Retaliation: The Economics of Reciprocity." *Journal of Economic Perspectives* 14: 159–181.

Fernandez, Roberto, and Roger Gould. 1994. "A Dilemma of State Power: Brokerage and Influence in the National Health-Policy Domain." *American Journal of Sociology* 99: 1455–1491.

Ferrary, Michel, and Mark Granovetter. 2009. "The Role of Venture Capital Firms in Silicon Valley's Complex Innovation Network." *Economy and Society* 38: 326–359.

Festinger, Leon, Stanley Schachter, and Kurt Back. 1948. *Social Pressures in Informal Groups*. Cambridge, MA: MIT Press.

Fine, Gary A., and Sheryl Kleinman. 1979. "Rethinking Subculture: An Interactionist Analysis." *American Journal of Sociology* 85: 1–20.

Firth, Raymond. [1939] 1975. *Primitive Polynesian Economy*. London: Routledge.

Fligstein, Neil. 1990. *The Transformation of Corporate Control*. Cambridge, MA: Harvard University Press.

Fligstein, Neil, and Doug McAdam. 2012. *A Theory of Fields*. New York: Oxford University Press.

Foddy, Margaret, and Toshio Yamagishi. 2009. "Group-Based Trust." pp. 17–41 in *Whom Can We Trust?*, edited by Karen Cook, Margaret Levi, and Russell Hardin. New York: The Russell Sage Foundation.

Fourcade, Marion, and Kieran Healy. 2007. "Moral Views of Market Society." *Annual Review of Sociology* 33: 285–311.

France, Anatole. 1894. *The Red Lily*. London: John Lane.

Frank, Robert. 1985. *Choosing the Right Pond*. New York: Oxford University Press.

Freedman, Maurice. 1959. "The Handling of Money: A Note on the Background to the Economic Sophistication of Overseas Chinese." *Man* 59: 65.

Friedland, Roger, and Robert Alford. 1991. "Bringing Society Back In: Symbols, Practices, and Institutional Contradictions." pp. 232–263 in *The New Institutionalism in Organizational Analysis*, edited by W. W. Powell and P. J. DiMaggio. Chicago: University of Chicago Press.

Friedman, Milton. 1953. *Essays in Positive Economics*. Chicago: University of Chicago Press.

Frigant, Vincent, and Damien Talbot. 2005. "Technological Determinism and Modularity: Lessons from a Comparison between Aircraft and Auto Industries in Europe." *Industry and Innovation* 12: 337–335.

Fukuyama, Francis. 1995. *Trust*. New York: Free Press.

Gambetta, Diego. 1988. "Can We Trust Trust?" pp. 213–237 in *Trust: Making and Breaking Cooperative Relations*, edited by D. Gambetta. New York: Basil Blackwell.

Gambetta, Diego, and Heather Hamill. 2005. *Streetwise: How Taxi Drivers Establish Their Customers' Trustworthiness*. New York: The Russell Sage Foundation.

Gartrell, David. 1982. "On the Visibility of Wage Referents." *Canadian Journal of Sociology* 7: 117–143.

Geertz, Clifford. 1978. "The Bazaar Economy: Information and Search in Peasant Marketing." *American Economic Review* 68: 28–32.

Gerlach, Michael. 1992. *Alliance Capitalism: The Social Organization of Japanese Business*. Berkeley, CA: University of California Press.

Gladwell, Malcolm. 2014. "Sacred and Profane: How Not to Negotiate with Believers." *The New Yorker* (March 31). Accessed at http://www.newyorker.com/magazine/2014/03/31/sacred-and-profane-4

Glaeser, Edward, David Laibson, Jose Scheinkman, and Christine Soutter. 2000. "Measuring Trust." *Quarterly Journal of Economics* 115(August): 811–846.

Goffman, Erving. 1974. *Frame Analysis: An Essay on the Organization of Experience.* Cambridge, MA: Harvard University Press.

Gould, Roger V. 1989. "Power and Social Structure in Community Elites." *Social Forces* 68: 531–552.

Gould, Roger, and Roberto Fernandez. 1989. "Structures of Mediation: A Formal Approach to Brokerage in Transaction Networks." *Sociological Methodology* 19: 89–126.

Gould, Steven Jay, and Richard Lewontin. 1979. "The Spandrels of San Marco and the Panglossian Paradigm: A Critique of the Adaptationist Programme." *Proceedings of the Royal Society of London* B205: 581–598.

Grace, Randolph C., and Simon Kemp. 2005. "What Does the Ultimatum Game Mean in the Real World?" *Behavioral and Brain Sciences* 28: 824–825.

Graeber, David. 2001. *Toward an Anthropological Theory of Value.* New York: Palgrave.

Granovetter, Mark. 1973. "The Strength of Weak Ties." *American Journal of Sociology* 78: 1360–1380.

———. 1983. "The Strength of Weak Ties: A Network Theory Revisited." *Sociological Theory* 1: 201–233.

———. 1985. "Economic Action and Social Structure: The Problem of Embeddedness." *American Journal of Sociology* 91: 481–510.

———. 1990. "The Old and the New Economic Sociology: A History and an Agenda." pp. 89–112 in Beyond the Marketplace: Rethinking Economy and Society, edited by R. Friedland and A. F. Robertson. New York: Aldine.

———. 1992. "The Nature of Economic Relations." pp. 21–37 in *Understanding Economic Process: Monographs in Economic Anthropology, No. 10,* edited by Sutti Ortiz and Susan Lees. Lanham, MD: University Press of America.

———. 1995. *Getting a Job: A Study of Contacts and Careers.* Chicago: University of Chicago Press.

———. 2002. "A Theoretical Agenda for Economic Sociology." pp. 35–59 in *The New Economic Sociology: Developments in an Emerging Field,* edited by M. F. Guillen, R. Collins, P. England, and M. Meyer. New York: Russell Sage Foundation.

———. 2003. "Ignorance, Knowledge, and Outcomes in a Small World." *Science* 301(5634): 773–774.

———. 2005. "The Impact of Social Structure on Economic Outcomes." *Journal of Economic Perspectives* 19: 33–50.

———. 2007. "The Social Construction of Corruption." pp. 152–172 in *On Capitalism,* edited by Victor Nee and Richard Swedberg. Stanford, CA: Stanford University Press.

———. 2009. "Comment on 'Capitalist Entrepreneurship' by T. Knudsen and R. Swedberg." *Capitalism and Society* 4(2): 1–11.

Granovetter, Mark, and Charles Tilly. 1988. "Inequality and Labor Processes." pp. 175–221 in *Handbook of Sociology,* edited by N. Smelser. Newbury Park, CA: Sage Publications.

Granovetter, Mark, and Patrick McGuire. 1998. "The Making of an Industry: Electricity in the United States." pp. 147–173 in *The Laws of the Markets,* edited by Michel Callon. Oxford: Blackwell.

Granovetter, Mark, and Richard Swedberg. 2011. *The Sociology of Economic Life,* 3rd ed. Boulder, CO: Westview Press.

Grusky, David, and Jesper Sorensen. 1998. "Can Class Analysis Be Salvaged"? *American Journal of Sociology* 103(5): 1187–1234.

Guiso, Luigi, Paolo Sapienza, and Luigi Zingales. 2006. "Does Culture Affect Economic Outcomes?." *Journal of Economic Perspectives* 2: 23–48.

———. 2008. "Trusting the Stock Market." *Journal of Finance* 63: 2557–2600.

———. 2011. "Civic Capital as the Missing Link." pp. 418–480 in *Handbook of Social Economics,* edited by Jess Benhabib, Alberto Bisin, and Matthew Jackson. North-Holland: Amsterdam.

Gulati, Ranjay, and Maxim Sytch. 2007. "Dependence Asymmetry and Joint Dependence in Interorganizational Relationships: Effects of Embeddedness on a Manufacturer's Performance in Procurement Relationships." *Administrative Science Quarterly* 52: 32–69.

Gulati, Ranjay, Maxim Sytch, and Adam Tatarynowicz. 2012. "The Rise and Fall of Small Worlds: Exploring the Dynamics of Social Structure." *Organization Science* 23(2): 449–471.

Haidt, Jonathan, and Selin Kesebir. 2010. "Morality." pp. 797–832 in *Handbook of Social Psychology,* 5th ed., edited by S. Fiske, D. Gilbert, and G. Lindzey. Hoboken, NJ: Wiley.

Hall, Peter. 2010. "Historical Institutionalism in Rationalist and Sociological Perspective." pp. 204–224 in *Explaining Institutional Change,* edited by James Mahoney and Kathleen Thelen, New York: Cambridge University Press.

Hall, Peter, and David Soskice. 2001. *Varieties of Capitalism: The Institutional Foundations of Comparative Advantage.* Oxford: Oxford University Press.

Hamilton, Gary. 2000. "Reciprocity and Control: The Organization of Chinese Family-Owned Conglomerates" pp. 55–74 in *Globalization of Chinese Business Firms,* edited by H. W.-C. Yeung and K. Olds. New York: St. Martin's.

Han, Shin-Kap. 2008. "Breadth and Depth of Unity among Chaebol Families in Korea." *Korean Journal of Sociology* 42: 1–25.

Hanneman, Robert A., and Mark Riddle. 2005.*Introduction to Social Network Methods.* Riverside, CA: University of California, Riverside. (published in digital form at http://faculty.ucr.edu/~hanneman/)

Hansmann, Henry, and Reinier Kraakman. 2004. "The End of History for Corporate Law." pp. 33–68 in *Convergence and Persistence in Corporate Governance,* edited by Jeffrey Gordon and Mark Roe. New York: Cambridge University Press.

Hardin, Russell. 2001. "Conceptions and Explanation of Trust." pp. 3–39 in *Trust in Society,* edited by K. Cook. New York: Russell Sage Foundation.

———. 2002. *Trust and Trustworthiness.* New York: Russell Sage Foundation.

Haveman, Heather, and Hayagreeva Rao. 1997. "Structuring a Theory of Moral Sentiments: Institutional and Organizational Coevolution in the Early Thrift Industry." *American Journal of Sociology* 102: 1606–1651.

Hedstrom, Peter. 2005. *Dissecting the Social: On the Principles of Analytical Sociology.* New York: Cambridge University Press.

Hedstrom, Peter, and Richard Swedberg, editors. 1998. *Social Mechanisms: An Analytical Approach to Social Theory.* New York: Cambridge University Press.

Hempel, Carl. 1965. *Aspects of Scientific Explanation.* New York: Free Press.

Hendry, Joy. 1996. "The Chrysanthemum Continues to Flower: Ruth Benedict and Some Perils of Popular Anthropology." pp. 106–121 in *Popularizing Anthropology,* edited by J. MacClancy and C. McDonaugh. London: Routledge.

Henrich, Joseph, Robert Boyd, Samuel Bowles, Colin Camerer, Ernst Fehr, and Herbert Gintis. 2004. *Foundations of Human Sociality: Economic Experiments and Ethnographic Evidence from Fifteen Small-Scale Societies.* Oxford: Oxford University Press.

Henrich, Joseph, Robert Boyd, Samuel Bowles, Colin Camerer, Ernst Fehr, Herbert Gintis, Richard McElreath, Michael Alvard, Abigail Barr, Jean Ensminger, Natalie Smith Henrich, Kim Hill, Francisco Gil-White, Michael Gurven, Frank W. Marlowe, John Q. Patton, and David Tracer. 2005. "'Economic Man' in Cross-Cultural Perspective: Behavioral Experiments in 15 Small-Scale Societies." *Behavioral and Brain Sciences* 28: 795–855.

Herrigel, Gary. 1996. *Industrial Constructions: The Sources of German Industrial Power.* New York: Cambridge University Press.

———. 2005. "Institutionalists at the Limits of Institutionalism: A Constructivist Critique of Two Edited Volumes from Wolfgang Streeck and Kozo Yamamura." *Socio-Economic Review* 3: 559–567.

———. 2010. *Manufacturing Possibilities: Creative Action and Industrial Recomposition in the United States, Germany, and Japan.* New York: Oxford University Press.

Hirschman, Albert. 1977. *The Passions and the Interests.* Princeton: Princeton University Press.

———. 1982. "Rival Interpretations of Market Society: Civilizing, Destructive, or Feeble." *Journal of Economic Literature* 20: 1463–1484.

Hirshleifer, Jack. 1985. "The Expanding Domain of Economics." *The American Economic Review* 75(6): 53–68.

Homans, George C. 1950. *The Human Group.* New York: Harcourt, Brace and Company.

———. 1971. *Social Behavior: The Elementary Forms.* New York: Harcourt, Brace Jovanovich.

Hucker, Charles. 1975. *China's Imperial Past: An Introduction to Chinese History and Culture.* Stanford, CA: Stanford University Press.

Jackson, Matthew. 2010. *Social and Economic Networks.* Princeton, NJ: Princeton University Press.

Jacobides, Michael, and John Paul MacDuffie. 2013. "How to Drive Value Your Way." *Harvard Business Review* 91: 92–100.

Jacobides, Michael, John Paul MacDuffie, and C. Jennifer Tae. 2016. "Agency. Structure, and the Dominance of OEMs: Change and Stability in the Automotive Sector. *Strategic Management Journal* 37: 1942–1967.

James, Harold. 2006. *Family Capitalism*. Cambridge, MA: Harvard University Press.

Joas, Hans. 1996. *The Creativity of Action*. Chicago: University of Chicago Press.

Johnson, Simon, and James Kwak. 2010. *13 Bankers: The Wall Street Takeover and the Next Financial Meltdown*. New York: Pantheon.

Kahneman, Daniel. 2011. *Thinking, Fast and Slow*. New York: Farrar, Straus and Giroux.

Kahneman, Daniel, Jack Knetsch, and Richard Thaler. 1986a. "Fairness as a Constraint on Profit-Seeking: Entitlements in the Market." *American Economic Review* 76: 728–741.

———. 1986b. "Fairness and the Assumptions of Economics." *Journal of Business* 59: S285–S300.

Kaplan, David A. 1999. *The Silicon Boys and Their Valley of Dreams*. New York: William Morrow.

Kaplan, Sarah. 2008. "Framing Contests: Strategy Making under Uncertainty." *Organization Science* September–October: 729–752.

Katz, Elihu, and Paul Lazarsfeld. 1955. *Personal Influence: The Part Played by People in the Flow of Mass Communications*. New York: Free Press.

Keister, Lisa. 2000. *Chinese Business Groups: The Structure and Impact of Interfirm Relations during Economic Development*. New York: Oxford University Press.

Kennedy, David M. 1975. "Overview: The Progressive Era." *The Historian* 37(3): 453–468.

Kim, Eun Mee. 1997. *Big Business, Strong State: Collusion and Conflict in South Korean Development 1960–1990*. Albany, NY: SUNY Press.

Kiong, Tong Chee. 1991. "Centripetal Authority, Differentiated Networks: The Social Organization of Chinese Firms in Singapore." In *Business Networks and Economic Development in East and Southeast Asia*, edited by G. Hamilton. Hong Kong: Centre of Asian Studies, University of Hong Kong.

Kirzner, Israel. 1973. *Competition and Entrepreneurship*. Chicago: University of Chicago Press.

Kontopoulos, Kyriakos. 1993. *The Logics of Social Structure* New York: Cambridge University Press.

Krippner, Greta, Mark Granovetter, Fred Block, Nicole Biggart, Tom Beamish, Youtien Tsing, Gillian Hart, Giovanni Arrighi, Margie Mendell, John Hall, Michael Burawoy, Steve Vogel, and Sean O'Riain. 2004. "Polanyi Symposium: A Conversation on Embeddedness." *Socio-Economic Review* 2: 109–135.

Krueger, Anne. 1974. "The Political Economy of the Rent-Seeking Society." *American Economic Review* 64(3): 291–303.

Kurlansky, Mark. 2002. *Salt: A World History*. New York: Walker.

Lamoreaux, Naomi. 1994. *Insider Lending: Banks, Personal Connections, and Economic Development in Industrial New England*. New York: Cambridge University Press.

LaPorta, Rafael, Florencio Lopez-de-Silanes, Andrei Shleifer, and Robert Vishny. 1997. "Trust in Large Organizations." *American Economic Review* 87(2): 333–338.

LaPorta, Rafael, Florencio Lopez-de-Silanes, and Andrei Shleifer. 1999. "Corporate Ownership around the World." *Journal of Finance* 54(2): 471–517.

Lawler, Edward, and Jeongkoo Yoon. 1996. "Commitment in Exchange Relations: A Test of a Theory of Relational Cohesion." *American Sociological Review* 61(1): 89–108.

Lazerson, Mark, and Gianni Lorenzoni. 1999. "The Firms That Feed Industrial Districts: A Return to the Italian Source." *Industrial and Corporate Change* 8: 235–266.

Leibenstein, Harvey. 1976. *Beyond Economic Man: A New Foundation for Microeconomics.* Cambridge, MA: Harvard University Press.

Leifer, Eric. 1991. *Actors as Observers: A Theory of Skill in Social Relationships.* London: Routledge.

Lepore, Jill. 2014. "The Disruption Machine: What the Gospel of Innovation Gets Wrong." June 23 (http://www.newyorker.com/magazine/2014/06/23/the-disruption-machine).

Levy, Marion J., Jr. 1954. "Contrasting Factors in the Modernization of China and Japan." *Economic Development and Cultural Change* 2: 161–197.

Lewis, Michael. 2010. *The Big Short: Inside the Doomsday Machine.* New York: W. W. Norton.

Lie, John. 2001. *Multiethnic Japan.* Cambridge, MA: Harvard University Press.

Light, Ivan. 1972. *Ethnic Enterprise in America.* Berkeley, CA: University of California Press.

Lim, Linda Y. C., and L. A. Peter Gosling. 1983. *The Chinese in Southeast Asia. Volume 1: Ethnicity and Economic Activity.* Singapore: Maruzen.

Lincoln, James, and Michael Gerlach. 2004. *Japan's Network Economy: Structure, Persistence, and Change.* New York: Cambridge University Press.

Lindquist, W. B., and I. D. Chase. 2009. "Data-Based Analysis of Winner-Loser Models of Hierarchy Formation in Animals. *Bulletin of Mathematical Biology* 71: 556–584.

Locke, Richard. 1995. *Remaking the Italian Economy.* Ithaca, NY: Cornell University Press.

———. 2001. "Building Trust." Paper presented at annual meeting of the *American Political Science Association.*

———. 2013. *The Promise and Limits of Private Power: Promoting Labor Standards in a Global Economy.* New York: Cambridge University Press.

Lounsbury, Michael. 2007. "A Tale of Two Cities: Competing Logics and Practice Variation in the Professionalization of Mutual Funds." *Academy of Management Journal* 50: 289–307.

Lukes, Steven. 1974. *Power: A Radical View.* London: Macmillan.

Luo, Jar-Der. 2011. "*Guanxi* Revisited: An Exploratory Study of Familiar Ties in a Chinese Workplace." *Management and Organization Review* 7(2): 329–351.

Lynch, Gerard. 1997. "The Role of Criminal Law in Policing Corporate Misconduct." *Law and Contemporary Problems* 60: 23–65.

Macaulay, Stewart. 1963. "Non-Contractual Relations in Business: A Preliminary Study." *American Sociological Review* 28: 55–69.

MacDuffie, John Paul. 2013. "Modularity-as-Property, Modularization-as-Process, and 'Modularity'-as-Frame: Lessons from Product Architecture Initiatives in the Global Automotive Industry." *Global Strategy Journal* 3: 8–40.

MacDuffie, John Paul, and Susan Helper. 2006. "Collaboration in Supply Chains: With and Without Trust." pp. 417–466 in *The Firm as a Collaborative Community: Reconstructing Trust in the Knowledge Economy*, edited by Charles Heckscher and Paul Adler. New York: Oxford University Press.

Mahoney, James, and Katherine Thelen, editors. 2009. *Explaining Institutional Change: Ambiguity, Agency, and Power.* New York: Cambridge University Press.

Malinowski, Bronislaw. 2014 [1922]. *Argonauts of the Western Pacific.* New York: Routledge.

———. 1944. *A Scientific Theory of Culture and Other Essays.* Chapel Hill, NC: University of North Carolina Press.

Mann, Michael. 1986. *The Sources of Social Power: A History of Power from the Beginning to a.d. 1760.* Cambridge, UK: Cambridge University Press.

———. 1993. *The Sources of Social Power: The Rise of Classes and Nation-States, 1760–1914.* Cambridge, UK: Cambridge University Press.

March, James G., and Herbert Simon. 1993. *Organizations.* 2nd ed. New York: Wiley.

Marchetti, P., and M. Ventoruzzo. 2001. "Corporate Law." pp. 2803–2810 in *International Encyclopedia of the Social and Behavioral Sciences,* edited by N. Smelser and P. Baltes. London: Elsevier.

McAdams, Richard. 1997. "The Origin, Development, and Regulation of Norms." *Michigan Law Review* 96: 338–433.

McCloskey, Donald. 1983. "The Rhetoric of Economics." *Journal of Economic Literature* 21: 481–517.

McDonald, Forrest. 1962. *Insull.* Chicago: University of Chicago Press.

McEvily, William, and Marco Tortoriello. 2011. "Measuring Trust in Organizational Research: Review and Recommendations." *Journal of Trust Research* 1: 23–63.

McGuire, Patrick, and Mark Granovetter. 1998. "Business and Bias in Public Policy Formation: The National Civic Federation and Social Construction of Electric Utility Regulation, 1905–1907." Paper presented at the 1998 meeting of the American Sociological Association.

Merton, Robert K. 1947. *Social Theory and Social Structure.* Glencoe, IL: Free Press of Glencoe.

———. 1957. *Social Theory and Social Structure.* Rev. ed. Glencoe, IL: Free Press of Glencoe.

Meyer, John, and Brian Rowan. 1977. "Institutionalized Organizations: Formal Structure as Myth and Ceremony." *American Journal of Sociology* 83: 340–363.

Meyer, John, John Boli, George Thomas, and Francisco Ramirez. 1997. "World Society and the Nation-State." *American Journal of Sociology* 103: 144–181.

Meyer, Marshall, and Lynne Zucker. 1989. *Permanently Failing Organizations.* Newbury Park, CA: Sage Publications.

Mills, C. Wright. [1956] 2000. *The Power Elite.* New York: Oxford University Press.

Mintz, Beth, and Michael Schwartz. 1985. *The Power Structure of American Business.* Chicago, IL: University of Chicago Press.

Mizruchi, Mark. 2010. "The American Corporate Elite and the Historical Roots of the Financial Crisis of 2008," in *Markets on Trial: The Economic Sociology of the U.S. Financial Crisis,* edited by Michael Lounsbury and Paul Hirsch. *Research in the Sociology of Organizations* 30: 103–139.

———. 2013. *The Fracturing of the American Corporate Elite.* Cambridge, MA: Harvard University Press.

Mizruchi, Mark, and Blyden Potts. 1998. "Centrality and Power Revisited: Actor Success in Group Decision Making." *Social Networks* 20: 353–387.

Mokyr, Joel. 2005. "Long-Term Economic Growth and the History of Technology." pp. 1113–1180 in *Handbook of Economic Growth*, Vol. 1, Part B, edited by Philippe Aghion and Steven Durlauf. Amsterdam: Elsevier.

Molm, Linda. 2001. "Theories of Social Exchange and Exchange Networks." pp. 260–272 in *Handbook of Social Theory,* edited by George Ritzer and Barry Smart. London: Sage Publications.

———. 2003. "Theoretical Comparisons of Forms of Exchange." *Sociological Theory* 21(1: January): 1–17.

Mnookin, Robert, and Lewis Kornhauser. 1979. "Bargaining in the Shadow of the Law: The Case of Divorce." *Yale Law Journal* 88(5): 950–997.

Nagel, Ernest. 1961. *The Structure of Science.* New York: McGraw Hill.

Nelson, Joel. 1966. "Clique Contacts and Family Orientations." *American Sociological Review* 31: 663–672.

Nelson, Richard, and Sidney Winter. 1982. *An Evolutionary Theory of Economic Change.* Cambridge, MA: Harvard University Press.

Nishiguchi, Toshihiro, and Alexandre Beaudet. 1998. "The Toyota Group and the Aisin Fire." *Sloan Management Review* 40: 49–59.

Obstfeld, David. 2005. "Social Networks, the *Tertius Iungens* Orientation, and Involvement in Innovation." *Administrative Science Quarterly* 50: 100–130.

Obstfeld, David, Stephen Borgatti, and Jason Davis. 2014. "Brokerage as a Process: Decoupling Third-Party Action from Social Network Structure." *Research in the Sociology of Organizations* 40: 135–159.

Okun, Arthur. 1980. *Prices and Quantities.* Washington D.C: Brookings Institution.

Orwell, George. 1945. *Animal Farm.* London: Secker and Warburg.

Ostrom, Elinor. 2003. "Toward a Behavioral Theory Linking Trust, Reciprocity, and Reputation." pp. 19–79 in *Trust and Reciprocity: Interdisciplinary Lessons from Experimental Research,* edited by E. Ostrom and J. Walker. New York: Russell Sage Foundation.

O'Sullivan, Mary. 2005. "Typologies, Ideologies, and Realities of Capitalism." *Socio-Economic Review* 3: 547–558.

Ouchi, William. 1981. *Theory Z.* Reading, MA: Addison-Wesley.

Padgett, John, and Christopher Ansell. 1993. "Robust Action and the Rise of the Medici." *American Journal of Sociology* 98: 1259–1319.

Padgett John, and Paul MacLean. 2006. "Organizational Invention and Elite Transformation: The Birth of Partnership Systems in Renaissance Florence." *American Journal of Sociology* 111: 1463–1568

Padgett, John, and Walter Powell. 2012. *The Emergence of Organizations and Markets.* Princeton, NJ: Princeton University Press.

Parsons, Talcott. 1937. *The Structure of Social Action: A Study in Social Theory with Special Reference to a Group of Recent European Writers.* Glencoe, IL: Free Press of Glencoe.

———. 1959. "General Theory in Sociology." In *Sociology Today: Problems and Prospects,* edited by R. K. Merton, L. Broom, and L. S. Cottrell Jr. New York: Basic Books.

———. 1961. "An Outline of the Social System." pp. 30–79 in *Theories of Society,* edited by Talcott Parsons, Edward Shils, Kaspar Naegele, and Jesse Pitts. Glencoe, IL: Free Press of Glencoe.

———. 1963. "On the Concept of Political Power 107(3: June 19): 232–262." *Proceedings of the American Philosophical Society* 107: 232–262.

Parsons, Talcott, and Neil J. Smelser. 1956. *Economy and Society: A Study in the Integration of Social and Economic Theory.* Glencoe, IL: Free Press of Glencoe.

Patterson, Orlando. 1982. *Slavery and Social Death: A Comparative Study.* Cambridge, MA: Harvard University Press.

Pempel, T. J. 2005. "Alternative Capitalisms Confront New Pressures to Conform." *Socio-Economic Review* 3: 569–575.

Penrose, Edith. [1959] 1995. *The Theory of the Growth of the Firm.* Oxford: Oxford University Press.

Perrow, Charles. 1986. *Complex Organizations: A Critical Essay.* 3rd edition. New York: Random House.

Pettit, P. 2001. "Consequentialism Including Utilitarianism." pp. 2613–2618 in *International Encyclopedia of the Social and Behavioral Sciences,* edited by N. Smelser and P. Baltes. New York: Elsevier.

Pfeffer, Jeffrey. 1981. *Power in Organizations.* Boston: Pitman.

Pfeffer, Jeffrey, and Gerald Salancik. 1978. *The External Control of Organizations: A Resource Dependence Perspective.* New York: Harper and Row.

Piore, Michael, and Charles Sabel. 1984. *The Second Industrial Divide: Possibilities for Prosperity.* New York: Basic Books.

Popkin, Samuel. 1979. *The Rational Peasant: The Political Economy of Rural Society in Vietnam.* Berkeley, CA: University of California Press.

Portes, Alejandro, and Julia Sensenbrenner. 1993. "Embeddedness and Immigration: Notes on the Social Determinants of Economic Action." *American Journal of Sociology* 98: 1320–1350.

Posner, Eric. 1996. "Law, Economics, and Inefficient Norms" *University of Pennsylvania Law Review* 144: 1697–1744.

———. 2000. *Law and Social Norms.* Cambridge, MA: Harvard University Press.

Posner, Richard. 1998. "Social Norms, Social Meaning, and Economic Analysis of Law: A Comment." *Journal of Legal Studies* 37(2: Pt. 2): 553–565.

Prahalad, C. K., and Gary Hamel. 1990. "The Core Competence of a Corporation." *Harvard Business Review* 68: 79–91.

Putnam, Robert. 1993. *Making Democracy Work: Civic Traditions in Modern Italy.* Princeton, NJ: Princeton University Press.

Rao, Hayagreeva, Philippe Monin, and Rodolphe Durand. 2003. "Institutional Change in Toque Ville: Nouvelle Cuisine as an Identity Movement in French Gastronomy." *American Journal of Sociology* 108: 795–843.

Reagans, Ray, and Ezra Zuckerman. 2008. "Why Knowledge Does Not Equal Power: The Network Redundancy Tradeoff." *Industrial and Corporate Change* 17: 903–944.

Reddy, William. 1984. *The Rise of Market Culture: The Textile Trade and French Society, 1750–1900.* Cambridge, UK: Cambridge University Press.

Ricardo, David. 1821. *On the Principles of Political Economy and Taxation.* 3rd ed. London: John Murray, Albemarle-Street.

Robbins, Lionel. 1932. *An Essay on the Nature and Significance of Economic Science.* London: Macmillan.

Roe, Mark. 1994. *Strong Managers, Weak Owners: The Political Roots of American Corporate Finance.* Princeton, NJ: Princeton University Press.

Roosevelt, Franklin D. 1932. "Campaign Address on Progressive Government at the Commonwealth Club in San Francisco, California." Text at http://www .heritage.org/initiatives/first-principles/primary-sources/fdrs -commonwealth-club-address

Rosenberg, Nathan. 2000. *Schumpeter and the Endogeneity of Technology: Some American Perspectives.* London: Routledge.

Rostow, W. W. 1960. *The Stages of Economic Growth: A Non-Communist Manifesto.* Cambridge, UK: Cambridge University Press.

Rousseau, Denise, Sim Sitkin, Ronald Burt, and Colin Camerer. 1998. "Not So Different after All: A Cross-Discipline View of Trust." *Academy of Management Review* 23: 393–404.

Sabel, Charles. 1982. *Work and Politics: The Division of Labor in Industry.* New York: Cambridge University Press.

———. 1993. "Studied Trust: Building New Forms of Cooperation in a Volatile Economy." *Human Relations* 46: 1133–1171.

Sahlins, Marshall. 1972. *Stone Age Economics.* Hawthorne, NY: Aldine.

Samuelson, Paul. 1947. *Foundations of Economic Analysis.* Cambridge, MA: Harvard University Press.

Saxenian, Annalee. 1994. *Regional Advantage: Culture and Competition in Silicon Valley and Route 128.* Cambridge, MA: Harvard University Press.

Schotter, Andrew. 1981. *The Economic Theory of Social Institutions.* New York: Cambridge University Press.

Schumpeter, Joseph. 1911. *The Theory of Economic Development.* Leipzig: Duncker and Humblot.

Scott, James C. 1976. *The Moral Economy of the Peasant: Rebellion and Subsistence in Southeast Asia.* New Haven, CT: Yale University Press.

Scott, John. 2010. *What Is Social Network Analysis?* London: Bloomsbury.

———. 2013. *Social Network Analysis.* 3rd ed. Newbury Park, CA: Sage Publications.

Scott, John, and Peter Carrington. 2011. *Sage Handbook of Social Network Analysis.* Newbury Park, CA: Sage Publications.

Scott, W. Richard. 2014. *Institutions and Organizations: Ideas, Interests, and Identities.* 4th ed. Los Angeles, CA: Sage Publications.

Sen, Amartya. 1977. "Rational Fools: A Critique of the Behavioral Foundations of Economic Theory." *Philosophy and Public Affairs* 6: 317–344.

Shapiro, Susan. 1984. *Wayward Capitalists: Target of the Securities and Exchange Commission.* New Haven, CT: Yale University Press.

Sheingate, Adam. 2010. "Rethinking Rules: Creativity and Constraint in the U.S. House of Representatives." pp. 168–203 in *Explaining Institutional Change: Ambiguity, Agency, and Power,* edited by James Mahoney and Kathleen Thelen. New York: Cambridge University Press.

Shenon, Philip. 1984. "Margolies Is Found Guilty of Murdering Two Women." *New York Times* (June 1).

Silver, Allan. 1989. "Friendship and Trust as Moral Ideals: An Historical Approach." *European Journal of Sociology* 30: 274–297.

———. 1990. "Friendship in Commercial Society: Eighteenth-Century Social Theory and Modern Sociology." *American Journal of Sociology* 95: 1474–1504.

Simmel, Georg. [1908] 1950. *The Sociology of Georg Simmel,* translated by K. Wolff. New York: The Free Press.

Simon, Herbert A. 1997. *Administrative Behavior.* 4th ed. New York: The Free Press.

Smith, Adam. [1776] 1976. *An Inquiry into the Nature and Causes of the Wealth of Nations.* Oxford: Oxford University Press.

Snow, David, D. Rochford Jr., S. Worden, and R. Benford. 1986. "Frame Alignment Processes, Micromobilization and Social Movement Participation." *American Sociological Review* 51(August): 464–481.

Solomon, Richard L. 1964. "Punishment." *American Psychologist* 19: 237–253.

Sorge, Arndt. 2005. *The Global and the Local: Understanding the Dialectics of Business Systems.* New York: Oxford University Press.

Spence, A. Michael. 1974. *Market Signaling: Informational Transfer in Hiring and Related Screening Processes.* Cambridge, MA: Harvard University Press.

Stark, David. 1986. "Rethinking Internal Labor Markets: New Insights from a Comparative Perspective." *American Sociological Review* 51: 492–504.

———. 2009. *The Sense of Dissonance: Accounts of Worth in Economic Life.* Princeton, NJ: Princeton University Press.

Sternberg, Robert J., and Karin Sternberg. 2017. *Cognitive Psychology.* 7th ed. Boston: Cengage Learning.

Stigler, George. 1946. *The Theory of Price.* New York: Macmillan.

Stinchcombe, Arthur. 1968. *Constructing Social Theories.* New York: Harcourt, Brace and World.

Stovel, Katherine, Benjamin Golub, and Eva Meyersson Milgrom. 2011. "Stabilizing Brokerage." *PNAS* 108: 21326–21332.

Stovel, Katherine, and Lynette Shaw. 2012. "Brokerage." *Annual Review of Sociology* 38: 139–158.

Strauss, George. 1955. "Group Dynamics and Intergroup Relations." pp. 90-96 in *Money and Motivation: An Analysis of Incentives in Industry,* edited by William F. Whyte. New York: Harper and Row.

Streeck, W. 2005. "Rejoinder: On Terminology, Functionalism, (Historical) Institutionalism, and Liberalization." *Socio-Economic Review* 3: 577–587.

———. 2011. "E Pluribus Unum? Varieties and Commonalities of Capitalism." pp. 419–455 in *The Sociology of Economic Life,* 3rd ed., edited by M. Granovetter and R. Swedberg. Boulder, CO: Westview Press.

Streeck, W., and K. Yamamura. 2001. *The Origins of Non-Liberal Capitalism: Germany and Japan in Comparison.* Ithaca, NY: Cornell University Press.

Sturgeon, Timothy J. 2002. "Modular Production Networks: A New American Model of Industrial Organization." *Industrial and Corporate Change* 11: 451–496.

Sunstein, Cass. 1996. "Social Norms and Social Roles" *Columbia Law Review* 96: 903–968.

Swedberg, Richard. 2003. *Principles of Economic Sociology.* Princeton, NJ: Princeton University Press.

Swidler, Ann. 1986. "Culture in Action: Symbols and Strategies." *American Sociological Review* 51: 273–286.

Taira, Koji. 1970. *Economic Development and the Labor Market in Japan.* New York: Columbia University Press.

Tarbell, Ida M. 1904. *The History of the Standard Oil Company.* New York: McClure, Phillips and Company.

Thompson, E. P. 1971. "The Moral Economy of the English Crowd in the Eighteenth Century." *Past and Present* 50: 76–136.

Thornton, Patricia, and William Ocasio. 1999. "Institutional Logics and the Historical Contingency of Power in Organizations: Executive Succession in the Higher Educational Publishing Industry, 1958–1990." *American Journal of* Sociology 105: 801–843.

Thornton Patricia, William Ocasio, and Michael Lounsbury. 2012. *The Institutional Logics Perspective: A New Approach to Culture, Structure, and Process.* Oxford: Oxford University Press.

Tocqueville, Alexis de. [1856] 1955. *The Old Regime and the French Revolution.* New York: Doubleday.

Tolbert, Pamela, and Lynne Zucker. 1983. "Institutional Sources of Change in the Formal Structure of Organizations: The Diffusion of Civil Service Reform, 1880–1935." *Administrative Science Quarterly* 28: 22–39.

Tversky, Amos, and Daniel Kahneman. 1981. "The Framing of Decisions and the Psychology of Choice." *Science* 211(January 30): 453–458.

Tyler, Tom. 2001. "Why Do People Rely on Others? Social Identity and the Social Aspects of Trust." pp. 285–306 in *Trust in Society*, edited by K. Cook. New York: Russell Sage Foundation.

———. 2006. *Why People Obey the Law*. Princeton, NJ: Princeton University Press.

Useem, Michael. 1984. *The Inner Circle: Large Corporations and the Rise of Business Political Activity in the U.S. and the U.K.* New York: Oxford University Press.

Vaisey, Steven. 2009. "Motivation and Justification: A Dual-Process Model of Culture in Action." *American Journal of Sociology* 114(6 May): 1675–1715.

Veblen, Thorstein. 1899. *The Theory of the Leisure Class*. New York: Macmillan.

Walker, James, and Elinor Ostrom. 2003. "Conclusion." pp.381–387 in *Trust and Reciprocity*, edited by Elinor Ostrom and James Walker. New York: The Russell Sage Foundation.

Wasserman, Stanley, and Katherine Faust. 1994. *Social Network Analysis: Methods and Applications*. New York: Cambridge University Press.

Watts, Duncan, and Steven Strogatz. 1998. "Collective Dynamics of 'Small-World' Networks." *Nature* 393: 440–442.

Weber, Max. [1921] 1968. *Economy and Society*, translated by Guenther Roth and Claus Wittich. New York: Bedminster Press.

Wellman, Barry. 1979. "The Community Question: The Intimate Networks of East Yorkers." *American Journal of Sociology* 84: 1201–1231.

Whitford, Joshua. 2002. "Pragmatism and the Untenable Duality of Means and Ends." *Theory and Society* 31: 325–363.

———. 2005. *The New Old Economy: Networks, Institutions, and the Organizational Transformation of American Manufacturing*. New York: Oxford University Press.

———. 2012. "Waltzing, Relational Work, and the Construction (or Not) of Collaboration in Manufacturing Industries." *Politics and Society* 40: 249–272.

Whitford, Joshua, and Francesco Zirpoli. 2014. "Pragmatism, Practice, and the Boundaries of Organization." *Organization Science* 25(6): 1823–1839.

———. 2016. "The Network Firm as a Political Coalition." *Organization Studies* 37: 1227–1248

Wiebe, Robert. 1967. *The Search for Order: 1877–1920*. New York: Hill and Wang.

Williamson, Oliver. 1975. *Markets and Hierarchies*. New York: Free Press.

———. 1991. "Comparative Economic Organization: The Analysis of Discrete Structural Alternatives." *Administrative Science Quarterly* 36: 269–296.

———. 1993. "Calculativeness, Trust, and Economic Organization." *Journal of Law and Economics* 36: 453–486.

Wilson, Edward O. 1975. *Sociobiology*. Cambridge, MA: Harvard University Press.

Woodward, Joan. 1965. *Industrial Organization: Theory and Practice.* New York: Oxford University Press.

Wright, Gavin. 1999. "Can a Nation Learn? American Technology as a Network Phenomenon." pp. 295–326 in *Learning by Doing in Markets, Firms, and Countries.* edited by N. Lamoreaux, D. Raff, and P. Temin. Chicago: University of Chicago Press.

Wrong, Dennis. 1961. "The Oversocialized Conception of Man in Modern Sociology." *American Sociological Review* 26: 183–196.

———. 1995. *Power: Its Forms, Bases and Uses.* New Brunswick, NJ: Transaction Publishers.

Yamamura, K., and W. Streeck. 2003. *The End of Diversity?: Prospects for German and Japanese Capitalism.* Ithaca, NY: Cornell University Press.

Zeitlin, Maurice, and Richard Ratcliff. 1988. *Landlords and Capitalists: The Dominant Class of Chile.* Princeton, NJ: Princeton University Press.

Zelizer, Viviana. 2005. *The Purchase of Intimacy.* Princeton, NJ: Princeton University Press.

Zucker, Lynne. 1986. "Production of Trust: Institutional Sources of Economic Structure, 1840–1920." *Research in Organizational Behavior* 8: 53–111.

Index

Action: affectual, 20; commitment impact on, 21–22; conceptions of, 11–15; consequences of, 20; cultural patterns of, 175–177; economic, 21–22, 79, 227n2; egocentric, 21; and human nature, 11–14, 74–76, 149–150; of individuals, 10; influence on, 28; justification of, 139, 187; limitation of, 1; nature of, 11; noneconomic, 21–22; null hypothesis, nature of, 11; optimum strategy of, 110–112; problem-solving, 192–193; rationality impact on, 1, 26, 34–35; resources for, 184–193; signal, 41; types of, 20–21; utility of, 59–60
Adaptation: for domination, 54; stories of, 6–7
Adaptive story, 6–7, 10, 43, 150
Advantage, in social networks, 23–24, 44
American Industrials, family-based, 85, 87–89
Analysis: cost-benefit, 35; of individuals, 14; levels of, 3; meso-level of, 5; static, 8–9
Anthropology, 30–31, 228n7; and human nature, 28–29
Apparel industry, 145–146
Applied rational choice theory, 3–4
Approval, in socialization, 23
Arguments, of reductionism, 12

Atomization: competition and, 13; from internalization, 13–15; from self-interest, 13
Authority: abuse of, 49; centralization of, 44, 87–88; dependence and, 100; of economics, 129; entitlement and, 97–98; hierarchy and, 92; lack of, 129; laws and, 98–99; legitimate, 103, 109, 126, 160; obligation of, 50–51; parental, 98; patriarchy, 90, 176; personal, 99; property owner, 195; in social networks, 131–132; structure of, 111, 129–130
Automobile industry, 151; codification of rules in, 159–160; computer industry as comparison to, 157–160; core competencies in, 160–161; deinstitutionalization of, 156–157; design improvements in, 163–166; globalization of, 156; institutional theory of organization in, 162–163; integrality in, 163; modularization in, 156–170; structure in, 166–167, 169–170; trust in, 167–169
Autonomy, in social network, 107–108

Baldwin, Carliss, 158
Barth, Frederick, 112–115
Becker, Gary, 2, 4

Behavior: consequences of, 24; in culture, 10–11; desirable, 41; expectations of, 65; guilt and shame impact on, 30–31; habits and, 28; incentive impacting, 32; individual, 11, 18–19; in institutions, 189, 196–197; interests impacting, 73–74; mental state impacting, 26–27; motivation in, 20–21; norms impacting, 76; predictable, 74; prediction of, 74–75; professional standards of, 34; rationalization of, 59–60; reinforcement of, 4; traditional view of, 49–54
Benedict, Ruth, 30–31
Bewley, Truman, 47
Biernacki, Richard, 153–154
Biology, 7–8
Bonaparte, Napoleon, 202–203
Brokerage: power from, 106–126, 232n8; roles of, 110, 118–119; structural holes and, 106
Burawoy, Michael, 44–45
Business: corporate governance in, 189; cultural patterns in, 177–178; family dynamics in, 87, 176, 231n8; groups, structure of, 87–89; history of ethics, 34; partnership system, 176–179
Business History Review, 188

Capitalism: development of, 198–201; human nature and, 138; institutional, 2; institutional logics of, 138; transition to, 154; varieties of, 55, 188–189, 191–192
Case studies: institutions, rise and fall of, 156–170; institutions after turmoil, war, and revolution, 193–203
Causality, 3–4; of culture, 14
Chaebol, 131, 132, 176; structure, 169
Cheating, 29, 81–82
Christensen, Clay, 161
The Chrysanthemum and the Sword (Benedict), 30–31
Clark, Kim, 158
CME. *See* Coordinated market economies
The Communist Manifesto (Marx), 181–182

Community welfare, 85–86
Competition, 13, 228n8
Consequences, 22, 24, 74, 106, 144; of action, 20; economic, 140; of forcing actors, 83; history and, 6; of macro-level changes, 54; national, 118; noneconomic institutions with, 19; of norms, 45; of power, 55; reputational, 67; of selection, 43; social networks and, 15; of status hierarchy, 95; of structure, 108
Consequentialist behavior, 31
Control: of agenda and discourse, 100–103, 127–128, 232n5; of industry, 195–196; over resources, 50, 92–95, 98, 121, 126, 134
Cooley, Charles, 64–65
Cooperation, 1; incentive for, 75; from interests, 77; rationality of, 58–59; beyond self-interest, 36–38; socialization for, 56
Coordinated market economies (CME), 188–189
Core competencies, 160–161
Corporate governance, 189
Cost-benefit analysis, 35
Costs and benefits: of breaking criminal laws, 29; group, from norms, 44; personal relationships, 60–61; resources, 61–62
Crenson, Matthew, 101
Criminality: benefits of, 29; human nature and, 61–62
Cuisine industry, 142–143
Culture, 5, 54–55; behavior in, 10–11; causality of, 14; consensus, 27–28; constructs of, 154; contrast of, 145–150; evolution of, 38; globalization of, 155; high trust, 85; influence on, 11; low trust, 85; modernization of, 154–155; national, 187–188; patterns, in business, 177–178; patterns, of action, 175–177; of politics, 151–153; social context of, 135–136; of trust, 96–97; trust impacted by, 84–85

David, Paul, 9
Decision dilemmas, 58–59, 230n1
Decision-making: in groups, 104–105; moral, 31
Deinstitutionalization, 156–157
Dependence, 92–97, 104; authority and, 100. *See also* Path dependence
Dewey, John, 27, 28, 187, 211, 227n2,
Division of Labor in Society (Durkheim), 22
Dobbin, Frank, 151–152
Domination: adaptation for, 54; power of, 92
Dualism, 227n3
Durkheim, Emile, 4, 22
Dynamics, 204–205; family business, 87, 176, 231n8; study of, 8

Economic imperialism, 2, 4
Economic norms, 28–29
Economic outcomes, 2, 9, 23, 79, 91
Economic power, 103–104, 110, 152–153; control of agenda and discourse, based on, 100–102, 232n5; dependence, based on, 92–97; legitimacy, based on, 97–100; macro-level perspectives on, 126–135
Economics, 228n6, 229n16; action, norms impact on, 35–36; consequences, 140; goals, 22–23; history of, 13–15, 20–21; of information, 57; norms in, 28–29; rational action in, 21–22, 79, 227n2; rationality of, 108. *See also* Noneconomic
Egocentricity, 21
Electricity industry, 182–183
Elite: corporate, 118–122; power of, 116–126, 118, 232n10
Ellickson, Robert, 33; on disputes, 38–40; on norms, 40–44
Embeddedness, 15; relational, 17–18; in social networks, 17–20; structural, 18–19, 65–66; temporal, 19–20
Emerson, Richard, 94–95
Emotions, 229n1; human nature and, 31, 62–64; judgment impacted by, 48;

norms impacted by, 29–30, 42–43; personal relationships from, 61–62; psychology of, 32–35; values impacted by, 35
The End of Diversity?: Prospects for German and Japanese Capitalism (Streeck and Yamamura), 190
Entitlement, 97–98
Entrepreneurship, 228n5; as market connectors, 180–184; power of, 112–116; resources and, 5–6; trust in, 79
Equilibria, socialization as, 37
Esteem, 230n6; for minority members of group, 43; norms arise for, 40
Ethics, 33–34
Evolution: biology of, 7–8; of culture, 38; norms, 26; stories of, 6
Evolutionary game theory, 38
Exchange, 233n2,3,4; commitment, 231n5; complex, 115–116; history of, 69–70; power in spheres of, 105, 112–116; of reciprocity, 105, 232n7; of resources, 16–17, 50–51, 67, 96, 100, 103–107; theory with social identity, 109–110
Experiments: hierarchy, 104; with modularization, 163–170; moral psychology, 31–32, 35; Ultimatum Game, 36–38
Explaining Institutional Change (Mahoney and Thelen), 136

Family, 233n1; accepted norms of, 173–174; business dynamics of, 87, 176, 231n8; industrials, based in, 85, 87–89; Marx on, 181–182; role conflict in, 172–173; trust of, 71–72, 78–79, 87–89
Financial services industry, 158
Force of norms, 32–34
Forging Industrial Policy (Dobbin), 151–152
Foundations of Economic Analysis (Samuelson), 21
France, Anatole, 93

Freedom, price of, 94
Friedman, Milton, 7
Friendship: Marx on, 181–182. *See also* Personal relationships
Functionalism, 5–8; history of, 8–12; Parsons on, 137; prerequisites for, 136–137

German historical school, 13
The Global and the Local (Sorge), 193–194
Globalization: of automobile industry, 156; of culture, 155
Goals: economic, 22–23; noneconomic, 22–23
Gould, Roger, 109–110
Government policy: limits of, 195; trust in, 83
Groups: business, structure of, 87–89; decision-making in, 104–105; identity of, 82; minority members, esteem for, 43; norms as beneficial to, 44, 82; norms as harmful to, 44–45; obligation to, 67; rituals and symbols of, 34; social context of, 135–136; trade between, 108–109; trust in, 65–68; of working women, 186
Guilt: behavior impacted by, 30–31; moral dilemma and, 32–33; norms impacted by, 31

Habits, 28
Harvard Business Review, 158
Herrigel, Gary, 193–194
Hierarchy, 198–200; authority and, 92; experiments of, 104; power of, 129–132; status, 95
Hirschman, Albert, 12, 21, 56–57
Hirshleifer, Jack, 4–5
Historic accident, 79–80
History: of business ethics, 34; of China, 200–201; consequences and, 6; of economics, 13–15, 20–21; of exchange, 69–70; of functionalism, 8–12; institutional, 5–7, 193–199; of interactions, 17; of organization, 140–141; personal, 18–19; of power,

133–134; of regulation, 128; of science, 4–5; of Wall Street, 101–102
Hobbes, Thomas, 12, 14; on centralization of power, 52
Human action, 139, 149; conception of, 76; conceptions of, 11, 14; oversocialized views of, 14
Human nature, 3, 230n3; action and, 11–14, 74–76, 149–150; anthropology and, 28–29; baggage of, 19; capitalism and, 138; criminality and, 61–62; emotions and, 31, 62–64; identity of, 23; institutions and, 157–158; learning and, 37; motivation of, 22; norms and, 35–36; of parsimony, 4–5; problem-solving and, 139–140, 147; psychology and, 43; rationality and, 57; sharing and, 43; social setting and, 11–12; taboo, 35–36, 230n2
Hume, David, 83–84

Identity: group, 82; in human nature, 23; individual, 174–175; personal relationships impacted by, 64–65; social, 67
Incentive: behavior impacted by, 32; for cooperation, 75; financial, as motivation, 48
Individual economic action, 1, 17, 227n2
Individualism, 77
Individuals: action of, 10; analysis by, 14; behavior of, 11, 18–19; characteristics, power from, 103–104; identity of, 174–175; motivation of, 20; social context of, 135–136; strategy among, 51–52
Industrial society, 75
Industry: apparel, 145–146; control of, 195–196; cuisine, 142–143; electricity, 182–183; financial services, 158; information technology, 145–148, 157–160; innovation in, 147–148; machine shops, 186–187; organization of, 141, 158–159; railway, 151; steel, 194–197; textile, 153–154; thrift, 142; venture capital financing, 183–184. *See also* Automobile industry

Influence: on action, 28; cultural, 11; of norms, 35, 38; on social network, 18–19

Information technology industry, 145–148

The Innovator's Dilemma (Christensen), 161

Institutional alternatives, after turmoil, war, and revolution, 193–203

Institutional logics, 28, 55, 136, 139–145, 150–154, 188; of capitalism, 138; conflict of, 173–174

Institutional solutions, 7, 57, 191, 198, 202

Institutions, 1–2, 54–55; behavior in, 189, 196–197; capitalism of, 2; forms of, 198–199; history of, 5–7, 193–199; human nature and, 157–158; intersection of, 24; legal system, protection of, 69; macro-level of, 91, 118, 136–137; problem-solving of, 190–191, 201–203; rise and fall of, 156–170; role conflict in, 172–173; schemata of, 172–175; spheres and, 137–138; theory of organization, 140–141, 162–163; trust in, 68–70, 75–76, 84–85. *See also* Deinstitutionalization

Interests: behavior from, 73–74; cooperation from, 77; power from, 103; trust of, 76

The International Motor Vehicle Program, 161

Intersections, 126, 172, 179; of economic with noneconomic aspects of society, 15; institutional, 24, 172, 186; social structural, 112; of sociocultural categories, 14

Judgment, 1; emotions impact on, 48

Justification: of action, 139, 187; conflict of, 186–187; modes of, 185; of value, 185–186

Kirzner, Israel, 112–115

Kluckhohn, Clyde, 28

Legal system, 69

Leviathan (Hobbes), 14

Liberal market economy (LME), 188

Lie, John, 145

LME. *See* Liberal market economy

Machine shop industry, 186–187

Macro-level: in industrial society, 75; institutions at, 91, 118, 136–137; power, perspectives on, 125–134; trust at, 85–86. *See also* Meso-level

Madoff, Bernard, 68

Mahoney, James, 136

"Managing in an Age of Modularity" (Baldwin and Clark), 158

Manipulation, of markets, 115

Manufacturing Consent (Burawoy), 44–45

Manufacturing Possibilities (Herrigel), 193–194

Marginalism, 13

Markets: entrepreneurship, connectors of, 180–184; interactions, norms as, 37; labor, 24; manipulation of, 115; personal relationship impacted by dominance of, 83–84; price gouging, 41–42, 46

Markets and Hierarchies (Williamson), 57

Marshall, Alfred, 13

Marx, Karl, 13; on family and friendship, 181–182

Marxism: on market power, 92–93; on worker cooperation, 187

Mead, George Herbert, 64–65

De Medici, Cosimo, 110–112, 126, 184–185, 232n9

Mental constructs, norms and values as, 1, 27

Mental states, behavior impacted by, 26–27

Merton, Robert K., 33

Meso-level: of analysis, 5, 227n4; of moral economy, 52–53

Mill, John Stuart, 13

Mills, C. Wright, 117–119

Modern economics, 7, 227n2

Modernization: of culture, 154–155; theory, 87

Modularization: of automobile industry, 156–170; experiments with, 163–170; of financial services industry, 158

Moral economy, 31, 46; disruption of, 54; meso-level of, 52–53; reference transactions in, 47–48, 67–68; subsistence ethic, 50–51, 53–54

The Moral Economy of the Peasant: Rebellion and Subsistence in Southeast Asia (Scott), 50

Morality, 231n6; commitment of professional communities, 49; decision-making, 31; dilemmas, psychology of, 154; judgments, 49–50; psychology, 31, 35, 41; shame and guilt as, 32–33

Mosca, Gaetano, 117

Motivation: of behavior, 20–21; financial incentives as, 48; for goods and services, 22; identification of, 61–63; individual, 20; learning mechanisms for, 37

Multiethnic Japan (Lie), 145

Mysticism, 227n3

New economic sociology, 15, 227n4

New Institutional Economics, 7

Noneconomic: goals, 22–23; institutions, with consequences, 19

Norms, 27, 89–90; action impacted by, 34–35; behavior from, 76; as beneficial for group, 44, 82; consequences of, 45; dynamics of, 204–205; economic, 28–29; economic action, impacted by, 35–36; Ellickson on, 40–44; emergence of, 38; emotions impact on, 29–30, 42–43; for esteem, 40; evolution, 26; exclusionary, 43; family, 173–174; force of, 32–34; functional, without mechanism, 40; group benefitting from, 44; as harmful to group, 44–45; human nature and, 35–36; inefficiency identification of, 43; inefficient, 43; influence of, 35, 38; malleability of, 51–52; market interactions, 37; market pricing, 41–42, 46; mental constructs, 27; moral judgments impact on, 49–50;

Parsons on, 28; problem-solving, 39–40; of reciprocity, 46–47, 49–50, 66, 70; role of, 1; self-interest, 45–46; shame, guilt impact on, 31; social context of, 135–136; social networks and, 15–16; in sociology, 28–29; theoretical work on, 38–39; trust based on, 70–72; welfare impacted by, 39, 44–45

Null hypothesis, 3, 4; of economic rationality, 108; of human nature, 3–4; of individualism, 77; on nature of action, 11; of parsimony, 45–46; of self-interest, 73; of socialization, 45

Occupations, 33–34

OEM. *See* Original equipment manufacturer

Opportunity, 112

Order, 12

Organization, 231n2, 232n2; history of, 140–141; of industry, 141, 158–159; institutions, theory of, 140–141, 162–163

Original equipment manufacturer (OEM), 156, 160–163

The Origins of Non-Liberal Capitalism (Streeck and Yamamura), 189–190

Outcomes, 2

Ownership, 130–131

Pareto, Vilfredo, 117, 229n17, 230n2

Parsimony: human nature of, 4–5; null hypothesis of, 45–46; trust impacted by, 60–61, 72–73

Parsons, Talcott, 12, 14, 228n11, 229n13; on functional prerequisites, 137; on power as centralized, 52; on power of money, 97–98; on social consensus, 80; on values and norms, 28

Partnership system, 176–179

The Passions and the Interests (Hirschman), 56–57

Path dependence, 9–10

Patriarchy, 90, 176

Personal relationships: based on sympathy, 84; benefits of, 60–61;

deception in, 81; emotions in, 61–62; identity impact on, 64–65; markets impact on, 83–84; as necessity, 84; trust in, 62–65; of victim-offender, 64

Political science, 28, 46, 95, 100, 127

Politics, culture of, 151–153

Pollution, 101, 103

Popkin, Samuel, 51–53

Positivistic, 12

Power, 1, 89–90, 232n11; in animals, 104; from brokerage, 106–126, 232n8; centralization of, 52; from control of agenda and discourse, 100–103, 127–128, 232n5; from dependence, 92–97, 104; domination as, 92; dynamics of, 204–205; of elite, 116–126, 118, 232n10; of entrepreneurship, 112–116; in hierarchy, 129–132; history of, 133–134; from individual character-istics, 103–104; from interests, 103; invisibility and, 102; legitimacy-based, 97–100; macro-level perspectives on, 125–134; Marx on, 92–93; of money, 97–98; through ownership, 130–131; from resources, 108–110, 129–134; seizure of, 110–111; small worlds and, 116–126, 122–123; social exchange impacted by, 94–95; from social network position, 104–105, 232n6; social structure and, 103; in spheres of exchange, 105, 112–116; varieties of, 91–92; Weber on, 91–93, 96–97

The Power Elite (Mills), 117

Pragmatist epistemology, viii, 22, 144, 149, 172

Pragmatist view, 28, 139, 147, 154, 187, 189, 192, 194, 202, 203, 227n2

Prisoners' Dilemma, 63

Problems, of order, 12

Problem-solving, 171–172; action as, 192–193; human nature and, 139–140, 147; institutions for, 190–191, 201–203; norms for, 39–40; social movement, 143–144

Professional communities: elite in, 118–122; ethics in, 33–34; moral commitment of, 49; recruitment in,

social network, 179–180; small worlds in, 123–125

Psychology: behavioral, 94–95; cognitive, 138; of emotions, 32–35; moral, 31, 35, 41; of moral dilemmas, 154; social, 16, 105, 112, 141; of social sciences, 3–5; of trust, 58–59, 67

Railway industry, 151

Rational action, 1, 26, 34–35, 227n2

Rationality: of cooperation, 58–59; economics, 108; human nature and, 57; trust and, 59–63

Rationalization, 59–60

The Rational Peasant (Popkin), 51

Reciprocity: exchange of, 105, 232n6; norms of, 46–47, 49–50, 66, 70

Reductionism, 4–5; arguments of, 12

Redundancy, 108

Relational embeddedness, 17–18

Relationships. *See* Personal relationships

Renaissance men, 102, 179

Reputation, 41, 61–63, 83, 87, 141; bad, 81–82; consequences, 67; establish, 172; power of, 77

Resources, 179–186; acquisition of, 84, 95–96; benefits from, 61–62; commit-ment of, 85–86; control over, 50, 92–95, 98, 121, 126, 134; entrepreneurship and, 5–6; exchange of, 16–17, 50–51, 67, 96, 100, 103–107; for guiding action, 184–193; human, 140–141, 162; investment of, 71–72, 79–80; power from, 108–110, 129–134; scarcity of, 1–2, 96

Ricardo, David, 13, 228n12

Risk: protection against, 69; of trust, 58, 72–73

Robbins, Lionel, 2

Robust action, 110, 184

Roe, Mark, 152

Role conflict: in family, 172–173; in institutions, 172–173

Rules, 98–100

Sacred values, 35, 74

Samuelson, Paul, 21

Scarcity, 1–2

Scott, James, 50

The Search for Order (Wiebe), 142–143

Self-interest: atomization from, 13; cooperation beyond, 36–38; norms, 45–46; null hypothesis of, 73; realization, 27

Shame: behavior impacted by, 30–31; as moral dilemma, 32–33; norms impacted by, 31

Silver, Allan, 83–84

Simmel, Georg, 93–94, 106–107

Skinner, B. F., 4

Small worlds: collapse of, 133; power in, 122–123; in professional communities, 123–125

Smith, Adam, 13, 21, 83–84

Social capital, 82

Social consensus, 80

Social context: of culture, 135–136; of individuals, 135–136

Social exchange, 23, 63, 104–105; power impacting, 94–95; theory, 67

Social identity, 67, 82, 109–110

Social institutions, 4, 15, 25, 76; capitalist, 138; definition of, 136; discussion of, 135–136; individual action impacted by, 12; intersecting, 179; like polity, 97; theory of, 6

Socialization: approval in, 23; for cooperation, 56; as equilibria, 37; labor markets impacted by, 24; null hypothesis of, 45; obedience as, 11–12

Social movement, 143–144

Social networks, 227n4; advantage in, 23–24, 44; authority in, 131–132; autonomy in, 107–108; for community welfare, 85–86; consequences and, 15; contours of, 45; density of, 229n15; embeddedness in, 17–20; influence on, 18–19; norms, 15–16; occupations, 33–34; power from position in, 104–105, 232n6; professional recruitment in, 179–180; redundancy within, 108; reputation in, 81; as small worlds, 116–118; structural holes in, 16–17, 110–112; weak ties in, 16

Social psychology, 16, 105, 112, 141

Social sciences, 3–5

Social setting, 11–12

Social structure: intersection, 112; mechanism, 54; power and, 103

Sociobiology, 6

Sociological exchange theory, 94, 104–109

Sociology, 135–136, 227n1, 232n1; norms in, 28–29

Solution: institutional, 6–7; understanding of, 8

Sorge, Arndt, 193–194, 197–200

Spheres: of exchange, 105, 112–116; institutions and, 137–138

Standard and Poor's, 87, 124

Stark, David, 185–187

Static analysis, 8–9

Status hierarchy, 95

Steel industry, 194–197

Stigler, George, 13

Stories: adaptive, 6–7, 10, 43, 150; of evolution, 6

Strategy: action, as optimum, 110–112; among individuals, 51–52

Streeck, Wolfgang, 189–190, 192

Strong Managers: Weak Owners (Roe), 152

Structural embeddedness, 18–19, 65–66, 231n7

Structural holes: bridge over, 114–115; brokerage and, 106; in social networks, 16–17, 110–112

Structure: of authority, 111, 129–130; in automobile industry, 166–167, 169–170; of business groups, 87–89; trust from, 82

The Structure of Social Action (Parsons), 12

Systems theory, 5, 227n3

Technology, as path dependence, 9–10

Temporal embeddedness, 19–20

Tertius gaudens, 106–107

Tertius iungens, 106–107, 118

Textile industry, 153–154

Thelen, Kathleen, 136

"The Methodology of Positive Economics" (Friedman), 7
Theory: applied rational choice, 3–4; evolution game, 38; exchange, with social identity, 109–110; institutional, of organization, 140–141, 162–163; of modernization, 87; systems, 5, 227n3
The Theory of Price (Stigler), 13
The Theory of the Leisure Class (Veblen), 43
Thompson, E. P., 27; on paternalism, 46
Thrift industry, 142
Trust, 1, 55, 89–90, 230n3; aggregation of, 81; in automobile industry, 167–169; concept of, 56–59; conditions for, 72–80; cultural impact on, 84–85; culture of, 96–97; dichotomy of, 78; dynamics of, 204–205; enforceable, 231n9; in entrepreneurship, 79; of family, 71–72, 78–79, 87–89; in government policy, 83; in groups, 65–68; high level of, 71, 78–79, 85, 146; institutional sources of, 68–70, 75–76; institutions impact on, 84–85; of interests, 76; in leader, 86–87; low level of, 71, 78–79, 84–85; at macro level, 85–86; from norms, 70–72; parsimony impact on, 60–61, 72–73; in personal relationships, 62–65; psychology of, 58–59, 67; rationality in, 59–63; risk of, 58, 72–73; as social capital, 71; of strangers, 80; from structure, 82

Ultimatum Game (UG), 36–38, 230n4
Utilitarianism, 12, 59–60

Value-rational action, 20
Values: as broad concept, 27; emotions impact on, 35; justification of, 185–186; as mental constructs, 27; Parsons on, 28
Veblen, Thorstein, 43
Venture capital financing industry, 183–184

Wall Street, 101–102
Weak ties, strength of, 16, 107
Weber, Max, 1–2, 20, 231n3,4; on power, 91–93, 96–97
Wiebe, Robert, 142–143
Williamson, Oliver, 52, 57
Wilson, E. O., 4
World Values Survey (WVS), 70, 78, 150
Wrong, Dennis, 11–12
WVS. *See* World Values Survey

Yamamura, Kozo, 189–190

Zucker, Lynne, 62, 66, 69, 75, 140
Zuckerman, Ezra, 108